# Networking IBM PCs
## A Practical Guide

Michael Durr

Que Corporation
Indianapolis

*Networking IBM PCs: A Practical Guide.*
Copyright© 1984 by Michael Durr.

All rights reserved. Printed in the United States of America. No part of this book may be used or reproduced in any form or by any means, or stored in a data base or retrieval system, without prior written permission of the publishers except in the case of brief quotations embodied in critical articles and reviews. Making copies of any part of this book for any purpose other than your own personal use is a violation of United States copyright laws. For information, address Que Corporation, 7999 Knue Road, Indianapolis, Indiana 46250.

Library of Congress Catalog No.: LC 84-60133

ISBN 0-88022-106-2

88 87 86      8 7 6 5

Interpretation of the printing code: the rightmost double-digit number is the year of the book's printing; the rightmost single-digit number, the number of the book's printing. For example, a printing code of 83-4 shows that the fourth printing of the book occurred in 1983.

*Editor*
Virginia D. Noble, M.L.S.
*Editorial Director*
David F. Noble, Ph.D.

# About the Author

## Michael Durr

Michael Durr received both his B.A. in Business and Technical Communications and his M.A. in Marketing Communications from California State University. He has worked as a Communications Security Specialist in the U.S. Navy and as Senior Editor of *Personal Computer Age*. Author of numerous magazine articles and coauthor of *Understanding the Law* (SRA, 1980), Michael Durr frequently lectures on networking and microcomputer communications and is a regular contributor to the magazine *Micro Communications*. *Networking IBM PCs* is based on many years of experience in communications, communications security, communications systems installation, and local area network analysis and review.

# Dedication

To LaVerne Z. Durr

# Table of Contents

**Preface** .................................................. xi
**Trademark Acknowledgments** ........................ xiii

**Chapter 1      Overview** ............................... 1
    What Is a Local Area Network? ........................ 2
    Components of the Network ........................... 3
    Arguments for and against Networking ................. 4
    Managing Resources .................................. 7
    The Alternatives ..................................... 8
    Multiprocessor versus Single-Processor ................ 8
    Network Applications ................................. 9
    The Network as a Communications Carrier ............ 11
    Data Safety and Security ............................. 12
    Network-Caused Problems ........................... 13
    Goals of This Book .................................. 14

**Chapter 2      Standards** ............................. 15
    Protocols and the OSI Model ......................... 16
    Hardware Layers .................................... 19
    High-Level Protocols ................................ 20
    Topologies .......................................... 20
    Access Schemes ..................................... 24
    Future Standards .................................... 26
    Network Cables ..................................... 27

**Chapter 3      The Operating System** ................. 29
    The Network Operating System ....................... 30
    Utilities ............................................. 30

  Presenting Devices .................................35
  Who Controls the Network? .........................38
  Multitasking Servers ..............................39

**Chapter 4  Locking ............................... 43**
 The Concept of Locking ................................44
 Types of Locks ........................................44
  Automatic File Locking ............................45
  Manual File Locking ...............................46
  Transactions ......................................46
  Record Locking ....................................46
 Deadlock ..............................................47
 Locking Shareable Files................................47

**Chapter 5  Hardware-Independent**
      **Operating Systems ...................... 51**
 Novell's NetWare ......................................52
 SofTech Microsystems' Liaison .........................53
 Digital Research's DR Net .............................55
 Lantech Systems' uNETix-DFS ...........................57

**Chapter 6  Evaluation ............................ 59**
 The Plan...............................................60
 Access Methods ........................................60
 Diagnostics and Control ...............................62
 Cost ..................................................62
 Documentation .........................................63
 Environment ...........................................63
 Topology ..............................................64
 Interface Requirements ................................64
 Internetting ..........................................65
 Network Cabling........................................65
 Network Speed .........................................66
 Fault Tolerance........................................66
 Data Security .........................................67
 Real Products .........................................67
 Multiple Machine Types ................................68
 Applications ..........................................68
 Multitasking ..........................................68

**Chapter 7    Leading Networks........................ 69**
    3Com ................................................70
    Corvus Systems, Inc. ...................................72
    The Destek Group .....................................75
    Novell, Inc. ...........................................77
    Gateway Communications, Inc. .........................79
    Tecmar, Inc. ..........................................80
    Ungermann-Bass, Inc. .................................82
    Interlan, Inc. .........................................84
    Nestar Systems, Inc....................................85
    Davong Systems, Inc...................................88
    Orchid Technology ....................................91

**Chapter 8    Applications Software .................... 95**
    Disk Sharing Only .....................................96
    Read-Only Applications Software ......................97
    A Multiuser Approach.................................98
    Categories of Network Software........................99
    Upgrading Single-User DBMS Software................101
    No Central Resource .................................101
    Equal Access to Data .................................102
    Keeping Track of File Activity ........................104
    Defining Users.......................................106
    Efficient Use of the Network ..........................107
    Software: Application or Tool? ........................108
    Languages on the Net ................................108

**Chapter 9    Administration.......................... 111**
    The Network Manager ...............................112
    The Initial Planning ..................................112
    File Organization ....................................114
    Assigning Users......................................115
    Directories ..........................................116
    Files on the Network .................................117
    Naming Conventions ................................119
    Backup .............................................120
    Backup Procedure ...................................121
    A Device Log .......................................122

**Chapter 10      Performance** .......................... **125**
   Reducing the Load ...................................125
   Caching ............................................127
   File Structure ......................................128
   Multiple Servers ....................................130
   Hard Disk Storage ..................................131
   Drive Technology ...................................132
   Faster CPUs .......................................133
   The Cable as a Bottleneck ...........................134
   High-Performance Peripherals ........................136

**Chapter 11      Security** ............................. **139**
   Networks and Security...............................140
   Risk Analysis.......................................140
   Levels of Security ..................................142
      Physical Security ...............................142
      Personal Identification ..........................143
         Passwords .................................143
         Security in Login ............................144
      Encryption ....................................145
         Encryption Keys .............................146
         On-Line Coders .............................147
      The Diskless PC................................147
      Protection against Cable Radiation..................149
      Call-Back Security ..............................150

**Chapter 12      Installation** .......................... **151**
   The Installation Log.................................152
   Cable Distribution ..................................152
   Planning Ahead ....................................154
   Cable Handling.....................................154
   Cable Connectors ..................................157
   Fire-Retardant Cable ................................159
   Cable Testing.......................................160
   Fault Tolerance.....................................160
   Interference .......................................161
   Grounding .........................................163

**Chapter 13     Maintenance and Diagnostics .......... 167**
    Network Control Center ............................. 168
    Local Area Network Diagnostics ..................... 168
    NetWare Diagnostics ............................... 170
    Diagnostics in Hardware ............................ 172
    The Role of the Network Manager ................... 173
    Network Monitoring ................................ 174
    Looking Ahead ..................................... 175

**Chapter 14     Internetting ......................... 177**
    Internet Hardware ................................. 178
        Bridges ....................................... 178
        Gateways ..................................... 181
    Internet Protocol .................................. 181
    X.25 for Wide Areas ............................... 182
    X.25 Options ...................................... 183
    An X.25 Gateway Processor ........................ 184
    Baseband-to-Broadband Bridging .................... 185
    Internet Addressing ................................ 187
    Selecting a Bridge or Gateway ...................... 188
    Remote Connections and Communications ............ 188

**Chapter 15     The Mainframe Connection .......... 191**
    3270 Emulation .................................... 192
    Evaluating an Emulator ............................ 193
    Protocol Converters ............................... 195
    Networking with the Emulator ...................... 196
    Using the Emulator-Equipped PC ................... 198
    Backup on the PC ................................. 201
    Downtime Equals Loss ............................. 202
    IBM's Micro-to-Mainframe Machines ................. 202
    For the Future .................................... 203

**Chapter 16     Electronic Mail ..................... 205**
    Defining Electronic Mail ........................... 205
    Using Electronic Mail ............................. 207
    Evaluating Electronic Mail ......................... 208

    An Intraoffice Study ................................211
    Interoffice Mail .....................................212
    Other Applications .................................212

**Glossary** ........................................... 215

**Vendor Directory** ................................. 225

**Index** .............................................. 231

# Preface

The pace of modern technology often thrusts industries into major changes, with little or no preparation or direction. The rapid development of the microcomputer is an example of one such change in the computer industry. Local area networking is another. Both these developments have been greeted with mixed emotions, especially in business applications. The most common criticism of local area networks is, who needs them? Some people have even described networks as "a technology looking for an application."

In this book I have tried to address these issues without getting entangled in the theory of networking. Many books are already available on packet size and formats, error-checking schemes, and communications software programming. To me, what is needed is practical information on using the local area network.

Local area networks have finally become prepackaged turnkey systems that a consumer can buy in a store. After purchase, the performance of the network almost totally depends on how you set it up and manage it. You don't need a degree in computer science to pick a good network, nor do you need to hire a technician to set it up. This book shows you how to select, install, use, and manage a local area network.

*Networking IBM PCs: A Practical Guide* is an application book designed for the person who is setting up a local area network for the first time or looking for ways to improve the performance of an existing network. That performance depends almost totally on how you make use of and manage the network's flexibility to keep up with changes in office size and the increased use of computers. I've included enough network theory for the reader to understand the network manager's role.

To a large extent, this book has been a group effort. Not surprisingly, I couldn't have completed the project without much help from the network industry. All the network companies have been accommodating in lending computers, network hardware, and software for evaluation. If you've read *Personal Computer Age* magazine for the past couple of years, you've seen some of the articles that have resulted from these evaluations.

In addition to equipment, network designers and engineers have given dozens of interviews and helped me develop most of the applications that appear here. Knowledgeable users have been harder to find, but I did locate a few whose experiences proved invaluable.

Industry expertise, criticisms, and concepts form the largest part of this book. The recommendations are based mostly on currently used procedures or are the compiled ideas of an evolving industry concerned with making the best use of its products. Of course, local area networking is not so mature a development that everything is "cut and dried." Disagreement exists not only about the best way to design and use a network, but also about a number of basic definitions.

In particular, I wish to acknowledge the following individuals for their information and the generous use of their equipment: Anixter Cable's Jay Myers; Gateway Communications' Larry Stephenson and Dave McMaster; Gateway Computer's Martin Swartz; Mountain Computer's Eric Swartz; Novell's Craig Burton, Dale Neibaur, Mark Hurst, Kyle Powell, and Drew Major; Orchid Technology's Robert Davi; Software Connections' Buck Gee; Ungermann-Bass' Richard Eisener; 3Com's Robert Metcalfe and Don Moore; James Glass; and Dwayne Walker.

Finally, I wish to thank *Personal Computer Age* Publisher Jack Crone and the entire staff of the magazine for their encouragement and friendship.

# Trademark Acknowledgments

IBM is a registered trademark of International Business Machines Corporation.

1-2-3 is a trademark of Lotus Development Corporation.

ARCnet is a registered trademark of Datapoint Corporation.

Apple is a registered trademark of Apple Computer, Inc.

Corvus Concept is a trademark of Corvus Systems, Inc.

CP/M, CP/NET, CP/M-86, and DR NET are registered trademarks of Digital Research, Inc. Concurrent CP/M-86 and MP/M-II are trademarks of Digital Research, Inc.

Cypher is a registered trademark of Cypher.

DataCryptor II is a registered trademark of Racal Milgo Information Systems.

Datapoint is a registered trademark of Datapoint Corporation.

ELAN is a trademark of Tecmar, Inc.

EtherSeries, EtherNet, EtherMail, and EtherPrint are trademarks of 3Com Corp.

G/NET is a trademark of Gateway Communications.

Intel is a registered trademark of Intel Corporation.

Interlan is a registered trademark of Interlan, Inc.

LANOS is a copyright of the Destek Group.

MicroPro is a registered trademark of MicroPro International Corporation.

MS-DOS, Microsoft, and Microsoft BASIC are trademarks of Microsoft Corporation.

Microrim is a trademark of Microrim, Inc.

Mountain is a trademark of Mountain Computer, Inc.

Motorola and MC68000 are registered trademarks of Motorola, Inc.

MultiLink is a trademark of Davong Systems, Inc.

Net/One Personal Connection is a trademark of Ungermann-Bass, Inc.

Net/Plus is a trademark of Interlan, Inc.

NetWare and NetWare/S are trademarks of Novell, Inc.

Omninet is a trademark of Corvus Systems, Inc.

PCnet, PCnetPlus, and BLOSSOM are trademarks of Orchid Technology.

p-System is a trademark of SofTech Microsystems, Inc.

Printronix is a registered trademark of Printronix, Inc.

R:base is a trademark of Microrim, Inc.

Rainbow is a trademark of Digital Equipment Corporation.

RM/COBOL is a trademark of Ryan McFarland Corporation.

Telenet is a registered trademark of GTE Telenet Communications Corporation.

Tymnet is a registered trademark of Tymnet, Inc.

TI Professional Computer is a trademark of Texas Instruments, Inc.

Touch-Tone is a registered trademark of American Telephone & Telegraph.

Transcriptor is a trademark of Merritt Software.

UNIX is a trademark of AT&T.

VisiCalc is a registered trademark of VisiCorp. VisiWord is a trademark of VisiCorp.

Xerox is a registered trademark of Xerox Corporation.

WordStar is a registered trademark of MicroPro International Corporation.

Z80 is a registered trademark of Zilog, Inc.

Que Corporation has made every attempt to supply trademark information about company names, products, and services mentioned in this book. Trademarks indicated above were derived from various sources. Que Corporation cannot attest to the accuracy of this information.

# 1
# Overview

A large aerospace corporation recently had its data processing department reviewed by a government agency. One of the recommendations made by the agency was that no IBM PCs should be used *unless they were linked into a local area network*. Because a large part of this company's business came from the government, we can safely assume that the recommendation was followed. Although this example illustrates a somewhat heavy-handed approach to keeping up with technology, the agency's recommendation is certainly a prudent one that many businesses, large and small, could profit from.

When first introduced, the microcomputer was a revolutionary development, bringing quick and convenient computing right down to the desktop level. As a tool of business, however, the microcomputer had some serious deficiencies. In effect, it offered only half a solution to the problem of office automation. The other half is the local area network—the indispensable partner of the microcomputer in the office.

Most of *Networking IBM PCs* deals with how to set up and organize this powerful combination: the microcomputer and the local area network. But first let's examine what a local area network is and why it is essential to the successful use of microcomputers in the office.

# What Is a Local Area Network?

A local area network is a communications system much like a telephone system. Any connected device can use the network to send and receive information. For the time being, that information on IBM PC networks is almost exclusively data, although the technology is now available for carrying voice and video signals also.

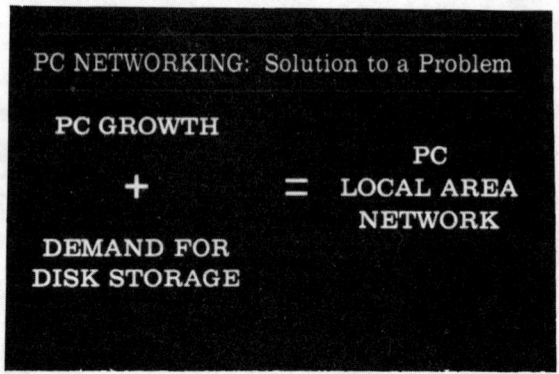

*Fig. 1.1. Demand for hard disk sharing, together with the growth of PC use, spurred the development of the local area network. Courtesy of Software Connections.*

As the name implies, a local area network is used to cover relatively short distances. Usually a local area network will be limited to a department or perhaps a single building. Whether used in large corporations or small businesses, local area networks tend to be small for functional reasons, which we'll discuss in later chapters. The most common network for IBM PC users contains from 3 to 12 PCs, various data storage devices, printers, and other specialized peripherals.

An important characteristic of local area networks is speed; they deliver data fast. A person passing and receiving data over a local area network ideally experiences the same rapid response time as if the data were coming from a local machine rather than from some place out on the network. To get this kind of response time, most local area networks operate at 1 to 10 megabits per second (Mbit/sec).

Besides being fast, local area networks must be both adaptable and reliable. They should have a flexible architecture that permits PC workstations to be located wherever they are needed. PCs or peripherals should easily be added or removed from the system without any extended interruption in the operation of the network.

One of the major benefits of a stand-alone personal computer is that if it breaks down or malfunctions in some way, the effect is limited. The rest of the office work is not interrupted. Likewise, when personal computers are linked into a local area network, the system should retain this kind of reliability. The failure of a single PC should not cause the entire network to shut down.

Finally, a local area network is essentially a peer-to-peer (micro-to-micro) network with distributed intelligence. The personal computers attached to the network can use the computing power of other intelligent devices, as in a host-to-terminal network, but the personal computers can also use their own computing power and talk as equals.

The network just described might be called a small, high-performance local area network for IBM Personal Computers. In common usage the term *local area network* implies a much broader definition than the one suggested here. A local area network often means everything from large corporate terminal networks to those based on PBX telephone systems. In this book, however, the use of "local area network" or simply "network" carries with it the more limited definition provided in this section.

# Components of the Network

A local area network is a system made from building blocks that can be added and shaped as needed. One of these components is the *cable*. Each device on the network is attached to a transmission cable so that messages can be sent from one device to another. For the interface, a piece of hardware, usually a circuit board, is placed between the cable and the PCs and peripherals. This board is logically called the *network interface card,* or NIC.

*Central mass storage* is provided in the form of a hard disk that contains files and programs which are shared by people using the network. Although a central disk is a common feature, it may not be present in all networks. Some architectures permit the random use of any storage device on the network, including local floppy disk drives. On these networks shareable data may be distributed all over the network.

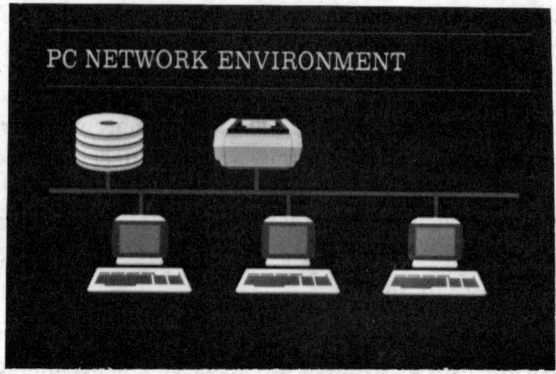

*Fig. 1.2. The local area network. Most local area networks consist of 3 to 12 PCs sharing a hard disk for central storage, a dot-matrix printer, and perhaps a letter-quality printer. Courtesy of Software Connections.*

A network is a multiuser system because more than one person at a time can send requests to a single microprocessor (machine). The shared machine, together with a software program, handles the requests and distributes the network resources, such as data files and printer time. Both the machine and its software are referred to jointly as the *server*. Separate software programs handle the printer (print server), files (file server), and virtual diskettes (disk server). All server programs may run on a single machine, which is often an IBM PC/XT.

PCs on the network continue to use their own local operating systems—for example, PC DOS, CP/M-86, or p-System. Since these operating systems make no provision for using a network, appropriate software must be added. This software is called the *network operating system*.

# Arguments for and against Networking

Probably the most important consideration for someone contemplating a network is whether to network at all. To make this decision, a potential buyer must examine the features that networking brings to the office and weigh their advantages against the cost of networking.

Sharing expensive peripherals is often promoted as the primary reason to network. But is this a sufficient reason? In considering the cost benefits of sharing, you may find some impressive arguments against networking. With today's more affordable technology, you can easily dedicate inexpensive peripherals and not bother with a network. Small, PC-mounted hard disk drives are getting less expensive as their capacities increase. As a result the local hard disk is becoming commonplace and is frequently dedicated to a local PC.

Floppy diskette technology has not stood still either. The 3.2 megabyte (M) floppy, now a reality, is being shipped by several companies. And because the standard-capacity, 360 kilobyte (K) floppy now has enough storage for many uses, the larger storage capacity of a hard disk is often not needed.

Printers are now more affordable, too. Some dot-matrix printers are so inexpensive that many companies dedicate a separate machine for each office use: a labels printer, an invoice printer, and so on.

Then we come to the question of sharing itself. Do most office users really want to share? A large part of the appeal and acceptance of the personal computer has been that it *wasn't* shared, that it was indeed available for personal use. Waiting in a queue to get computing time on a mainframe or to have a document printed is just not something that most people relish.

Sharing also raises another possible disadvantage. You may like the idea of having a large and fast hard disk, and sharing it may seem to be an ideal way to justify the expense. But when three or four people start using that hard disk, its speed can quickly go back to that of a local floppy drive.

These are serious considerations but only part of the picture. When viewed as a system, networking has some powerful arguments in its favor. In most cases organizations with multiple PCs should network them for the following reasons:

1. Sharing of peripherals reduces their per-user cost. Often, a higher-quality peripheral can be justified as a "shared resource," with the result that speed and quality are improved and mean-time-between-failure (MTBF) is increased. Sharing in a properly designed network improves the reliability of the entire system. When a device fails, another one is ready to fill the void while repairs are being made.

2. Better response time can be achieved through networking. The speed with which a request is answered is a crucial

factor in computing. After all, most jobs performed by a computer can be done with pencil and paper. When you buy a computer, you're buying speed more than capability.

Keep in mind that better response time through networking is in no way guaranteed. In fact, inefficient use of the network will quickly result in unacceptably poor response. The elements needed for superior performance, however, are part of most networks. If properly implemented, a PC network will be more efficient than stand-alone computers or networked terminals and will equal or surpass stand-alone computer performance.

3. The peripherals attached to a network tend to be faster than those dedicated to stand-alone PCs. The cable speed (bandwidth) of all the local area networks discussed in this book far exceeds the speed capability of the PC with its 8088 microprocessor. For many applications the PC, not the network, is the bottleneck. But since a local area network is by definition a multiple processor system, the possibility exists for sharing the processing load across several microprocessors, which is similar to parallel processing. You may not be able to speed up the PC itself, but you can speed up the results.

4. Often overlooked in an evaluation of networking is its organizational benefit. Departments, companies, corporations, and institutions are all organizations, which imply interaction and teamwork. Without networking, the personal computer has been a powerful but isolated device. Its output has been difficult to integrate into the organization mainstream, so its value has been limited. In some instances the isolated personal computer has even created serious threats of data loss.

Networking is a communications mechanism that ties the isolated PC into the organization. In a networking environment, being able to communicate and share data encourages continuity and compatibility so that administrative chores can be systematized. For example, the task of backing up the data can be assigned to a particular individual, rather than left as an afterthought to each employee.

## Managing Resources

Flexibility is a distinct advantage of a local area network. Microcomputers can use another computer's processing power instead of their own. Peripherals can be shared or dedicated. And as we shall see later, local area network users have options that can be tailored to achieve the right balance of performance and cost efficiency for the needs of a particular network.

Where computers are concerned, we sometimes tend to get too heavily involved in the "miracles" of a computer system. In a business, however, the primary consideration is usually the net cost of the output. The manager of a computing system manages three resources for cost efficiency: processors, peripherals, and personnel.

The use of any one of these resources can be reduced through an increase in the use of one or both of the other two. For instance, the processor, which is the IBM PC itself, was brought into businesses to increase the efficiency of personnel. The same job can be done with more people and fewer processors, or with fewer people and more processors. Likewise, more peripheral power, such as faster printers and hard disks, reduces the load on the processors. Additional peripherals also reduce personnel downtime, incurred as people wait in turn for a report to be printed or for data to be delivered to the local PC from the hard disk.

The relative cost of each of these three resources changes continually. A few years ago, units of processing power were quite expensive. Now the evolution of the microprocessor has perhaps made processing the least expensive of the three resources, certainly less expensive than personnel. For this reason, using intelligent, processor-equipped personal computers as workstations is both possible and cost effective.

As processors have declined in cost, so have peripherals. Each character-per-second printer output and each byte of hard disk storage are much less expensive than they were even several months ago.

In the computing system, personnel time has become the most expensive resource, and the cost gap is widening. Generally, this expense justifies purchases of PCs and high-performance peripherals.

The ideal balance of resources is unique to each organization. High performance is relative, as are the hourly costs of personnel. A local network exploits the low cost of processors, permitting a single-user environment for computing. At the same time, the total cost of system peripherals is reduced by the creation of a multiuser environment for peripheral sharing. But most important, the network lets you tailor the system performance to your organization's individual needs.

## The Alternatives

For a person wishing to network several PCs, communicate among them, and share peripherals, a number of alternatives are available. One of these is to use a PBX system instead of a high-speed local area network. A PBX network is a relatively low-speed system using telephone wires for the connection. This system may prove entirely satisfactory for some applications, such as batch file transfers, in which a file is pulled down from the central hard disk and processed locally on the PC. When an application requires repeated, frequent access of the remote disk, however, only a high-speed local area network can provide the needed performance.

Another choice facing a potential buyer is whether to select a broadband or baseband system. Then the buyer must choose from among the various access schemes and, finally, from among the specific vendors. Types of systems, access schemes and their options, and other computer terms will be defined and discussed in later chapters.

One point about selection should be made at this time. No single network currently available, or even proposed, is ideal for all network applications because network technology does not lend itself to cross-optimization. Thus, a "shake-out" of technologies is unlikely. Baseband networks, for example, will not supplant broadband networks.

## Multiprocessor versus Single-Processor

One alternative to a microcomputer local area network is a terminal network, now common in mainframe and minicomputer systems. Recently, terminal networks have "migrated" to the microcomputer world, where terminals are designed to run with an IBM PC/XT as host. A terminal network may cost only one-third as much as a micro network, but with a corresponding degradation in performance. Terminal networks are also less dependable, relying totally on a single microcomputer to keep the system running.

The 8088 microprocessor chip that provides central processing unit (CPU) power to the IBM PC/XT is not an especially fast processor compared to many other microprocessor chips. Although the 8088 is more than adequate for most single-user applications, it quickly becomes bogged down in a multiuser environment. For this reason many microcomputer network designers add microprocessors to handle many of the network tasks, although each workstation may already have its own dedicated microprocessor.

In addition, mainframe and minicomputer systems are notorious for poor response time. In fact, user dissatisfaction with time-sharing, host-to-host terminal systems has been one of the driving forces behind the acceptance of the desktop microcomputer. Even in a lightly used application, an XT-hosted system comes to a virtual standstill. As more users are added to the system, the host's computing power is further diluted.

With a local area network, each PC retains local processing capability. As long as there is any sharing (of processor, peripheral, or communication lines), performance degradation is a potential problem. But in a typical network of under 12 workstations, degradation is uncommon. When it does occur, it is responsive to a number of procedural and hardware remedies.

Local area networking is also highly reliable because the entire system does not depend on a single processor. In the peer-to-peer environment of a local network, the failure of any single PC will not shut down the entire system. Other PCs and peripherals can continue to be used while repairs are made. But with a terminal-to-host system, the failure of the host halts all processing and any business operations that rely on the system.

# Network Applications

The micro network was first created strictly as a cost-reduction tool for sharing expensive peripherals, thus reducing the overall cost of managing the resources of a computer system. The technology that evolved, however, resulted in broader implications for micros in a networking environment.

In 1979 the price of the hard disk, or Winchester, storage device dropped significantly. Almost immediately, personal computer users wanted to attach their PCs to these fast, convenient peripherals. Still, many people didn't need the high capacity offered by the hard disk, so manufacturers were asked to provide a means of letting several micros share a hard disk.

This request led to the introduction of a multiplexer device from Corvus, called Constellation, which was the forerunner of today's microcomputer networks. Constellation used a simple polling scheme to regulate PC access to the central hard disk. Users could share a single hard disk, dividing among themselves its storage capacity and cost.

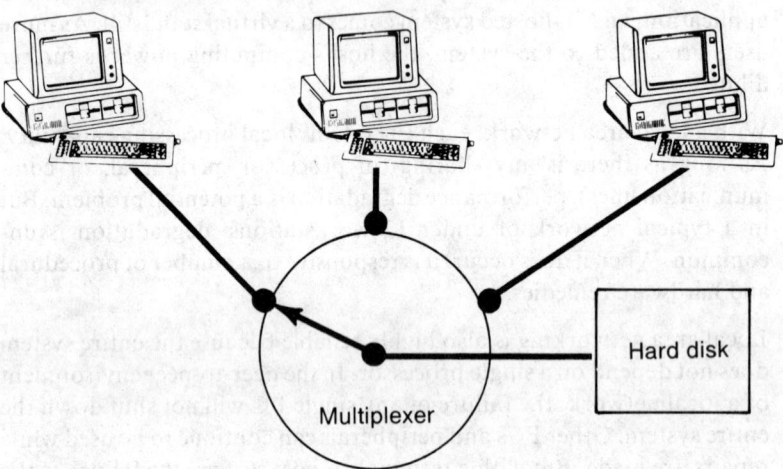

*Fig 1.3. The forerunner of microcomputer networking was the multiplexer, a simple scheme that allowed several computers to access the same hard disk. Disk use and data integrity remained the responsibility of individuals using the system.*

With Constellation, the same hard disk could be shared among users; the next logical step was to share files on that disk. Thus, the relatively simple sharing of equipment turned into the more complex process of sharing information. In fact, many people tried sharing files before the protections were in place for such activity. Some major problems had to be resolved concerning how files could be shared. Solutions have taken several years, and some are still undergoing refinement.

The path that started with peripheral sharing was therefore moving steadily toward true multiuser systems with peer-to-peer communications. And now that micro networks are becoming multiuser systems, these networks can benefit from experiences in mainframe computer environments.

The first multiuser system really came into being when more than one person could load a batch of cards into a mainframe. The mainframe computer processed the batch jobs, and data was distributed to the different users. Later, "dumb" terminals and distributed systems were introduced to improve input methods. Obviously, a motivational force quite different from the one behind microcomputer networking created Ethernet and the other mainframe networks. Today the lines of distinction are beginning to merge as the two forces come together.

Most of the developments we see now in local area networks are the result of work that has gone into local terminal networks over the last ten years. All this activity has brought us to a point in networking technology where we're now able to do things that were once possible only in host-to-terminal networks. In addition, wholly new applications made possible by PCs and local networks are being developed. Two examples are voice management and shared local processing.

# The Network as a Communications Carrier

When most people think of networking or plan a network, they still think of a local area network as simply a device-sharing scheme. Device sharing is certainly one of networking's benefits, but it's far from the total picture.

Local area networks, as defined earlier, are communications devices. Messages, letters, memos, and whole files can be sent from one PC to another. Beyond this use, a local area network can be connected to wide area networks through gateways so that users can communicate with other local networks, data base services, and remote PCs.

Communicating and sharing information have a side benefit that may actually be the best inducement of all for networking: a network promotes an organized computing environment. In many businesses, even a small one, the personal computer can be a disruptive force. It may encourage a kind of "maverick" behavior among users because everyone does things differently. The text files generated by one user are not readily usable by another because each person has a different word processor. Formats of company documents tend to vary from machine to machine, and the list goes on.

What is more, if information generated on a personal computer must be read by other machines or stored on a mainframe, much of the work may need to be redone to move it to a new system. Such an endeavor reminds us of the building of the classic Tower of Babel, in which cooperative work became hampered through problems of communication. Is it any wonder that many data processing professionals have resisted personal computers? The network, however, with its shared central storage and channels of communication, requires user cooperation, which results in better organization and continuity of effort.

## Data Safety and Security

One company purchased a DEC VAX minicomputer and a multiuser terminal network to handle the company's computing needs. Then someone calculated that if the VAX went down, the company would lose $30,000 to $40,000 per day. If the hard disk crashed, the loss would be catastrophic. To guard against these dangers, a second VAX was purchased, along with a hard disk backup system. The company thus spent considerable money to build a manageable and reliable computing facility.

Not long after these purchases were made, company employees started requesting personal computers. Management said no. The company believed that personal computers threatened the "manageable and reliable computing facility" it had so carefully constructed. But, as has happened in many other companies, employees brought in micros anyway. No one had any control over what software was put on the machines. Just one key employee having a micro could copy company files onto a diskette and walk away with hugh amounts of valuable data. Eventually, the company decided to install a local area network, primarily to regain control over the data.

Networks permit distributed processing and central storage. Distributed processing is a performance enhancer, but central storage is crucial to data control. On a network, data can be protected through a supervisor-administered backup system. Access to data can be limited and monitored with multiuser protection schemes, such as user passwords, which are available on most networks.

In effect, microcomputer networks are capable of providing a microcomputer environment with many of the security and data integrity protections common to multiuser terminal networks. At the same time, micro networks offer special controls that are necessary to handle intelligent workstations.

## Network-Caused Problems

Despite the many benefits that local area networks can bring to an office, they can also be a source of problems that are specifically network-related. One of these is the accidental loss of data that may occur when two or more people share the same data *at the same time*. For example, in a system with multiple PCs accessing a hard disk, two users may need to work on a single file on the hard disk, and they may routinely do so without problems. But what if they try to work on the same file at the same time? When they finish their work, they store the file—under the same file name—in the same disk space. Under these circumstances, the user who stores the file last will overwrite and destroy the other's work. Any changes or additions made by the user who first stored the file are lost.

On local area networks, stand-alone machines designed for single users are being shoved into a multiuser environment with no tiller, or steering connection, to coordinate data access. A local area network's software must therefore be sophisticated enough to protect against the danger of accidental loss of data. As we shall see in later chapters, there are some subtle variations of this basic problem. In some cases the users themselves must provide protection unavailable through software.

Though networks prevent some security problems, they may create others. Anytime you put information on a transmission line, you are inviting security leaks. Someone can tap into the network by entering the cable at an accessible point. This intrusion can be a serious threat to companies with particularly valuable or marketable data.

A similar but more common threat may come from authorized network users. They can use their networked PCs to rummage through files on the central storage facility. Many safeguards exist, however, to protect against such threats. The subject of security will be carefully examined in Chapter 11.

## Goals of This Book

This chapter has provided a brief overview of the potential power of local area networking, as well as its possible problems. Throughout the book you will find more extensive discussions of the strengths and weaknesses of various network systems and applications. By the time you finish Chapter 16, you should understand what a network can do. You should also know how to select and configure a network for your particular needs. Finally, you should understand how networks are installed and maintained for maximum reliability and performance.

# 2
# Standards

When we define "microcomputer local area network," we do so in terms of function. The network serves a restricted area, interconnects microcomputers and peripherals, offers fast response, and so on. Precise measurements and physical characteristics are conspicuously missing from the definition. As a consequence, any cable, cable layout, circuit board, and software combination that can function as a local area network can literally be called one.

Moreover, a good argument can be made for a company to use a variety of local area networks. Even though the technology is mature, no one has yet come up with the perfect local area network. In other words, no single combination of hardware technology is perfect for every use.

Part of the problem is that a local area network's basic function is communication. If manufacturers blindly go their own way, we may end up with local area networks that talk only to themselves. Having an oddball local area network is about as useful as having a proprietary local telephone system; neither is a solution for modern communications needs.

Companies with installed bases of PCs from various manufacturers want those PCs to use the same network as well as to communicate with one another. A company with a minicomputer or mainframe is seriously hampered if its local area network does not connect distributed micros to the main computing environment.

Networks need *internetting,* a process that allows them to talk to each other. Local area networks, in fact, should be compatible with worldwide communications systems that include wide area networks and cable TV.

From this discussion a question arises: How do you optimize networks for specialized applications by using whatever technology is appropriate, yet retain enough similarity for various networks to communicate?

# Protocols and the OSI Model

We can't settle on a single solution for local area networks, but we can agree on one structure. Most local area network manufacturers have accepted the importance of an established structure, and they now follow the International Standards Organization's (ISO) scheme for networking, referred to as the Open Systems Interconnection, or OSI model.

The OSI model does not establish or promote any particular standard. Its definitions are broad enough to include many standards. The structure does require enough similarity so that network-to-network interfaces, called *gateways,* can be built. These gateways let the networks communicate.

The OSI model contains the following seven layers:

> Layer 7. Application
> Layer 6. Presentation
> Layer 5. Session
> Layer 4. Transport
> Layer 3. Network
> Layer 2. Data-Link
> Layer 1. Physical

These layers are interdependent. Each one has a built-in interface to the adjacent layer. Layer 2 can pass data to layer 3 or layer 1, but layer 1 cannot communicate directly with layer 3. The model is hierarchical, with the following interdependent functions:

- *Layer 1*. The lowest layer defines the physical connection between the personal computer and the network communications system. This connection is partly mechanical, including the cables and connectors. It is also electrical, with specified modulation techniques and voltages. The most commonly used protocols at layer 1 are RS-232 and RS-422. (A *protocol* is a set of rules governing a specific way of communicating.)

- *Layer 2*. The data-link layer defines the formats used in the message units, as well as the means of controlling access to the network. Local area networks do not send messages as a continuous stream but break them up into one or more *packets,* or message units. Each packet carries the address of its source and destination, along with some error-detection mechanisms. At layer 2, functions are limited to a single point-to-point link. A widely used layer 2 protocol is Binary Synchronous Communications.

- *Layer 3*. The network layer defines the switching and routing of information between networks. Network management, which includes the relay of status information to PCs and the regulation of packet flow, is also established in layer 3.

- *Layer 4*. The transport layer defines the distribution of addresses on the network. If necessary, messages may be divided into smaller units. The procedure for accomplishing this task is determined at this layer. Error detection and recovery are also handled here.

    The network communications process is logically made up of two sets of services. One set, roughly corresponding to layers 1 through 4, is associated with providing communications service. The other set of services, corresponding to layers 5 through 7, pertains to the use of the communications. Layer 4 establishes the transfer mechanism between these two sets of communications services.

- *Layer 5*. The session layer defines the binding and unbinding of communication links, as well as the passage of data.

- *Layer 6.* The presentation layer defines the translation of formats and syntax from an application to the network.
- *Layer 7.* The applications layer defines the support for applications run on the PC and specifies the manner in which applications can enter the network. Many network utility programs are part of layer 7.

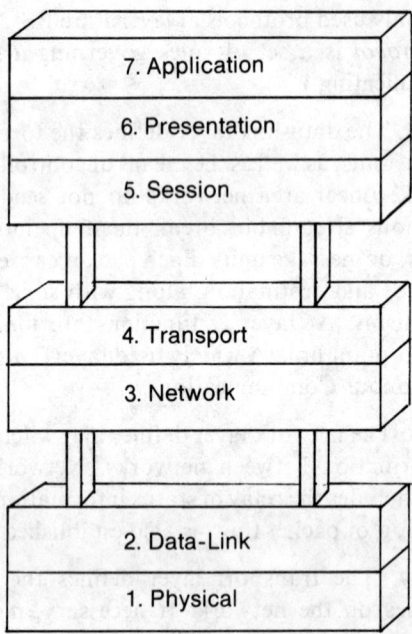

*Fig. 2.1. The OSI seven-layer model. The International Standards Organization's Open Systems Interconnection (OSI) model divides local area network architecture into seven layers. Each layer in the model is defined and provides rules for network design. Viewed another way, the bottom four layers define the network and how it functions. The top three layers define how the network is used.*

Some depictions of the OSI model contain an eighth layer to cover network management features. The traditional seven layers are stacked in their hierarchical configuration, and layer 8 runs vertically, interfacing with all 7 layers. This network management layer determines how the health of the network is to be monitored.

Layers 1 and 2 are the hardware layers. They provide the fundamental connection on which more sophisticated services are built. The topology (layout) and bandwidth (speed) of the network are determined in these layers.

At the hardware level the two dominant architectures for networking IBM PCs today are Ethernet and ARCnet. In the United States the 802 committee of the Institute of Electrical and Electronic Engineers (IEEE) is the primary group that sets network standards. At this writing, the standards for Ethernet (802.3) and ARCnet (802.4) have each been published. Other standards have been proposed but not formally defined.

Standards at the hardware level offer a number of positive advantages. Foremost of these is that data can easily be sent from one Ethernet network to another. Many companies, however, have chosen to modify these standards and develop what they feel are systems with superior performance. Some of these companies are working to have their systems accepted, each as another IEEE standard. Almost certainly the next standard to be published will be the IBM network, already known as 802.5. It will probably not be the last.

With so many "standards" at the same level, it may be appropriate to call them "schemes" rather than standards. Actually, the broad acceptance of the OSI model, coupled with the availability of many different communications gateways, has diluted the importance of a single hardware-level standard. This circumstance has freed up the network selection process and allowed buyers to look for other distinguishing criteria.

The situation is no less diverse in the software layers (layers 3 through 7) of the OSI model. Several middle-range protocols, commonly called level 4 protocols, are well entrenched. The level 4 protocol most commonly found on local area networks is XNS, Xerox Network Systems. XNS is oriented toward peer-to-peer communications, making it excellent for use in a microcomputer network.

Systems Network Architecture (SNA), is level 4 protocol from IBM. Essentially a host-to-terminal protocol, SNA is gradually being adapted by IBM to service distributed intelligent workstations. The importance of SNA (and the reason for including it here) is that it will probably be the level 4 protocol used by IBM in its local area network. Most network manufacturers who make gateway devices offer an SNA gateway so that PCs can communicate with IBM mainframe computers. Presumably, any local area network offering such a gateway will be able to talk with an IBM local area network, provided that it too uses SNA protocol.

Two other level 4 protocols are established but not widely used on local area networks. Internet Protocol/Transmission Control Protocol (IP/TCP), is an accepted protocol of the U.S. Department of Defense. Right now, its importance is limited to communications with military networks.

ECMA, the European Computer Manufacturers Association, is working with the International Standards Organization and the U.S. Bureau of Standards to develop its own level 4 protocol. As international data communications become more important, so will this protocol. For the moment, though, it's just one more element that prevents clear standards from evolving.

## High-Level Protocols

The upper layers of the OSI model (layers 5, 6, and 7) are still in the theoretical stage. Some confusion exists among manufacturers about how to implement these levels. Xerox has published high-level protocols, and even if they are not accepted by everyone, the mere existence of such protocols is a stabilizing influence in network development.

When we speak of the "network operating system," we are referring to these upper layers. From the user's point of view, they are extremely important because they control access to the network utilities. Most network administrative and procedural practices, such as access procedures and data organization, are handled at this level.

## Topologies

As mentioned earlier, the *topology,* or physical layout of the network, is defined in the hardware layers. The cost and flexibility of a network installation are partly affected by topology, as is system reliability.

Many network topologies are commonly used, but they all have certain similarities. Each local area network uses a cable to carry information. This cable must control the movement of information on the network so that messages can be passed in a reliable manner.

On most topologies signals are broadcast in all directions from the sending PC. Each device has its own assigned address, and software is used to program a device to accept messages with its address only and to ignore all others.

Local area networks ordinarily use one of four basic wiring arrangements: the Star, the Ring, the Distributed Bus, or the Token Bus.

The *Star* topology has a separate cable for each PC on the network. Each cable attaches to a central network processor. The Star is widely used in host-to-terminal networks, in **PBX** telephone systems, and in a few local area networks.

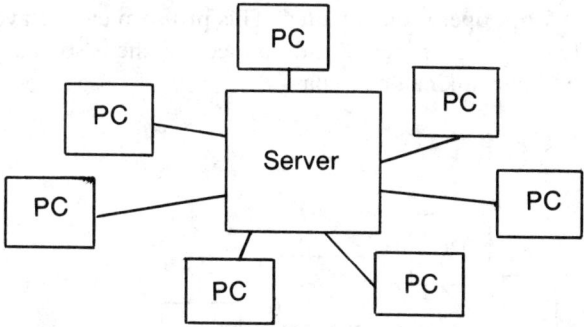

*Fig. 2.2. Star topology.*

In Star topology the central processor passes messages from their sources to their destinations—either another PC or a peripheral device. A message comes down from the server to the PC, and the PC acknowledges the message. If the PC doesn't acknowledge it, the server sends the message again. The advantages of a Star topology are that connecting the hardware is simple and sometimes existing telephone wires can be used as the transmission media.

The Star has several disadvantages for local area network use. Because each PC must be attached with its own dedicated cable to the central processor, a Star topology uses more wire than other topologies. Installation of an additional PC to the network is more difficult because a new cable must be installed from the processor to the PC.

Another cause of concern with the Star topology is that a single point of failure exists. In other words, if the central processor fails, the whole network stops. The network may use intelligent workstations, such as PCs, whose stand-alone operation isn't affected by the central processor. But network traffic must go through the central processor, and often no other workstation can assume the central processor's role if the processor fails.

The *Ring* topology is a closed system. The cable passes through each PC workstation and peripheral, and the ends are joined to form the ring. The Ring may be the network most subject to downtime since each device is a part of the network circuit. If a PC fails, the circuit is broken, and the network operation is halted. This problem can be avoided by running two rings in parallel and connecting them so that a down machine or cable link can be bypassed.

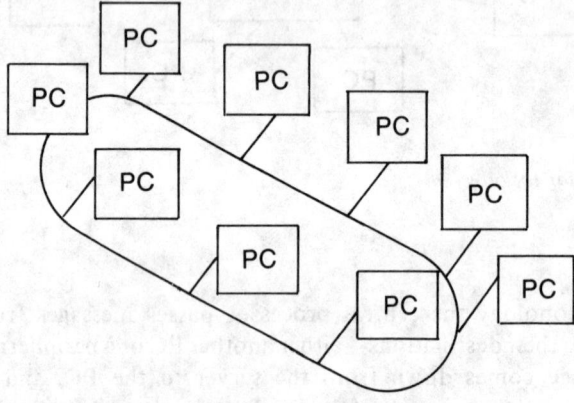

*Fig. 2.3. Ring topology.*

A *Distributed Bus* is the most widely used topology in local area networks. The bus is a single cable routed through the work area. Workstations and peripherals can be attached at any convenient point. A Distributed Bus topology is highly reliable and flexible. Failure of any networked device has no effect on network operation, but failure of the cable will shut down the network.

The *Token Bus* topology, also called a Distributed Star, is similar to the Distributed Bus in that both use a single bus. However, the Token Bus uses special bus interface devices called HUBs, which are attached to the bus at convenient points. Dedicated cable runs from these HUBs to the networked PCs.

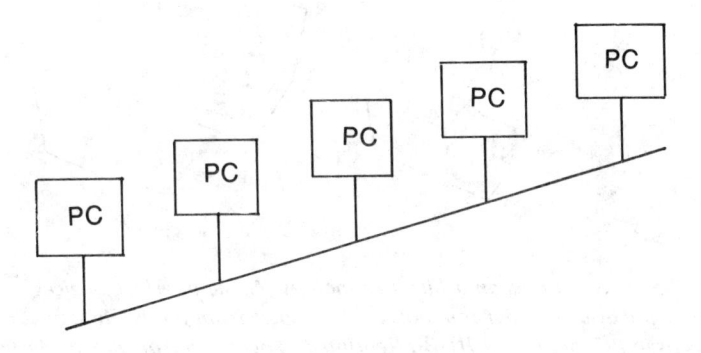

*Fig. 2.4. Bus topology.*

The *Star-Wired Ring* is another topology that should be mentioned, especially since IBM is proposing its use. Like the Token Bus, the Star-Wired Ring uses a combination of common and dedicated wires. Dedicated cables radiate from a central processor to each networked device. In addition, the Star-Wired Ring has a redundant processor that eliminates the single point of failure, which is a disadvantage of the Star network. The two processors are connected to each other by two parallel rings, thus providing backup redundancy also.

Although doubtlessly reliable, the Star-Wired Ring buys its reliability with a considerable expenditure of hardware and cable. If two PCs are in close proximity, attaching them to a single cable is more convenient

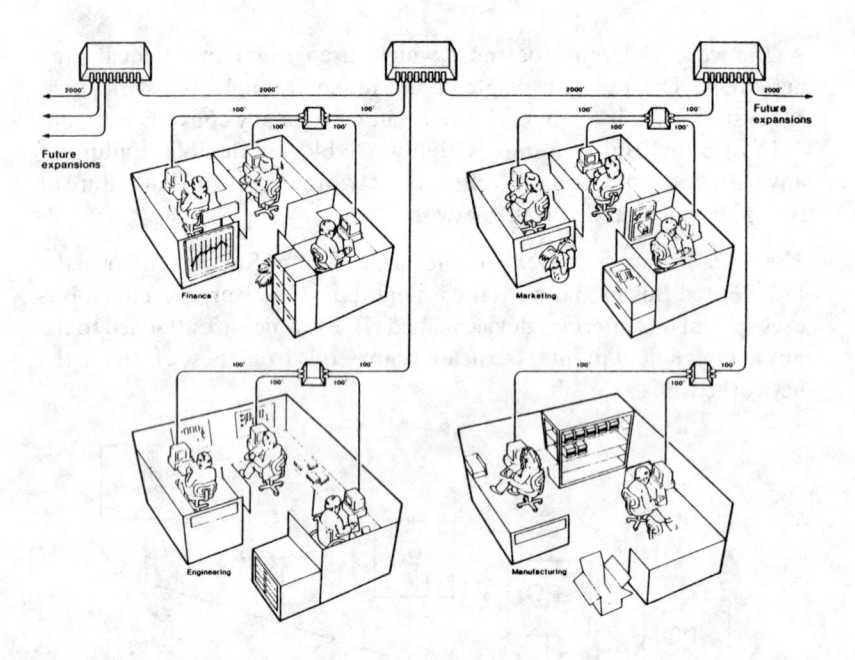

*Fig. 2.5. ARCnet uses an arbitrary topology. Cable interface devices, called HUBs, are attached to a common cable. Cables from the HUBs can connect directly to PCs or to other HUBs. Reprinted by permission of Davong Systems.*

than running dedicated wires from each PC out to a central processor. Indeed, Ethernet and the Distributed Bus were invented to solve the problem of excessive wiring that the Star-Wired Ring requires.

Personal computer local area networks currently tend to be small. In these systems the additional cost incurred with a Star-Wired Ring would probably rule out its use, except in situations where extremely high performance and high reliability are paramount.

# Access Schemes

As mentioned earlier, any topology that uses a common bus must have some means of regulating access to that bus. Otherwise, nothing would prevent two PCs from making simultaneous transmissions and ef-

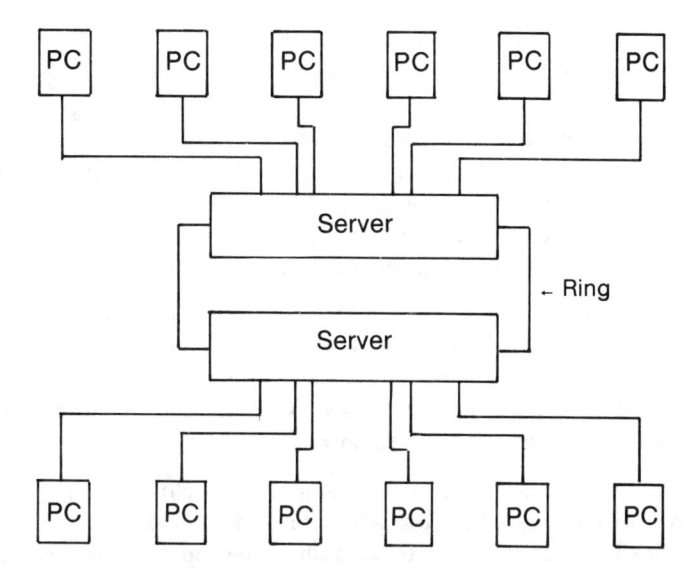

*Fig. 2.6. Star-Wired Ring topology.*

fectively blocking one another. Two access schemes are currently used: Carrier Sense Multiple Access (CSMA) and token passing. Access schemes are part of the hardware layers of the OSI model. Of the two major hardware layer protocols, CSMA is used by Ethernet, and token passing is used by ARCnet.

CSMA is referred to as a "contention scheme"; PCs aren't automatically given access to the network but must compete for an open time slot. With CSMA an attached PC monitors the network and transmits only when the PC hears no other signal.

Most CSMA networks also include Collision Detection (CD) as part of their access method. While a PC transmits, it continues to listen to the network to verify that the transmission is not being interrupted. If another PC were to transmit during this time, the resulting collision would be detected. Any PC that detects the collision sends a jamming signal, then retransmits after a predetermined interval.

Token passing is an access scheme whose function, like that of CSMA-CD, is the orderly use of the transmission medium. In a token-passing network, an access-granting message, called a *token,* is generated during system configuration and passed from PC to PC. Any PC wishing to transmit must wait until a free token is offered. The PC takes possession of the token and the network by altering a bit in the token. Then the PC can transmit. When the transmission is finished, the PC releases the token by resetting the bit to "free" status.

Token passing is defined as a "deterministic" access method. The maximum time a PC must wait before gaining access is predictable since each PC is offered a turn on a regular basis. CSMA-CD is a "probabilistic" access method; network control is acquired in a haphazard, first-come-first-served basis.

Both access schemes perform adequately. In close comparisons, however, differences in performance are evident. During low-traffic conditions or "bursty" activity with short periods of high use, the CSMA-CD scheme shows a slight performance edge. This occurs because the transmitting PC doesn't need to wait for a free token to arrive; a clear network is all that is required.

In heavy-traffic environments token passing will outperform CSMA-CD. Since a PC must have the token in order to transmit, collision/retransmission problems don't arise. On a CSMA-CD network, as the number of transmissions increases, so do the number of collisions, the necessary waiting periods, and retransmissions.

## Future Standards

Many people are concerned about the longevity of any technology. In an area as new as local area networking, this concern is heightened. Both CSMA-CD and token passing are well entrenched and will remain dominant into the 1990s, and probably long after that.

CSMA-CD, in particular, has developed a solid position by being the first standard to emerge. Xerox spent five years developing and debugging Ethernet and the CSMA-CD access method. Other manufacturers have spent millions of dollars crystalizing their complex protocols into simple chips. These chips are inexpensive, and they're available. What is more, the access method is suitable for office environments.

A parallel but somewhat later growth path has occurred for token-passing networks. Many manufacturers have adopted these systems and have large installed customer bases. These cannot be abandoned.

Neither of these standards will disappear. What will probably develop is an increased sophistication in internetting so that Ethernet and ARCnet can communicate with each other. The appearance of new access methods will increase the options, not narrow them.

## Network Cables

The cable used in the network is specified at the hardware level. Network manufacturers currently have a number of choices of cable. Like retail buyers, the manufacturers must weigh the cost of the cable, along with the transmission speed and maximum range of the network. Susceptibility to electrical interference and even security threats may be factors, too.

Local area networks for IBM PCs are now almost exclusively single-channel systems. But multichannel technology will become increasingly important, especially as smaller local area networks are tied into larger but still local communications systems.

The least expensive network cable is *twisted pair*, which is the same medium used in telephone wire. Physically, twisted pair is multistrand wire, insulated and frequently shielded to reduce the possibility of interference. Twisted-pair cable can support data transmissions up to approximately 1Mbit/sec. This cable is best suited to dedicated cable systems, such as a Star topology, and small department-level networks.

*Baseband coaxial cable* is the choice of most local area network manufacturers. A single-channel cable, baseband uses electrical frequency signals and handles high-speed data rates well, up to 10Mbit/sec. Baseband coax is relatively inexpensive and free from interference. But most important, baseband is easy to install and maintain. For the typical local area network, the end-user is fully capable of all the installation work. A baseband network has a maximum range of about 4,000 meters.

*Broadband coaxial cable* is a high-speed data medium that is similar to baseband. Broadband differs, however, in that it carries a radio frequency signal, which increases the bandwidth and permits multichannel capacity. Up to 24 channels may now be placed on a broadband cable, and the technology exists for as many as 100 channels in the future. Another advantage of broadband cable is its range. End to end, a broadband network can extend 50 kilometers.

In most instances the capacity offered by broadband coax isn't needed for direct PC connection or for local area networking. Broadband cable is more costly than baseband cable and requires expensive RF modems at each device interface. Because of the complexities of RF modems, broadband is somewhat difficult to install; most installations should be done by a professional. Once a broadband network is installed, it is quite reliable.

*Fiber-optic cable* is the newest technology to be used in local area networks. A light beam is carried through a glass thread running the length of the cable. The beam is modulated by the network to shape the signal.

Because light beams transmit messages, the system is immune to outside electrical interference. Cable-generated interference does not occur so that extremely fast and error-free data transfers are possible. Fiber-optic cable is a multichannel medium. For a given amount of space, the channel capacity of fiber-optic cable is enormous.

Fiber-optic cable has several disadvantages. First, it is expensive. Second, its connections are the most difficult of any network cable. Finally, fiber-optic cable cannot be tapped easily for additional workstations, as other cables can.

# 3
# The Operating System

Some network vendors like to describe their networks as "transparent to the user." In other words, you're not supposed to notice any differences between using the stand-alone PC and a networked machine. This idea is nonsense, of course, because many differences are obvious. For instance, with a network you have a list of new commands to control the computing system. You can communicate from your PC to other PC users on the network. New multitasking and multiuser features are also available to you. (*Multitasking* means that multiple jobs can be performed on a single processor; *multiuser* means that a single processor is shared among multiple users.)

The differences between a stand-alone PC and a networked machine are principally supplied by the network operating system. From the user's point of view, the network operating system is the single most critical element of networking. Functionality, ease of use, management, data safety, and security are all features of the operating system.

## The Network Operating System

A network operating system supports applications on the network in much the same way that a local operating system supports applications on the PC. Just as PC DOS and the other local operating systems have their own sets of required utilities, so do network operating systems.

Remember from the OSI model that the first two layers of a network are hardware layers. These layers define how the hardware components are connected and how a message gets onto the network. Layers 3 and 4 govern how devices are addressed and routed through the network. Layers 5, 6, and 7, taken as a group, form the network operating system. This system serves as an additional layer over a single-user operating system, such as PC DOS, and permits the PC to interact in a multiuser environment.

In a typical example Davong's MultiLink network uses ARCnet for the first two layers. Then for layers 3 and 4, MultiLink uses Xerox Network Systems (XNS) protocols. Above these layers Davong has its own implementation of disk sharing and printer sharing protocols that are the foundation of its network operating system. Although the lower layers are well defined by published protocols in general use, the top three layers are proprietary, as they are on most local area networks. You can see that network operating systems, without standards, are a varied lot.

Variety does not necessarily mean lack of compatibility for communicating with other networks. Davong, for instance, sends information in packets according to the ARCnet protocol and uses message addresses adhering to the XNS format. In Davong's proprietary network software, a strict request/response protocol is used. That is, a request for data from a hard disk is responded to with the data. This level of conformity is necessary in order for the network to interface with applications software and the local operating system. The differences occur in the way that the network operating system handles the local operating system and also in the utilities that the network operating system supports.

## Utilities

Network operating systems work in the background, supporting applications "transparently," just as the network industry claims. But

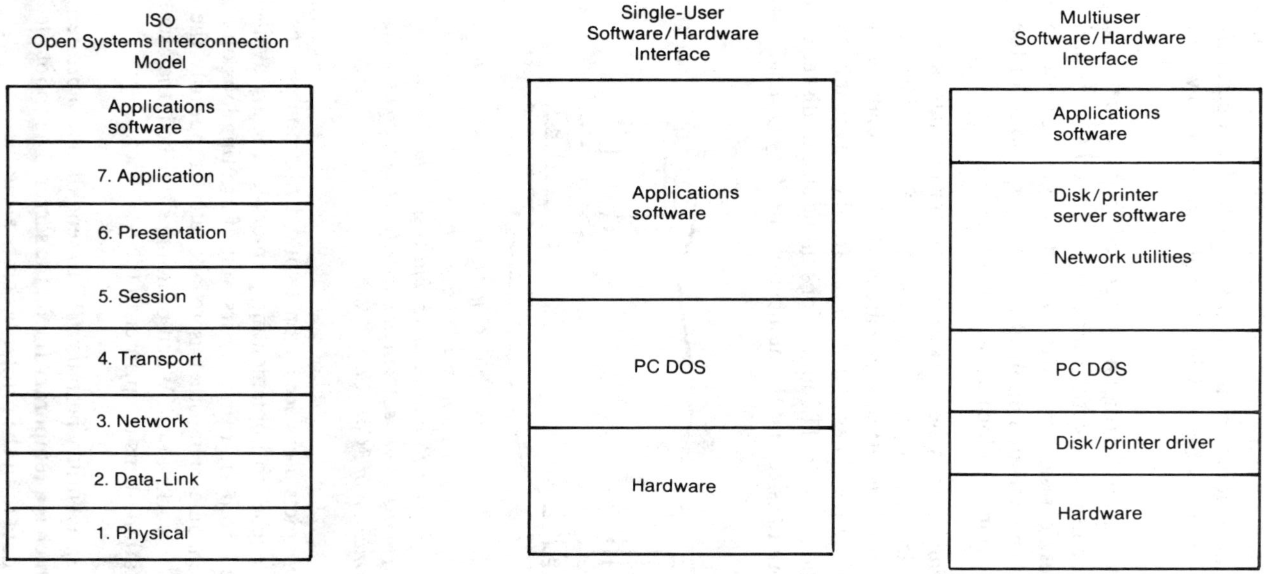

*Fig. 3.1. Hardware/Software Interfaces. Multiuser systems usually are built on single-user systems by adding software called drivers that route messages to remote disks and printers. Server software is added to handle network requests.*

you can see the operating system's utilities and, through them, you can get a glimpse of what is going on inside the system. The operating system limits the kinds of utilities possible and also governs how they can be implemented.

A *utility* is a special-purpose program integrated into the network operating system. The utility directly interfaces with the PC user and performs a discrete, useful task. You can think of utilities as the network operating system's own dedicated applications software. Some of the following utilities are found on local area networks:

1. *Disk serving* permits networked computers to share mass storage devices, usually a hard disk. A disk server divides the disk into virtual diskettes, which are electronic emulations of physical diskettes. These "diskettes" are then available to users on the network. The limitations in the size of diskettes control both file size and the number of directory entries.

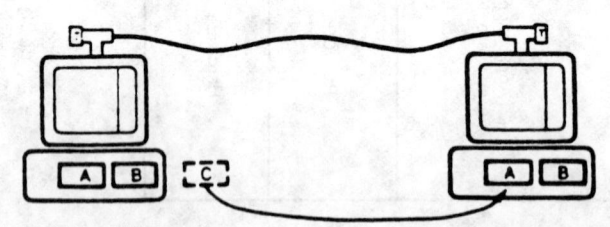

*Fig. 3.2. PC workstation #1 has a virtual drive C that is mapped to workstation #2's drive A. Whenever #1 requests information from drive C, the request is accepted as if it were a request to a local drive, but then redirected by the network operating system to #2's drive A. All this activity is transparent to the user. Reprinted by permission of 3Com Corp.*

2. *Print serving* lets users access a networked common printer. Two approaches to implementing printer sharing are available. One is to permit first in, first out of printing jobs on a queued schedule. The other is to allocate temporarily the printer to a workstation. When printing is finished, the user on that station opens the printer to the next user.

3. The *print spool* utility permits a PC to send data to a printer buffer, which is a temporary file on the server. The spool file holds the data until the printer becomes available.

# THE OPERATING SYSTEM

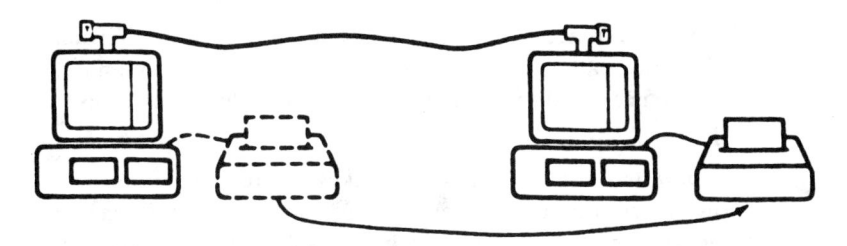

*Fig. 3.3. Printer requests from workstation #1 are responded to by a remote printer emulating a local device. Reprinted by permission of 3Com Corp.*

4. The *login* utility implements the procedure for entering the network environment. Ordinarily, a user supplies a name and a password. The PC is then mapped to that user's authorized directory and files. Some networks' login is station-dependent, meaning that privileges are granted to the station. Other networks have a user-dependent login, which means that privileges are granted to the user. In a user-dependent system a user can login at any PC and be able to use his own privileges, receive mail, etc.

5. *Password* utilities provide the mechanism to protect data from unauthorized use. Network access is limited to anyone with knowledge of a valid password, which is keyed to the login and is unique for each user. Beyond general-access protection, a password identifies a user profile.

Each user has a defined set of privileges regulating the use of data on shared disks. Full privileges may be *Read/Write,* which give the user the right to use and modify the file. Or privileges may be *Read-Only,* in which case the user has access to the information but cannot modify it. Finally, the user may have no rights at all to the file. Some networks refine these basic privileges by permitting additions but not deletions within the file, or by permitting creation of new files but not deletion of files.

6. The *file specification* utility is a mechanism of data protection similar to password privileges, except that here the restric-

tions are placed on the file instead of the user. Virtual diskettes, called *volumes,* may also be defined in this manner. File specification normally takes precedence over user privileges.

A *public* volume or file is one that can be read by authorized users but cannot be written to. A *private* volume or file can be accessed by only one person who has full privileges to that file. A *shareable* volume or file can be accessed simultaneously by multiple users. And a *nonshareable* volume or file can be opened by only one user at a time.

7. *Locking* is a network-associated utility that reserves a file, record, or field for a particular user. For example, anyone wanting to write to a file first locks the file, makes the changes, then unlocks the file. This process prevents possible overwriting when two people decide to update simultaneously the same file. A lock may be implemented as either a warning or a physical denial of access. (For a further discussion of locking, see Chapter 4.)

8. *Pipes* are temporary volumes used to communicate between applications programs running on different PCs. Piped messages are stacked in a queue so that the first message in is also the first message out. Pipes have many uses in a network, one of which is to provide a message center facility. Technically, a pipe is a tool, a kind of low-level utility that supports applications.

9. *Electronic mail* lets memos, letters, and files be sent from one workstation to another. An electronic mail utility maintains a record of users' addresses on the network and reports whether or not mail has been received. A simple editor is often part of the mail utility. (For a further discussion of electronic mail, see Chapter 16.)

10. *Configuration* is another important tool that lets the user issue commands to configure or reconfigure the virtual environment dynamically. For example, a user can ask to assign a drive F to a different virtual volume, or to switch between one file server and another without having to go through a manual configuration program. Most networks

permit the entire network to be reconfigured without interrupting service while users login and logout on the network.

11. The network *monitor* is a diagnostic utility that lets a user see the activity on the network. (This utility's name varies from network to network.) The monitor utility usually can list the stations that are active on the network and the available printers and can also display printer queues. In addition, the monitor may show the percent of network utilization and the status of files.

Network operating systems contain many more utilities than those described here. Like utilities in single-user systems, utilities are included in networks to perform copy, backup, restore, and directory functions, among others.

## Presenting Devices

Network software is commonly divided into two packages of programs, one for the server and one for the PC workstation. The server programs divide the shared hard disk into virtual diskettes, or volumes. These volumes can then be allocated to a user or an application. A server program manages the requests of multiple users so that the requests can be received simultaneously but answered sequentially.

The user software is equipped with a software driver to handle network commands. With the driver a link is established between a volume name (created for the user's directory) and the actual drive on the shared hard disk.

Ideally, the operating system for a network should present physical devices—whether they're hard disks, computers, or whatever—as additional parts of the same machine. Each device adds another drive letter. Then when the user asks for drive X, that device can be accessed.

This arrangement is usually set up as a configuration program when you bring up the network. You might designate drive B for user 4 to be physical drive F. Once set up, the applications software won't know the difference.

Sometimes the software must be aware of the network. Where data bases are concerned, software must be written to handle multiple users sharing a data base, with more than one person accessing it at the same time. At a rudimentary level the network operating system can handle this kind of activity. The problem is that often the network doesn't know what users are doing with the data they access, and the network is therefore unable to protect the data.

The operating system must be aware of users accessing files and also be able to make decisions that are more intelligent than those which are simply activity-based. In other words, during the process of an update, the system must be able to determine whether a person is a Read-Only or Read/Write user. This level of sophistication can be furnished by the operating system, but more frequently the function is provided by one of the multiuser applications programs. Whichever scheme is possible depends on the type of server being used by the network.

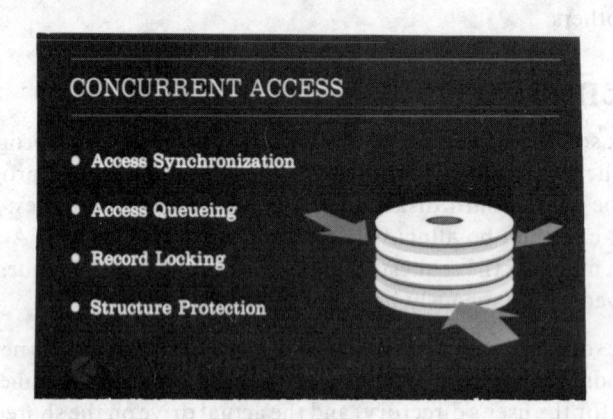

*Fig. 3.4. Concurrent access must be regulated so that modifications are accomplished with full data integrity. Courtesy of Software Connections.*

Two types of network servers are available: the disk server and the file server. With a disk server the control of the directories and files is distributed among the networked PCs. A file server, on the other hand, maintains central control.

The difference between these two servers is evident in shared file management. With a disk server each networked PC participates in disk management. The disk is accessed through a disk emulation process in which the shared disk is controlled by low-level system calls. In the case of a file server, all management of the shared disk is taken away from the local PC. The file server is responsible for opening the file properly and making sure that no other user is given the same disk space. The file server also manages a utility called *default file locking*. If one person attempts to open a file that is already open and also nonshareable at the file level, the file server will invoke a default file lock and prevent access.

To illustrate the hazard inherent in uncoordinated disk management, let's suppose that two users open the same file, an inventory that has 1K of data in it. When user A opens the file, an FCB (file control block) is passed to user A's PC. The FCB contains the time, date, file name, and file location on the disk. Part of the FCB contains the size of the file, which in this case is 1K, or 1,024 bytes.

Since two users opened the same file, both FCBs are identical. User A is just browsing and doesn't intend to update, but user B updates and adds 100 bytes of data. Now user B's FCB indicates 1,124 bytes, while user A's FCB remains at 1,024. Then user B closes his file. What is written to the disk, of course, is user B's FCB, which says that the file is 1,124 bytes. Next, user A closes his file, and user A's FCB changes the file size back to 1,024 bytes.

User B was doing record locking, while user A was in a Read-Only mode. But user B lost data because user A wrote an FCB that was of a different size. With a disk server the only way to avoid this problem is to reopen the file, make sure that the FCB is correct, then close it again. The default file locking utility, which is implemented in a file server, prevents this problem from occurring.

Some networks have a central processor that acts as a manager, except that it does not control the directories or files. The central processor has control of a resource called a volume, and the processor's task is to make sure that more than one does not mount a nonshareable volume. If the volume is shareable and two people decide to use it simultaneously, the disk server assumes no control and offers no protection. In this case the users themselves must synchronize the use of the volume if they are running a single-user application. A better solution is to run a multiuser applications program with protections built in.

On other networks the options are more limited because the networks don't have different kinds of volumes—no Read-Only or personal limiters. Whenever the user logs in, access is to a shareable Read/Write volume. The user's responsibility is to make sure that no one else has the password. Of course, this approach severely inhibits data sharing.

Some disk servers perform directory synchronization, which is similar to a file server's synchronization. These disk servers will make certain that one user is not handed the same vector space that another has already been given. This similarity in disk and file servers tends to blur the visible differences between the two servers. In an evaluation of network operating systems, the name applied to the server is therefore less significant than the functions it supports.

## Who Controls the Network?

The choice between disk server or file server suggests the more general question of how a network should be controlled. A disk server requires distributed control, whereas a file server implies central control. Personal computer networks have distributed intelligence. But should they also have distributed control? Or is centralized control preferable? Let's consider briefly each method of control.

For device sharing—say, of a hard disk or printer—an intelligent machine must be assigned organizational control. On most local area networks, the peripheral device is served by the PC to which it is attached. Control of the files and directories, however, may be either distributed among the local PCs or given to a central PC or another computer.

Supporters of distributed control point out that people choose personal computers because they want more autonomy; they want to get away from central control and the host-to-terminal environment. Distributed control also may be less expensive since a dedicated central processor is not required. Finally, distributed control definitely is more fault tolerant and, therefore, more dependable than central control with its single point of failure.

On the other hand, proponents of central control argue that a single network manager is needed to organize properly the multiuser activities on a local area network. Central control also may offer superior password protection and other network access schemes. And less software and network overhead is required with central control because only one device is performing a management function.

## Multitasking Servers

Servers are intelligent machines, usually personal computers. They run the server software, monitor requests to the shared peripheral, and perform a certain number of network administrative functions. If the server is restricted to performing server duties, it is called a "dedicated server." This server was usually a network requirement until mid-1982. At that time network operating systems became available with multitasking capability on the server. Without multitasking, a person who wanted to set up a small office of two or three PCs was forced to buy another PC just to handle server duties. Consequently, networking was impractical because of the cost.

Multitasking permitted the PC to be both a server and a PC workstation. The microprocessor on the server divided its time, normally running the network functions in background and the local PC functions in foreground. This kind of system was a tremendous breakthrough for the small office, where the system functioned well. Larger offices were also able to move slowly into local area networking. They could connect a few machines at low cost, and if the network proved itself, the system could be expanded.

All these benefits of multitasking continue today, but this kind of operating system has some limitations. Consider the varied functions that a multitasking server provides. It handles many chores. A server supports virtual diskettes, each with a designated owner. The names of the owners and their access rights are maintained by the server. And a server supports both login and password protection. In addition to all these functions, a single server often supports one or more printers and electronic mail systems. The load can become quite substantial even if three or four PCs are networked.

Providing these functions can easily use up an IBM PC/XT's processing power, leaving nothing for foreground processing. Then a person trying to use the server as a local workstation may discover that the system's response time is totally unacceptable. If you find yourself in such a predicament, you should stop using the server as a workstation during periods of high network traffic. You may have to dedicate the server because of performance considerations even though you have a multitasking operating system.

Multitasking on an IBM PC/XT server may present yet another problem. With the standard network operating system, the server does multitasking—but not multitasking on independent processes. Multitasking is done within processes that are working together. A multitasking environment in which any general task can run locally while another task is also running is much more complex.

If two applications are running on different PCs, the PCs treat the server as if it were a regular disk drive. The server is simply sitting and monitoring input ports, waiting for requests. If requests come at the same time, the server buffers or queues them. The server acts as the interface between the operating system and the PCs.

In its role as server, the PC/XT performs necessary duties for the network. But in a foreground/background environment, the server PC has no mechanism for protecting network operation from the foreground user because the 8088 microprocessor used by the IBM PC and PC/XT cannot partition areas of memory. Therefore, a careless foreground user can stop these network duties or interfere with them in several possible ways.

A foreground user can be running a program and have the program fail or crash. Either result freezes the foreground application or exits the application and puts the foreground into PC DOS (or whatever local operating system is in use). In this situation, most users automatically reboot the system by using Ctrl-Alt-Del. If that doesn't bring the machine back to life, they turn it off, wait a minute, then turn the power back on.

In a foreground/background environment, such actions are disastrous. Even though the foreground application has failed, the network operating system will still be running in background, supporting the network transparently. System reboots and power shutdowns are not isolated by foreground/background divisions; these actions affect everything running on the system, including the network. Rebooting the network without warning will cause unstored data to be lost and some opened files to be destroyed.

To protect against these problems, the foreground user in a multitasking system must be knowledgeable. This user must understand that safeguarding network operations is a primary duty. To carry out this duty, the foreground user should become aware of hazardous operations in order to avoid them. In other words, the knowledgeable user won't try to contend with the network but will recognize that the network takes first priority.

# 4
# Locking

For someone new to a multiuser environment, the potential hazards of information sharing may not be obvious. A careless user, however, can wreak havoc on files and possibly destroy thousands of dollars worth of data because the user is simply unaware of what takes place when files are shared.

Consider the following scenario. Carl and Frank both decide to work on the same file at the same time. Both men work for several hours. Carl finishes his work and writes the file back to disk. Then Frank finishes his work and writes the file back to disk. In many networks Carl's work will be completely overwritten when Frank stores his update. In other words, Carl's work will be lost.

A similar occurrence might take place with reservations for theater tickets. Two people call up for reservations. Agents using individual workstations check the central file. They read the reservation list simultaneously and find only four tickets available for the show. Caller 1 buys all four tickets. Caller 2, speaking to a different agent, buys the same four tickets.

In both these examples, sharing the same files results in lost or misreading of data.

## The Concept of Locking

What is needed to avoid this predicament is a reliable method for sharing the data, reading the data simultaneously by any number of users, successively manipulating the data, *but* preventing the simultaneous manipulation of the same data.

All these activities can be accomplished by *locking* files while they are being updated. In the most common example of locking, a user who wants to update a file requests the file in a "locked state," one in which no one else can use that file. When the update is completed, the lock is released, and other users can then access the file.

The term "lock" may be misleading here. The word is not used in a conventional sense to indicate a device that physically prevents entry. A lock on a file is a *semaphore,* which is a flag warning that the file is in use. The only way this semaphore will be seen is if an attempt is made to lock the file. A message will indicate that the file is already locked, in which case the user must wait until the lock is removed before a new lock will be acknowledged and set.

Even when the whole system is well designed by the programmer, it is far from secure. The most obvious danger is that untrained people will use the network without bothering to use the locking system. For this reason, users must first be told of the significance of locks and then be required to use them. Unfortunately, problems may still arise if informed users choose simply to ignore the locks. Not many solutions are available when this happens.

## Types of Locks

A good network operating system provides several types of data locks for programs using the network. The simplest type is *automatic file locking*. Here the network operating system and its locking utility are entirely transparent to programs running on a PC.

*Manual file locking* is another type of lock. With this method a user manually locks and unlocks files.

A third type of lock involves a *transaction*. The operating system manages file sharing so that sharing appears to be simultaneous to the users.

A final option is *record locking*. Only specific parts of a file—those the user wants to update—are locked. The rest of the file remains available to other users.

From a user's point of view, the easiest locking utility to use is automatic locking. The user requests files as if they were resident on a local drive. When a request is received by the operating system, the file is given to that user, and no one else can use or read the file.

With the other three types of locking, the user must be aware that the files are being shared. To some extent, users are partly responsible for protecting the data. They must therefore become aware of the hazards of sharing data and how to eliminate them.

## *Automatic File Locking*

Automatic file locking is enforced by the network operating system. This operation is typically a default mode. Unless otherwise instructed by the application, the operating system automatically locks a file for a user's private use when that user's application program opens a file. The file remains locked until the user closes it.

With automatic file locking, programs don't need to know how the network operating system works; they simply make normal requests to open files, close files, read data, and write data. The network operating system will perform all locking and unlocking. If a second user attempts to open a file already locked for use by the first user, the network operating system will offer to the second user the option of retrying or aborting.

Automatic file locking is suitable for a number of applications running on the network. Many programs, such as word processors and spreadsheets, are designed to allow only one user at a time to work on data stored in a file. As long as the data is required by only one person at a time, automatic file locking is appropriate. Software can be loaded and run from the network as if it were being run on local disks. Even though the software is designed for a single user, it does not need to be modified to run on the network.

## Manual File Locking

Manual file locking lets the user control the locking process. The entire file is locked, and the user can safely update any record within that file. Some network operating systems permit the user to lock several files at once. This feature is particularly useful when "window" programs or other coresident operations are used.

## Transactions

A transaction is the process of lock, read, modify, write, and unlock— all necessary steps for the safe use of shareable Read/Write files. This process is similar to automatic file locking in that both processes are activated automatically by the operating system. The automatic lock, however, restricts all use of the file to a single user. A transaction can be an adjunct to file reads. For example, several users may be reading a file. When one user wishes to modify the file, that user performs the transaction sequence. No other user can perform a transaction at the time of the first user's transaction. Compared to automatic file locking, a transaction typically reduces the lock time, which is the length of time other users are prevented from accessing the file.

## Record Locking

Another way to increase the amount of time during which data is available is to use record locking. With this method, only limited data (records) will be updated in the write operation of a single user. Record locking ties up only part of the information contained in a file, leaving the remaining data available to other users.

A strict pattern must be followed to use record locking properly. First, the user must identify each record in every shareable file that can possibly be affected by the updating call. After the user determines what records are needed and passes that information to the network, the appropriate records are locked. Then the user can execute the read, modify, and write cycles on those specific records.

Record locking is a more sophisticated scheme than other types of locking because other users aren't simply excluded from a particular physical area of the disk. A record-locking utility acts as a manager to coordinate multiple activities in the same area and to allocate the use of specific records to the station that "owns" them. Note that one program cannot use record locking while another program attempts to use other types of locking on the same file.

## Deadlock

Locks improperly used can cause a common problem, known as *deadlock,* in multiuser systems. A deadlock is a condition that can effectively halt network operations. Let's examine how it occurs.

Suppose that user A locks file 1 at the same time that user B locks file 2. Then, to complete a particular operation, user A needs file 2; and, conversely, user B needs file 1. Neither user can continue, however, and in a large office this deadlock can remain until the network supervisor unravels it. Obviously, the problem gets more critical when even more users become active on the network.

Deadlock can be prevented by having the first user lock all the files needed for a given update. Of course, care must be taken that this user does not monopolize network resources. Using transactional locks rather than manual file locks is one way to distribute file use more equitably.

## Locking Shareable Files

Although most files are appropriately used by only one person at a time, two kinds of files are frequently shared simultaneously. In the first, users require Read-Only access; in the second, they must have Read/Write access.

The first kind of shared file contains data that may need to be read by many stations, but this data is rarely, if ever, changed. An example of such a file is an applications program. When the network supervisor puts such a program on the network, the program should be flagged as shareable Read-Only. If the program must be altered, the supervisor can change the designation to Read/Write, make the appropriate change, then set the file back to Read-Only.

The second kind of shared file is one that contains data which may be read and written by programs running simultaneously on two or more PCs. The most common examples of this kind of file are large shared data bases and order-entry files. Running a data base in Read-Only status would prevent updating the data base. And using an automatic locking utility would be inefficient, like letting only one person at a time into a large public library. For this second kind of shared file, the network operating system needs to include one or more of the manual types of locking utilities.

To update shared files safely, you should follow a standard procedure. First, lock the file to be updated. If you use record locking, be sure to lock all the records you intend to alter. After locking the file, you must read the data you want to change. The file is then updated and written back to the network. The last operation in this cycle is for you to release the lock so that other users can access the file.

The reasons for most of these steps should be obvious by now. But let's look at an operation that may not seem necessary: the read-after-lock operation.

Let's suppose that users A and B, in a shared environment, are both reading a file. User A decides to modify the file, so he locks it, performs the update, writes the file to disk, and releases the lock. User B then decides to make a modification, unaware that the file has been modified since he last read it. User B locks the file, performs the update, and writes the file to disk.

Even though both updates were performed in a locked environment, user A's update was wiped out when user B overwrote the file. Furthermore, user B's update may be based on the old information and therefore invalid. Some new data has now been lost, and the data that was saved may be inaccurate.

This illustration demonstrates that you can safely read data simultaneously with other users. But when you wish to modify the data, you must clear your local memory to make certain you are not modifying old data. Then you must lock the file that is currently on disk, reread it so that you know what you are modifying, then make the modification. Finally, you must write the modified data back to the disk *before* you release the lock.

As already mentioned, you may occasionally want to access a file from the central network disk, then manipulate the file locally in a standalone mode. This practice should not be followed if you are working on a central data base or a shareable Read/Write file. The time you spend updating that file locally may be wasted since you must reread a *locked, centrally stored version of the data* before you can safely update that version.

Stand-alone operations should be reserved for the following files only: private files, such as notes and calendars; shareable Read-Only files, such as applications programs; and sequentially shareable files, such as spreadsheets.

Most network operating systems, along with multiuser applications software, provide several alternatives for sharing data. The network supervisor should evaluate each application run on the network and determine its best use. A written guideline explaining this use should be given to each user. The limitations of locks can be explained, and the point can be made that a lock is only a warning. The guideline should begin with a brief statement about the potential problems of using files in a shared environment. Providing such a statement should increase user compliance since users will know not only what the procedure is but also why it should be followed.

# 5
# Hardware-Independent Operating Systems

Hardware-independent network operating systems have become a major asset to local area networking. One vendor, SofTech Microsystems, accurately describes the reasons for such operating systems and the needs they should address:

1. No family of networking products can be expected to meet the needs of the entire marketplace.

2. A local area network should provide the means for its users to share applications programs, hardware resources, and information. But the network should not impose a set of management practices on the user organization.

3. Since the information system needs of an organization change very frequently, the network software products should allow very dynamic reconfiguration.

4. Networking communications hardware is available over a wide range of cost and performance characteristics, and

the capabilities of software networking products should accommodate this variety of networking hardware.

Operating systems that are not hardware-specific are going to be important to networks, just as operating systems that are manufacturer-independent are important to personal computers. A great deal of the success of personal computers can be attributed to the success of CP/M, p-System, and PC DOS because they are manufacturer-independent. The same thing will also be true for network operating systems.

In a hardware-independent network operating system, you not only can have a choice of software, but you can also choose the most appropriate hardware by considering cost, performance, and compatibility. After these decisions have been made, you can then select the operating system that will support your application. It may be that the operating system normally supplied with the network is your best choice. But now, in the maturing era of local area networking, at least you have a choice.

## Novell's NetWare

NetWare from Novell is a multiuser network operating system. It is currently available for several PC-based networks, including Novell's NetWare/S, 3Com's EtherSeries, Corvus' Omninet, Gateway Communications' G/NET, and Proteon's proNET.

NetWare uses the "file server" approach to networking. This server controls the directories and files on the network. Requests to access files are synchronized by the server so that reads and writes are done in an orderly manner.

PC DOS (V1.1. V2.0, and V2.1), MS-DOS, and CP/M-86 are supported by NetWare. No partitioning of the hard disk is required, however. All the operating systems can coexist and share the same directories and files. Printers are shared, and queues are supported. Files in the queue may be deleted, rerouted, or rearranged by priority.

NetWare also provides extensive locking utilities, including manual file locking and record locking. If no locking method is specified, a default file locking utility automatically protects users from opening files that are in the process of being updated.

In NetWare a "shell" structure is used for local operating systems. The shell sits between the application and the file server. A different shell is required for each operating system. PC DOS (or another local operating system), the shell, and the application are three distinct layers of the network system. When the application makes a DOS function call to ask for a directory on local drive A or B, the shell simply hands the request to DOS, and DOS does its normal work to display the directory of this local device.

However, if the application should request a directory of drive C, which is a shared device, the shell handles the request. It picks up the request; "packetizes" it to whatever method the hardware requires, such as Omninet or Ethernet; and sends it down to the file server. The file server does the work and sends back the information, and the shell then displays the data in a method that emulates whatever operating system you have. Here the file server is really doing the work; the PC is just requesting and imaging it. NetWare can shell CP/M-86 and PC DOS, V1.1 and V2.0. No partitions are necessary to support these various operating systems on the disk. The server supports both hierarchical and nonhierarchical files without partitions.

With NetWare you can create what are called search directories, which are searched sequentially. For example, if you call up WordStar and it's not found in your personal directory, the operating system will automatically look for the program in the first search directory. If WordStar is not in the first directory, the system will search the second and third directories, and so on. You can have up to 16 search directories, with different security levels for each one.

## SofTech Microsystems' Liaison

SofTech Microsystems' Liaison is a media-independent network operating system with full object-code compatibility between dissimilar personal computers. This network is based on the p-System portable operating system and supports only microcomputers running p-System.

On the Liaison a shared disk can become a central storage device for all applications programs. These programs can be accessed by all PCs on the network. Through p-System a Liaison network can include a diverse mixture of personal computers, all capable of talking to one another.

The system is portable across a wide range of local area network communications hardware.

Because Liaison is a member of the p-System product family, this network shares many of the qualities of p-System software. Applications programs for p-System are fully portable. Object-code applications can run without changes being needed on different personal computers. The Liaison operating system and multiuser software can similarly run on most networked PCs. In addition, a Liaison disk server can manage a library of programs that may be run on any personal computer on the network.

Features of Liaison include multitasking, virtual memory management, and automatic linking. Disk and printer server software programs can run on any computer in the network or on several machines simultaneously, depending on load requirements.

The disk server software manages disk storage on the network. The server is designed to provide shared access to the disk for any networked PC and can manage up to 480M of direct access storage. Each disk server can support up to 30 volumes.

Actually, the disk server is two programs: a server program run on the PC that acts as server for the hard disk, and a share utility that each networked PC runs in order to access the volumes managed by the server. A locking mechanism, used to coordinate disk access, allows programs to obtain exclusive use of files to prevent simultaneous updating.

The print server software manages the printers attached to the network. Each server can support up to two printers. Printer access may be on an exclusive basis, may be granted to a requesting workstation, or may be on a queued basis in which the printers' services are shared. Statistics and monitoring facilities are supported by the print server.

Any topology is suitable for Liaison. Essentially a peer-to-peer operating system, Liaison also supports either distributed or centralized network control. Under Liaison, programs consist of "clients" and "servers." A client is a program that uses services, and a server is a program that provides the services. In the multitasking environment of Liaison, a PC workstation can concurrently support both client and server functions.

Three types of services are performed: locator services, which establish both the addresses of devices and a connection; channel services, which support communication; and socket services, which may be used by programmers to reconfigure the network.

As part of the network monitoring statistics, a disk server records the total number of I/O requests received, the number of I/O errors that occurred, the number of requests by type (write, read, lock, etc.), the number of mounts and dismounts, and the start/stop time for the recording period.

Liaison supports the development and execution of distributed applications. A file server, disk server, or print server is essentially one type of application—an application that shares a device.

With Liaison a central control facility can be constructed, and users can be required to log onto the network to do the procedural tasks that are normal in time-sharing systems and most local area networks. But Liaison is primarily aimed at decentralized processing. Many local area network applications can and should be simplified. Liaison was designed as an open communications link, like a telephone system. Some controls are available for access, but these are implemented only as needed by the application.

To use the Liaison operating system, each networked personal computer must have at least one disk drive and 128K of memory. Also with Liaison, software maintenance costs are reduced because only one copy of each software program is required per network. Liaison runs on Omninet networks only.

## Digital Research's DR Net

DR Net from Digital Research is a portable network operating system that currently supports four local operating systems: CP/M, Concurrent CP/M, CP/M-86, and MP/M-II. DR Net runs on Ethernet, Omninet, and ARCnet networks.

One feature of DR Net is that multiple requesters can run on the same systems. For instance, under Concurrent CP/M-86, you can have virtual consoles all running network applications. You can configure a particular network environment so that drive F can be drive B on server X, and so on. Once you've reconfigured, the network is transparent.

Because a multitasking operating system operates as a requester, servers can be dropped anywhere on the network. The result is a "serverless" network, which is also hardware-independent. Every PC workstation acts both as a file server and a requester. A centralized resource, once required to do networking, is no longer needed. But if the user wants a centralized resource that controls a large hard disk, expensive letter-quality printers, and high-speed printers, then this kind of resource is also configurable with DR Net.

Like CP/Net, DR Net has a password system for logging onto a particular node. Also available is a standard password system for files, which is already used in Concurrent CP/M. In this password system, users must specify a password to open a file, modify it, or delete it, depending on the level of protection. In addition, DR Net offers another level of protection: the "private drive" concept. This level is optionally available to the local user. Users can protect specified disk drives by marking them "private," and then these drives cannot be accessed over the network. If an unauthorized user tries, the user will get a select error (as if the drive weren't there). DR Net, then, provides three levels of protection.

Under one configuration, each PC is a network manager. Alternately, the PCs can be configured so that any one PC can be only a workstation, only a dedicated server, or both a workstation and server simultaneously. The choice is up to the user.

At present, DR Net runs Concurrent CP/M-86. A CP/M-86 version will soon be released that will perform the requester function but not file service. In addition, Digital Research plans to support the old 8-bit nodes under Concurrent CP/M. Users will be able to mix 16-bit and 8-bit processors in their networks.

A print spooler is a highly useful network utility because it relieves the print server's CPU from the job of serving the printer directly. The print server can send a file to the print spooler in a high-speed file transfer operation and let the print spooler handle the slow process of feeding the printer.

The Digital Research spooler provides considerable versatility. It supports multiple printers on the network. The spooler also lets the user select how print jobs will be assigned. A particular printer can be specified, or the job can be flagged to go to the next available printer.

If you already have 3Com's EtherSeries set up in-house, you might consider DR Net because it provides a completely homogenous system. No special file servers or print servers are needed on DR Net.

DR Net supports multitasking network servers and a multitasking file system as well. A user can share files and do data base programs that can automatically update records in a cohesive manner. Record locking and automatic file locking are also available.

With DR Net, locking can be used to reserve the file for updating. When it is reserved, nobody else can read or write the file. Files are not listed as shareable, but the user can open them in a shareable mode. When a user updates a file that was opened as shareable, an automatic lock is placed on the file to prevent others from updating or even reading the file. As soon as the update is completed, the lock is removed, and others may use the file.

DR Net also has network status utilities. These keep track of the number and names of users logged into the network, any alterations to drive paths, and the names of files that are being updated and by whom. The idea is to make the system look as much as possible like a gigantic multiuser system with many CPUs and printers, all accessible from any workstation. The investment is nothing more than the cost of connecting the network.

A network operating system is foremost a distributed file system. It allows you to access transparently any drive in the network and any file on any drive in the network through existing applications programs, with no additional modification to the programs. The only thing the user must do is to preconfigure the system. It can be either preconfigured by the vendor or dynamically configured by the user.

## Lantech Systems' uNETix-DFS

Lantech Systems' uNETix-DFS is based on the uNETix operating system. uNETix-DFS is hardware-independent and currently runs on Ethernet, Omninet, and PerComNet. All versions of UNIX and PC DOS are compatible with uNETix.

Any user in the network can use data held in any location on the network without knowing the data's address. As a distributed network operating system, uNETix-DFS supports virtual files.

uNETix-DFS is also a multitasking system. Multiple window capability at each local PC permits data to be transferred and applications software to be integrated.

Lantech Systems' uNETix-DFS is a distributed file system that allows users to access files and devices on other systems in the network. Using the REMOTE MOUNT command, users can share peripherals, including printers and modems.

uNETix-DFS is fully compatible with the Plexus UNIX System Network Operating System. This compatibility permits the user to expand a microcomputer local area network to include Plexus minicomputers, without any software modifications.

Users can access remote devices transparently, as if they were local. A remote hard disk, for example, can be used with the same commands as a local disk. Single-user applications software can be run without change.

Finally, password and login routines protect networked data. A system security scheme protects each file and peripheral, and ownership of files determines user access. The modular design of uNETix-DFS allows the addition of new network services in the future.

# 6
# Evaluation

In the preceding chapters the essential features of the local area network were discussed. By now you should have a basic understanding of these features, as well as the hardware and software components that can be combined to create a local area network.

The OSI model, protocols, and access methods were also discussed earlier. These are complex technical topics, and even communications engineers seldom agree on which strategies are superior. If evaluating these topics is a prerequisite to selecting the right network, then the job is indeed difficult.

Networks are often evaluated from a technician's point of view. From this perspective many complex aspects of controversial technical issues must be resolved. But many of these are simply unimportant to the manager/buyer. Moreover, they tend to obscure the issues that are important. The alternate approach to networks is to ignore all the technical aspects and make a choice on functionality alone. In other words, if it works, it's okay.

The best approach, however, lies somewhere between these two extremes. The local area network shopper has many networks from which to choose, all with a wide range of features and prices. In most cases, the relative importance of these features is decided by the applications needed and the environment in which the network will be used. The right choice of network should be based on an assessment of features, weighted by their value to the user.

Network selection is a building process that starts with a detailed definition of applications that the network must handle immediately. You'll want to ensure as much as possible that the various terminals, word processors, workstations, and personal computers can communicate with each other, with the mainframe, and with peripherals. The networking plan should specify the kinds of personal computers, peripherals, interfaces, and applications that are common to the organization.

A growth plan of the organization will identify future applications. A physical description of the problems relating to the environment must also be developed. In effect, you decide actual and potential needs for both the present and the future. These criteria can then be used to make a network selection checklist.

# The Plan

An organization must have a plan for networking. This plan should begin by stating what the organization wants, how the organization will benefit, and what the benefits are worth. The plan thus becomes a benchmark for comparing the reality with the expectation. Finally, the plan, along with its goals, must be approved by management so that the evaluation process has a positive, defined terminus.

Without laying this kind of groundwork, you may spend valuable time in studying the field, evaluating products, and selecting vendors, only to have the choice overturned at the last minute. Because networking is continually evolving, new products and alternatives are announced almost weekly. Of course, next week's "miracle" will be even better than last week's.

# Access Methods

Most local area network architectures include a shared transmission medium, similar to a telephone party line. Although the cable is shared, messages cannot be sent simultaneously. If two messages should get on the cable at the same time, a collision will occur, necessitating the retransmission of both messages.

Access methods have been developed to govern the orderly, sequential use of the cable. Two principal access methods used in IBM PC local area networks are available. Both perform adequately and have been published as standards by the IEEE. In selecting an appropriate access method, the prospective buyer needs to consider three things: compatibility, support, and performance.

Carrier Sense Multiple Access with Collision Detection (CSMA-CD) is one of the two access methods. CSMA-CD is an integral part of the widely used Ethernet, a mainframe network protocol designed by Xerox. Ethernet was adapted to IBM PC local area networks by 3Com. Compatible systems are used by Ungermann-Bass, Interlan, and Tecmar. Ethernet-like systems with CSMA-CD are used by Corvus Systems, Orchid Technology, Gateway Communications, and Destek.

Token passing is generally associated with ARCnet, a mainframe network developed by Datapoint. Nestar Systems developed a token-passing network for the IBM PC, and Davong uses token passing in its network.

Besides the IBM PC-based networks, there are, of course, many other local area networks. These typically use either CSMA-CD or token passing.

In performance CSMA-CD has a slight edge during low-traffic conditions. Token passing is faster when network traffic is high. Thus, a word-processing shop may prefer CSMA-CD, but a manufacturing facility may want a token-passing network. However, the differences in network performance resulting from the choice of an access scheme are insignificant in most applications.

Compatibility and support are important evaluation criteria for every facet of computing, including access schemes. If an organization is currently using one access method—say, on its mainframe side—then staying with that method will be simpler and less expensive when the organization selects a local area network. CSMA-CD is generally more widespread than token passing. Likewise, more CSMA-CD hardware, such as gateways and bridges, is available.

## Diagnostics and Control

A network differs from a single stand-alone personal computer in that the network's environment is always changing. New users may be added, peripherals may be upgraded, peak loads may be adjusted, and new applications software may be tested and adopted. A broad range of performance is possible in any given local area network, depending on how these changes are implemented.

Repair and maintenance of the network are made much easier by diagnostic routines. Good diagnostics can spot faults in the network, report where they are occurring, and suggest why they have occurred.

Local area network diagnostics are still in the embryonic stage, but routines are developing fast. Network managers must be able to monitor the network and assess its performance on a frequent basis. This monitoring is an essential prerequisite to spotting performance degradation and correcting it. A record of who accesses the network can be used for everything from performance statistics to bill-backs to security monitoring.

Diagnostics and control are of little importance on very small networks with up to five workstations. As the network grows and supports increasing traffic, these features gain accordingly in significance.

Diagnostics, of course, are only a first step in repair work. Knowing who will actually perform the needed repairs is essential before the repairs are made. Repair options generally fall into three categories: repairs supplied by the retailer, a third-party, and the manufacturer. Since downtime on a network may have a serious negative impact on an organization, the repair options become a major factor in network evaluation.

## Cost

Present technology allows the building of a local area network that rates high on every performance measurement. Features that are listed as future capabilities, such as video and voice transmissions, can be implemented now. But the cost of such a network makes it impractical at this time.

This same kind of price/performance relationship extends to the local area networks evaluated in this book. As a general rule, the more expensive the network, the better its performance. Beyond that, performance of installed networks can almost always be enhanced at a cost. (Network performance is discussed in Chapter 10.)

Cost is a balancing criterion. It points up the importance of identifying needs before you go shopping for a network.

## Documentation

At first, local area networks were sold by manufacturers' representatives who sometimes worked through local retailers. Today, a direct sales effort is impractical because the market is larger, distributorships have grown, and networks are more refined. Usually, a buyer simply visits a local computer store and picks up a network, as if the buyer were getting just another multifunction card.

The photocopies of designer-written notes that once served as documentation won't do the job any longer. Network users need detailed instructions on every phase from installation to application. Installation, in particular, should be thoroughly explained, since a poor installation can cause intermittent problems that plague the network and eventually necessitate rewiring.

After reducing the field to a couple of network choices, the prospective network buyer should get the user's and technical manuals for each remaining candidate. Users who will be writing their own applications must have this data before making a decision. Other users will also find the manuals useful, primarily to build application scenarios and to evaluate the power and friendliness of the network.

## Environment

As part of the evaluation procedure, the planner should draw the proposed physical layout of the network, stipulating where each PC, mass storage device, printer, and other pieces of equipment will be placed. The planner should also draw the path that the wiring will need to follow to conform to possible topologies.

If the wiring must pass areas of high electrical interference, such as an elevator shaft, air conditioner system, or electrical transformer, specially shielded wiring may be required. Hostile conditions, like high heat or humidity, may necessitate special connectors, whose availability should be determined.

In terms of physical size, the local area network adds very little network-specific equipment. Still, the planner will need to make sure that everything required for the network will fit into the available space.

The most likely problem to arise is distance limitation. Distances vary greatly among networks and may be sufficient cause to eliminate certain networks from consideration. The vendor should help verify that the proposed installation is actually possible and that the end-to-end distances do not exceed the network's capabilities.

## Topology

The topology, or layout, of a local area network is a significant feature in the evaluation process. Topology affects flexibility, reliability, and cost of installation.

A general requirement of local area networks is flexibility. Devices may be added or removed on all networks, but some topologies make this procedure easier and less expensive than others. The advantage largely depends on the particular installation; candidate networks should be measured against the proposed layout, including possible expansion configurations.

Networks that require dedicated cables for individual devices are usually more expensive and more complicated to wire. Dedicated cables offer higher performance, however, since the line does not need to be shared. Closed topologies, such as Rings, tend to be less reliable than open topologies.

## Interface Requirements

The networks discussed in this book are designed for the IBM PC, PC/XT, and PC compatibles. Being part of this large family guarantees interface compatibility with machines in the mainstream of computing technology. Virtually all common interface protocols are available as add-on options to the IBM PC. As long as the network architecture permits the integration of these add-ons into the network, interfaces should present no problem.

If the network includes its own dedicated processor, that processor's interfaces should be compatible with desired peripherals. For example, if parallel interface printers will be part of the network, but network hardware supports only serial interfaces, some additional expense may be incurred in making an adaptation.

Regardless of any other consideration, the network should conform to the International Standards Organization's Open Systems Interconnection (OSI) model. This conformity is a prerequisite for future expansion and interconnection among networks.

## Internetting

Since most people have little experience with internetting, this capability may be overlooked in a list of features desired in a network. Yet internetting, or communication among networks, is a powerful, new application with many advantages.

Two "roads" lead to internetting. Either the network protocols are close enough to let the networks talk directly, or protocol converters and gateway devices are built to provide necessary translation. Internetting between a local area and a wide area network usually requires the gateway approach.

Gateways have a range of capabilities. The best gateway devices can pass a high percentage of application functionality along with the basic information. Gateways also have enough resident memory and intelligence to manage predicted data flow.

## Network Cabling

Cable type helps to determine both data rates and network range. Susceptibility to interference is wholly cable-dependent.

On large networks especially, the overall cost is heavily affected by the choice of cable. Baseband coaxial cable, for instance, is about five times as expensive as twisted-pair cable. Occasionally, cables that are already in place before the network is installed can be used. When telephone wires are available, they may be used on twisted-pair networks. Offices replacing 3270 terminals with personal computers are able to use the same 3270 baseband coax (RG-62) on some local area networks.

## Network Speed

Any network user wants the network to have good response time. Ideally, a network should come close to providing the same performance as a local hard disk. Network speed is usually given as raw bit rate. All networks that range from 1Mbit/sec to 10Mbit/sec are potentially capable of satisfactory speed. However, data rate is only one of the factors in network speed. The amount of traffic carried by the network can bring the system to a virtual standstill.

Some networks have network interface cards equipped with on-board coprocessors and memory. The coprocessor can unload some or all of the network processing from the PC's microprocessor. The additional memory can be used for speeding up disk transfers. These features can significantly improve network performance and reduce the effects of heavy traffic.

Some networks, notably IBM's PC Cluster and PBX systems, have data rates under 1Mbit/sec. These systems are useful for batch transfers of data but will not provide the transparent access to shared peripherals expected on a local area network.

## Fault Tolerance

The fault tolerance of a network refers to its ability to function even when part of the system fails. The worst arrangement is one in which all the devices and the network become one interdependent circuit, much like a string of Christmas tree lights. When one component goes, everything goes.

Fortunately, most local area networks are not that sensitive. A PC workstation can go down, but the rest of the network will continue to operate. Most networks, however, do have at least two points of failure: the network cable and the machine that runs the server software. These points of failure can be neutralized only with redundant systems, such as two cables in parallel or two servers. The additional cost of redundant components must be weighed against the potential loss due to network outage.

## Data Security

Cable and how it is installed are important for local area network security. Signal radiation can be limited by improved shielding. Cables may be routed and encased to make unauthorized taps difficult to accomplish. The most fundamentally secure type of cable is fiber-optic cable. This cable neither radiates signals nor can be tapped. All other types of cable are easily tapped, but certain grades of cable do keep radiation down to secure levels. The U.S. government rates specific cables according to their signal radiation. If data security is a factor in network evaluation, the network vendor should be asked to furnish evidence that the proposed cable passes government standards.

Network software may provide security features, such as passwords and multilevel access on a file-by-file basis. A wide range of security features are available on network operating systems and applications software. These features can furnish excellent protection against casual access and opportunistic intrusions. But to combat more serious threats, a potential network buyer should consider encryption and physical security devices from third-party sources.

## Real Products

One of the most important ratings of a network is the "reality" rating. Does the network exist now? Can you see one actually installed? Is it on the shelves? Most of the technology used in local area networks is well established. The actual implementation has often lagged behind. Virtually every maker of local area networks "intends" to have an electronic mail package, a mainframe gateway, an Ethernet gateway, and record locking. These manufacturers plan to extend their support to CP/M-86, p-System, and UNIX, and to machines other than the IBM PC and PC compatibles. Intentions are to support voice and video as well as data transmissions. The fact is, though, that the timetable for these introductions is usually a moving target.

In the meantime a network should be evaluated according to its demonstrable features. If your network must support both the DEC Rainbow and the IBM PC, and if these machines must be able to share data, then you should have these capabilities demonstrated during the presentation.

## Multiple Machine Types

An office with many different incompatible personal computers is possibly the most questionable candidate for networking. Why bring in a network if not everybody can use it? Remember that using the network means more than simply being able to share peripherals; users should also be able to share files and to communicate.

Most local area networks support one or more computers with expansion buses that are not IBM compatible; that is, they do not accept the same network interface card used on the PC. But only a few networks have operating systems that permit information sharing among dissimilar systems.

## Applications

One goal of network manufacturers is to enable any software that can run on the stand-alone PC to run on their networks also. This goal is not always possible since some single-user applications software cannot be accommodated by particular network operating systems. The same incompatibility is true of multiuser software. In fact, very little multiuser software can be used on every network because of network operating system idiosyncrasies. Just as in the selection of a personal computer, the prospective network buyer should make certain, through actual use, that the network can handle all desired applications.

## Multitasking

Some local area networks require a dedicated network processor. This processor may be a proprietary machine built just for this purpose, or an IBM PC or PC/XT. Other networks permit the server PC to do multitasking and use part of its processing power as a local workstation. If multitasking is considered an important network feature, the prospective buyer should make certain that the load on the server is low enough for it to be used as a workstation, too. As a general rule, for small networks with less than five or six PCs, multitasking is considered useful. For larger networks, it often is not.

# 7
# Leading Networks

Network features change dramatically with daily announcements of new products and features. The descriptions that follow are not intended to indicate merely the current features available on local area networks. You should get that information from the vendor at the time you are considering a purchase.

The purpose of these descriptions is threefold: (1) to provide a list of the major local area network producers, (2) to show how various network features are implemented on specific networks, and (3) to discuss the basic characteristics of most networks. These characteristics are not likely to change, and a discussion of them may help you to select the network features you would like to examine further.

In some descriptions a feature may be discussed in depth, such as how the hardware layers are implemented. In another description, only the name of the protocol used in the hardware layer may be provided. This approach eliminates redundancy.

3Com
1390 Shorebird Way
Mountain View, California 94043
(415) 961-9602

3Com's network, EtherSeries, follows the Ethernet standard (IEEE-802.3). The bit rate is 10Mbit/sec, and access is CSMA-CD. Software includes disk sharing, print sharing, and electronic mail. An SNA gateway is available.

The operating system presents networked devices, such as disks and other computers, as additional physical devices on the PC. To applications software, all these devices look like the same machine. During network configuration each device is given its own drive letter. Volumes can be as large as 32M. Three types of volumes are available: private, public Read-Only, and shared Read/Write. Volumes can be assigned their own passwords so that they can be shared with selected users.

*Fig. 7.1. 3Com EtherSeries. Photograph courtesy of 3Com Corp.*

Part of the EtherSeries design includes a network server, which manages all network resources, including volumes on the shared hard disk and printers. Multiple servers can be used on the network, with three types of servers being supported. The IBM PC/XT server can handle about eight users on the network. IBM PC/XT software supports multitasking so that the server can also be a workstation. The AP server is 8086-based and can serve about 30 users and manage 60M of disk storage. Large networks can use a DEC VAX as server.

The performance of Ethernet is high in bits per second, addressing, and data integrity. The speed, 10Mbit/sec, is one of the performance measurements. Because Ethernet has 48-bit addresses, which are set when it is manufactured, workstations are identified by a 48-bit number unique to any Ethernet card, including those on other Ethernet networks. A 32-bit CRC on all the packets provides error detection. All these features give Ethernet room to grow. As a 30-year standard, Ethernet has been built to handle VAXs, 4300s, and, with EtherSeries, IBM PCs. Right now, the 10Mbit/sec speed is more useful to larger machines and larger networks. As faster PCs with 80186 and 80286 processors become available, these new machines will also be able to exploit 10Mbit/sec.

3Com puts a packet buffer on the network interface card so that the IBM PC itself does not have to generate or handle data at 10Mbit/sec. The arrival or exit of the data goes through the packet buffer on the controller. This procedure is necessary to help the processor keep up with 10Mbit/sec.

EtherSeries permits IBM PC users to store information on a shared hard disk. The disk is divided into volumes that are like diskettes in function. The volumes are created with EtherSeries commands and linked by the user to a drive specifier on the PC. After the link is established, the volumes can be used with DOS or application programs just as if the volumes were diskettes. Fifteen commands let the manager create and maintain volumes and users; log in and out of the network; create, modify, and delete volumes; link volumes; create, modify, and delete users; and list a directory of users or volumes. An on-line help facility describes each of the commands.

Ethernet topology is thought of as being a bus. In fact, its topology has two variations. One is the classical Ethernet in which the coax runs down the center of the corridor with transceivers tapping into it and a transceiver cable dropping down into the office. On 3Com's PC products, a variation has been introduced in which the coax goes directly to the PC, thereby eliminating the separate transceiver and transceiver cable. The transceiver is placed on the network interface card. This variation is more convenient and also reduces cost.

Both topological variations have particular uses. For longer distances among larger numbers of machines, you may prefer the classical approach, which is somewhat more expensive. If you have a few machines in close proximity in a work group or department, you may prefer the second option, which is called thin Ethernet. This is 1/4-inch RG-58 cable that permits cable runs up to 305 meters. Thick Ethernet (classical Ethernet) is electronically identical but permits cable lengths up to 1,000 meters, using 3Com transceivers.

Printer sharing is accomplished through EtherPrint, the print server software. EtherPrint spools print requests so that each request is accepted even while the printer is in use. Jobs are printed on a first-come-first-served basis. Because jobs can be listed on the server monitor, the user can see where a job is and when it will be picked up. Jobs also can be deleted from the queue.

EtherMail is 3Com's electronic mail program. Messages that have been received can be answered, printed, filed, forwarded, or forwarded with annotation. A full-screen text editor is part of the EtherMail package, and a remote mail facility is also available. Using remote mail, a modem-equipped remote PC can link into the network by telephone.

3Com's EtherSeries is readily available from national retailers and is shipped reliably. 3Com has established nationwide service through Xerox's Americare Service Program. Americare can service all of 3Com's products, including boards and servers. Maintenance contracts are available.

Corvus Systems, Inc.
2029 O'Toole Avenue
San Jose, California 95131
(408) 946-7700

Corvus' network, Omninet, is a low-priced, moderate-performance network that permits IBM PCs to share a Corvus Winchester hard disk, files on the disk, and printers. PCs can also communicate with each other.

With over 60,000 network nodes already installed, Omninet is one of the most widely used networks. It was one of the first PC networks, a fact that has helped it gain a large installed base. Omninet also has considerable third-party support, both in hardware and software, with gateways, network operating system software, electronic mail, and other applications.

This network uses a proprietary 1Mbit/sec protocol with CSMA handling contention. No collision detection mechanism is used; however, a randomized transmit start time is implemented on each station to reduce the probability that two PCs will transmit simultaneously. Omninet's bus topology permits easy attachment or detachment of devices anywhere along the network. The medium is twisted-pair cable, with cable runs up to 4,000 feet.

A transporter card provides Omninet's interface, which plugs into any available slot in the PC. Network collision avoidance, error detection, error recovery, and duplicate-packet detection are handled by the transporter. Thus, overhead on the PC is decreased. Omninet uses a positive acknowledgment scheme to verify message receipt. If the acknowledgment is not received by the sending station, the transporter continues to retransmit until acknowledgment is received or a specified number of retries have been performed.

Any PC or peripheral connected to Omninet must be equipped with a transporter. This transporter has its own intelligence, a Motorola 6801 microprocessor, and a gate-array integrated circuit to control high-speed data transfers. Because of the 1Mbit/sec speed, which approximates the speed of the PC, data buffering is not mandatory on the network interface card. Network control is distributed on Omninet. Control is temporarily taken by any transporter with a message to send, as soon as the network is available.

The servers on Omninet are dedicated machines made by Corvus. At present, Omninet offers a disk server, a print server, and a gateway server for SNA.

The print server is a Z80-based device with two serial ports and one parallel port. This server also functions as a time server, spooling the requests it receives. When the server receives information to be printed, the server starts on that job and continues to poll the network for more requests.

Corvus has taken the base of its Concept computer and used that 68000 machine as a gateway box. The SNA gateway performs the functions of a 3274 cluster controller.

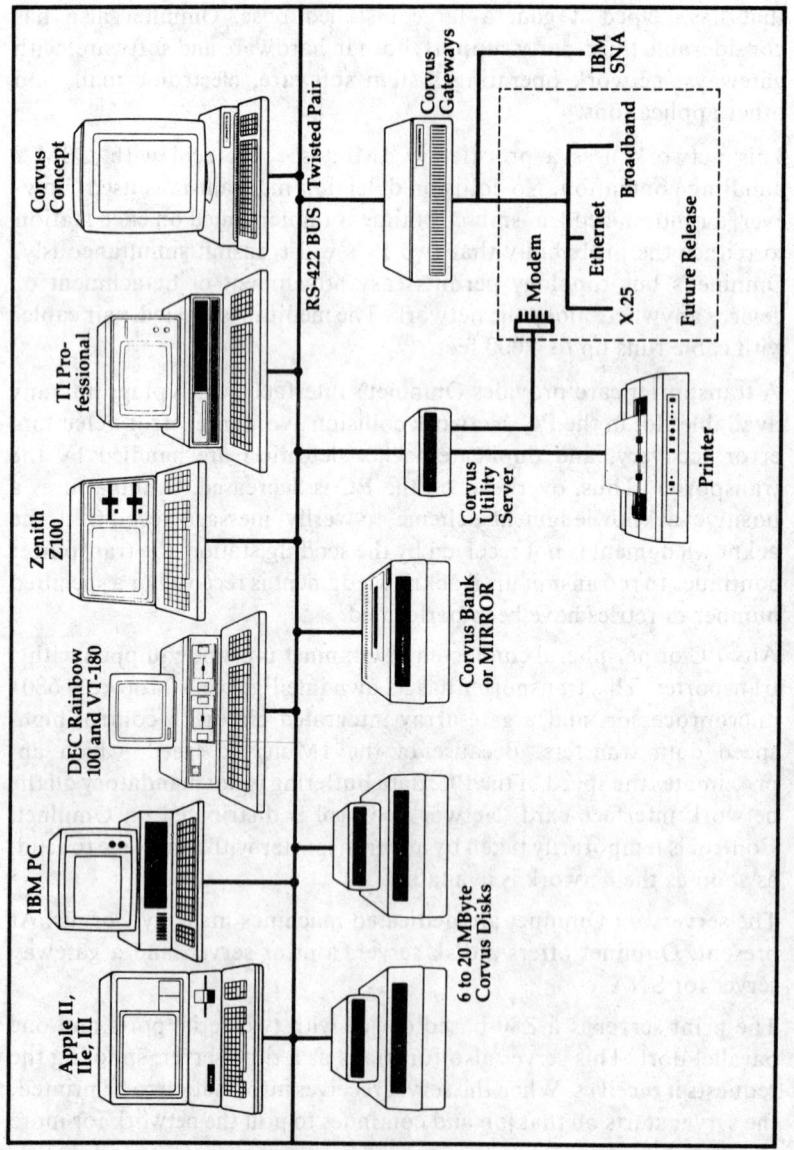

Fig. 7.2. Corvus Omninet. Reprinted by permission of Corvus Systems, Inc.

One of Omninet's most significant capabilities is that it supports many different machines on the same network: IBM PC, Corvus Concept, Apple II and III, DEC Rainbow, and TI Professional. Each computer uses its own single-user operating system without modification. These computers can also share peripherals on Omninet.

To a limited degree, Omninet permits not only peripheral sharing, but also information sharing between dissimilar operating systems. The hard disk is divided into volumes. Access to these volumes is restricted by passwords, with Read/Write or Read-Only privilege granted to the password holder. Current Corvus Winchesters are available in 6M, 11M, and 20M versions. These hard disks can be daisy-chained in any combination of four drives for up to 80M per disk server.

The Destek Group
830 C E. Evelyn Avenue
Sunnyvale, California 94086
(408) 737-7211

DESNET, from Destek, is a 2Mbit/sec network. It is configured in a bus topology and provided with CSMA-CD for contention. Destek has network application software that provides capabilities for transferring messages, records, or files throughout the network; and sharing common resources, such as printers or large disks. One or more stations may be designated as a central file server.

The standard medium is RG-59/U coaxial cable in baseband mode. The maximum cable length is 2,000 meters. An optional external tap will allow broadband, fiber optics, or internal modem media interconnections to be made.

Networked devices are attached to the network through a network interface card. The card contains a Z80A microprocessor. On-board firmware in the card implements most of layers 1 and 2 of the OSI model. Statistical information is maintained on each station, allowing the implementation of sophisticated network monitoring functions. Using the card and DESNET software, an IBM PC/XT or any PC on the network can be designated as a server.

Supported operating systems include PC DOS, MS-DOS, CP/M, and UNIX. DESNET allows device sharing and information sharing among these systems. The DESNET operating system, called LANOS, sits on

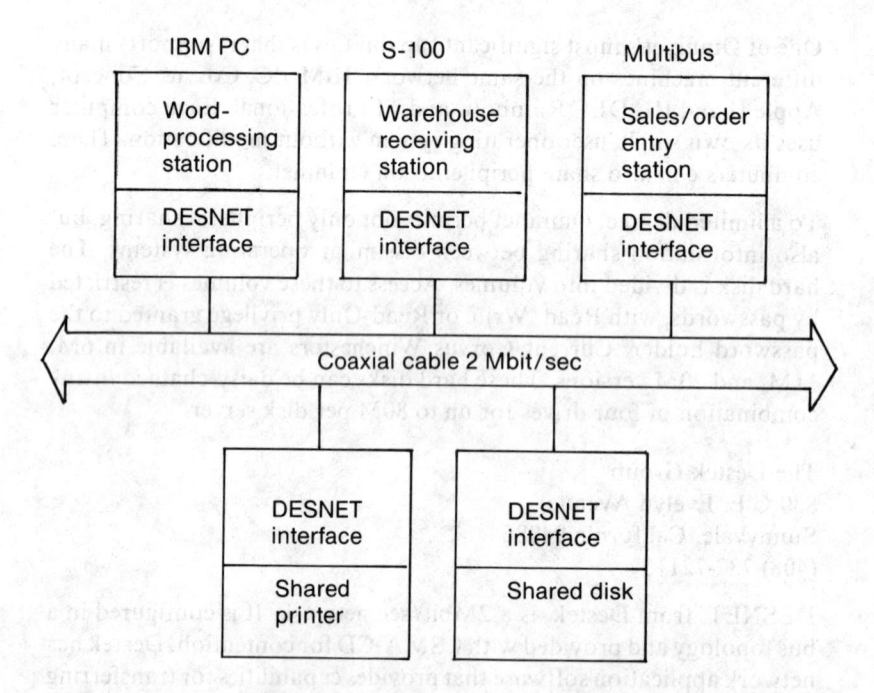

```
        IBM PC              S-100              Multibus
   ┌──────────────┐   ┌──────────────┐   ┌──────────────┐
   │    Word-     │   │  Warehouse   │   │ Sales/order  │
   │ processing   │   │  receiving   │   │    entry     │
   │   station    │   │   station    │   │   station    │
   ├──────────────┤   ├──────────────┤   ├──────────────┤
   │   DESNET     │   │   DESNET     │   │   DESNET     │
   │  interface   │   │  interface   │   │  interface   │
   └──────┬───────┘   └──────┬───────┘   └──────┬───────┘
◄─────────┴──────────────────┴──────────────────┴─────────►
                  Coaxial cable 2 Mbit/sec
◄─────────────┬──────────────────┬────────────────────────►
       ┌──────┴───────┐   ┌──────┴───────┐
       │   DESNET     │   │   DESNET     │
       │  interface   │   │  interface   │
       ├──────────────┤   ├──────────────┤
       │   Shared     │   │   Shared disk│
       │   printer    │   │              │
       └──────────────┘   └──────────────┘
```

*Fig. 7.3. Destek DESNET. Reprinted by permission of The Destek Group.*

top of the local operating system and provides the networking services. Networked resources are made to look like local devices so that existing single-user applications can run on the network.

Destek produces a number of local area networking board-level products for different processors or processor buses (such as the S-100, IBM PC, and Multibus). In addition, the company has a general purpose Network Interface Server that has an RS-232, IEEE 488, RS-422, or parallel interface available for it. These networking products allow the user to tie a wide range of dissimilar computers and peripherals to the same network.

With DESNET the user can connect processors of dissimilar architecture, thereby implementing a fully distributed, data processing network.

Novell, Inc.
1170 North Industrial Park Drive
Orem, Utah 84057
(800) 453-1267

The Novell network comes in two configurations: a Star topology called NetWare S and a bus topology called NetWare X. NetWare S has a dedicated 68000-based network server that can connect as many as 24 PCs. The server can be configured with from 256K to 1M of RAM; and a hard disk, with between 20M and 120M of storage. NetWare S uses shielded twisted-pair cable with a maximum range of 1,000 meters.

In addition, the network processor uses separate Texas Instruments 99-125 16-bit processors, one for communications and one shared between every two PCs in the network. This arrangement not only helps the 68000 keep up the speed, but also does not overburden the 68000 in communications.

NetWare S uses a Star topology and runs at .5Mbit/sec per station. This speed measurement is deceptive. In a Star topology the speed is calculated on a dedicated cable; no overhead exists for contention or for sharing. The dedicated cable, the 68000 processor, the TI 99-125 processors, and features of the operating system all enable the response time on NetWare S to be one of the fastest of any local area network.

Novell also sells NetWare X, with a speed of 1.43Mbit/sec and bus topology. NetWare X, which uses an IBM PC/XT as the server, must be configured with a minimum of 256K of RAM. The cable is RG-59/U coaxial, with a maximum length of 1,300 meters.

Netware S has five printer ports, all serial, from 50 to 19.2K baud. Netware X has three printer ports. One port is parallel, and two are serial.

NetWare provides multilevel password and privilege protection. The disk storage file structure is hierarchical. The levels are designated volume, root, and subdirectories. A user can have up to 7 volumes, 256 roots, and unlimited subdirectories. Commonly used files can reside in a default area. If a user requests a file, the operating system will go first to the area indicated. If the file is not there, the operating system will automatically search the default area.

The NetWare operating system makes a shell over the local operating system. This shell provides a translation service back to the file server.

## NetWare/S

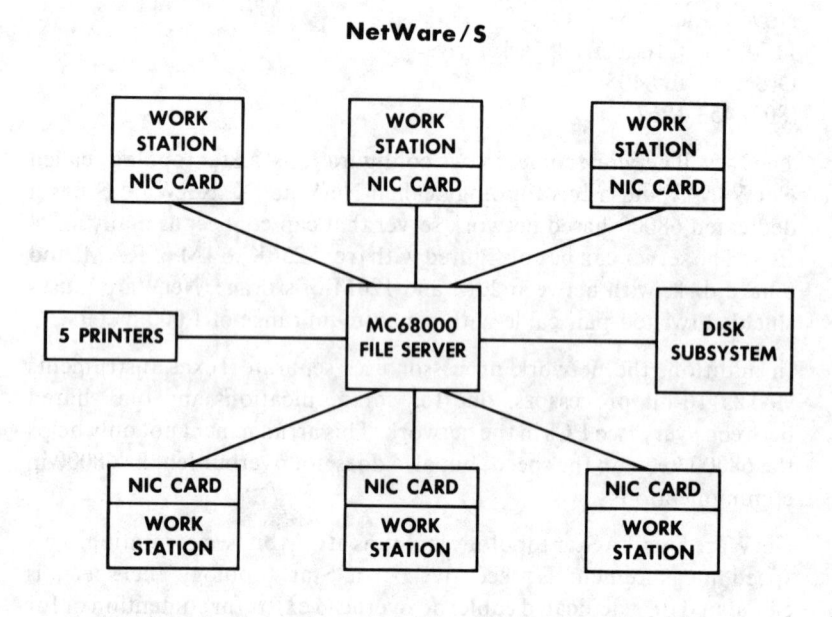

*Fig. 7.4. Novell, Inc., offers two network topologies. Reprinted by permission of Novell, Inc.*

In this way, a shell can be provided for dissimilar local operating systems; any systems can share and communicate on the same network. At present, Novell has shells for PC DOS V1.1, V1.2, and V2.0; CP/M; and CP/M-86.

A system's administrator is provided with considerable control in the NetWare operating system. Included are file usage, printer queue, and user access control. A monitor on the network processor can give continual file and status reports. The activity of each PC on the network is displayed on the monitor.

Password and privilege levels can be set up simply or very specifically to accommodate different user/file authorizations. Shared files are provided with an automatic locking system to protect against concurrent access problems. Manual file and record locks are also available.

NetWare's electronic mail is a full-service package. A user can receive, forward, forward with annotation, delete, and send messages. In addition, an express mail feature uses the PC's status line to notify users that mail is waiting. The mail editor is a full-screen editor.

Novell offers a factory service contract, part of which guarantees 24-hour turnaround for equipment sent to the factory for repair. Customers who elect not to be covered by the service contract may still get factory service. On-site, third-party service is provided by General Electric Instrumentation Service Co., which is available in most major cities.

Gateway Communications
16782 Redhill Ave.
Irvine, CA 92714
(714) 261-0762

G/NET is a low-cost but moderately high performance network. Its data rate is 1.43Mbit/sec, and the network uses a bus topology.

G/NET puts no overhead onto the personal computer itself. The G/NET board has its own CPU and memory. Network management functions are done on the board, and no cycle time or memory are required from the PC's processor. The board has a Z80B processor and 64K of RAM.

G/Net uses CSMA with both CD and CA. Collision avoidance is a pseudorandom number assigned to each physical station. Without collision avoidance, if two stations transmit simultaneously, then detect each other and pull back, they may come back at exactly the same time and get into a loop so that no messages can get through. With collision avoidance each station is assigned slightly different delay times to prevent successive collisions.

Error correction and detection logic are in the board's firmware. Positive acknowledgment of messages is required from the receiving station. If a message is not received, it is retransmitted nine times before the system times out and reports that the message cannot be sent. The likelihood of data being lost is thus reduced. G/NET does not have a transformer on the board. Instead, the network uses proprietary transceiver logic. Transceivers can oscillate and require tuning, but the logic is stable once it has been locked in.

Gateway's G/NET supports the Novell NetWare file server software, which allows PCs on G/NET to share up to 300M of disk storage and three parallel printers. The file server supports both DOS V1.1 and V2.0, CP/M-86, Concurrent CP/M-86, and UCSD p-System.

Along with G/NET, Gateway has an X.25 gateway, a 3270-emulation gateway, and an SNA gateway. The 3270 emulator resides on the PC, but only one emulator is needed per network. With a Gateway processor connected to G/NET, the IBM PC can communicate with wide area networks using either SNA or X.25 protocols.

G/NET allows the option of any one of three baseband coaxial cable media: RG-59/U, RG-11/U, or RG-62/U. A shunt is located at the end of the interface board. When the shunt is on, the board supports RG-59/U with a range of 4,000 feet, and RG-11/U with a range of 7,000 feet. When the shunt is removed, the board supports RG-62/U, which is the 3270 coax. If an installation replaces its 3270 terminals with PCs and the building is already wired for 3270 coax, the existing wiring can be used.

The G/NET board can be configured during installation. Both memory and I/O addresses can be changed to prevent a conflict with already installed boards.

Tecmar, Inc.
6225 Cochran Road
Cleveland, Ohio 44139
(216) 349-0600

The ELAN network uses the 3Com EtherSeries board and connectors and the same baseband coax. To this mature technology Tecmar has added a full-fledged voice I/O system. This includes voice mail, messaging, and voice-annotated text. Through a sophisticated voice recognition system, voice commands can be input to the computer, even remotely, by telephone. ELAN also has electronic mail that supports straight text, voicegrams, and voice and video mail.

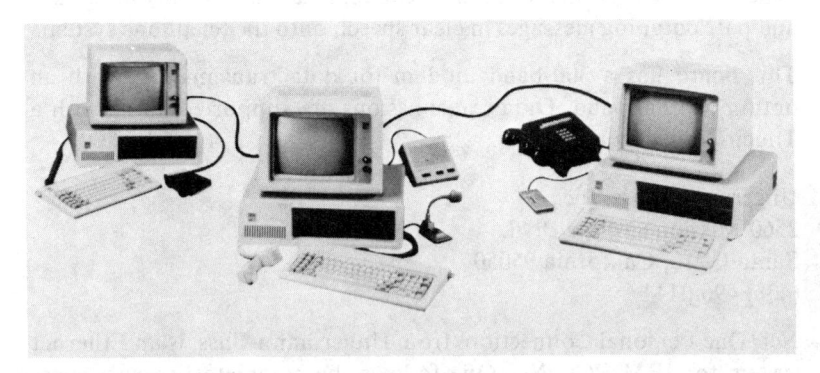

*Fig. 7.5. ELAN's Secretary, Executive, and Manager. Photograph courtesy of Tecmar, Inc.*

The network is served by an IBM PC/XT. Foregrounding and backgrounding are implemented on the network server, which eliminates the need for a dedicated processor. ELAN runs under DOS V2.0. Proprietary software is overlaid to support the network. The Tecmar system will work with Tecmar hard disks or a PC/XT hard disk.

With ELAN you can send files and transmit digital data through Ethernet. A second board is added by Tecmar that enables you to digitize your voice, store it, send it to other computers, and replay it.

Although a dedicated main server is not required, you must identify at least one machine on the network to service the network in background. Passwords, protection lists, notification of undelivered electronic mail, etc., are kept on that machine. The machine polls the network to find out who is logged in and performs other administrative network functions.

Two additional boards form the ELAN Voice System. One is a complete voice control board, which does both voice digitization and voice replay. Voice can be put into a file, and the file can be copied like a voice telegram anywhere over the net. Voice-annotated text lets the user add notes to a file with a microphone.

The second board is an FTC-approved RG-11 interface through telephone lines. A telephone set can be plugged into this interface. When the power is off, the telephone functions as a standard telephone. When the power is on, the audio voice circuit can digitize incoming calls and pass outgoing messages in clear speech onto the telephone system.

This board has a 300-baud modem for data transmission, with an option of 1200 baud. Data transmissions are supported along with a Touch-Tone decoder.

Ungermann-Bass, Inc.
2560 Mission College Blvd.
Santa Clara, California 95050
(408) 496-0111

Net/One Personal Connection, from Ungermann-Bass, is an Ethernet system for IBM PCs. Net/One follows the complete Ethernet specification, including a speed of 10Mbit/sec and CSMA-CD for contention handling.

Net/One uses an intelligent Ethernet-compatible network interface unit (NIU) for the IBM PC. The NIU allows IBM PC users to share information and resources, and integrates them with other corporate resources, such as IBM hosts, through IBM's Systems Network Architecture (SNA).

The NIU's on-board intelligence handles all communications tasks that would otherwise consume a large percentage of the host CPU's resources. In addition, this intelligence will allow PCs to utilize multitasking operating systems better, as these are introduced.

PCs configured with NIUs can run any applications programs under the MS-DOS operating system, without modification. Applications can also be shared across the network. Networking of applications is handled by adding five commands to PC DOS.

Net/One Personal Connection has a shared disk server and print server. Server software programs run on any of the PCs attached to the network. The disk server manages the shared access to all files and applications programs stored on one or more Winchester disks at the server station. Multilevel password protection is provided.

Printer server software permits the sharing of printers attached to a PC running the server software. Applications programs or keyboard-generated output can be redirected automatically to a networked printer through a spooler. This redirection frees the workstation to begin a new task without waiting for the print function to end. Workstations can simultaneously access multiple disk and print servers.

The print server has a complete spooling capability, page backup, and print over. The disk server supports volume sharing.

With the NIUs, PCs can be configured as diskless workstations. In such an environment PCs don't need any disk storage because both network and operating system software can be downloaded to diskless PCs on the network by a network disk server.

Ungermann-Bass has a bridge to connect baseband to broadband, baseband to baseband, and broadband to broadband, in Ethernet systems. SNA gateways are available that allow users to access mainframe-based applications programs. These gateways are PCs equipped with software that enables them to emulate IBM 3274 controllers or 3278 terminals, and 3287 printers.

Also with the NIU, PCs can be mixed in a high-speed network with information-processing devices from different manufacturers. This mixing is possible because the PC network maintains full compatibility with Net/One.

NIUs utilize the XNS protocols. In addition, an NIU supports both standard Ethernet and thin coaxial cable, and contains an optional on-board transceiver for use with the thin cable.

The Ungermann-Bass network interface unit (NIU) runs all network software, offloading the PC. This intelligent NIU enables PCs that are used as disk servers to give network users superior performance.

Ungermann-Bass has implemented its NIU in a PC-compatible board. For the print share and the file share, only a very small piece of code is required in the PC. The NIU has an 80186 chip with 128K of memory. When new PCs arrive that can do multiprocessing, controller boards will be required that are faster than those needed with the 8088 PC. Otherwise, the network burden will have to be carried by the new processor, which will effectively strip its power. The NIU has enough memory and processing power to handle multiprocessing and multi-functioning operating systems within the IBM PC.

Interlan
3 Lyberty Way
Westford, Massachusetts 01886
(617) 692-3900

Interlan's network is an Ethernet-compatible system called Net/Plus. With Net/Plus a PC is attached to a terminal server which, in turn, attaches to the network through an RS-232 link. A virtual circuit is created between any two RS-232 devices on Ethernet. With the common RS-232 interface, communications between dissimilar devices is possible.

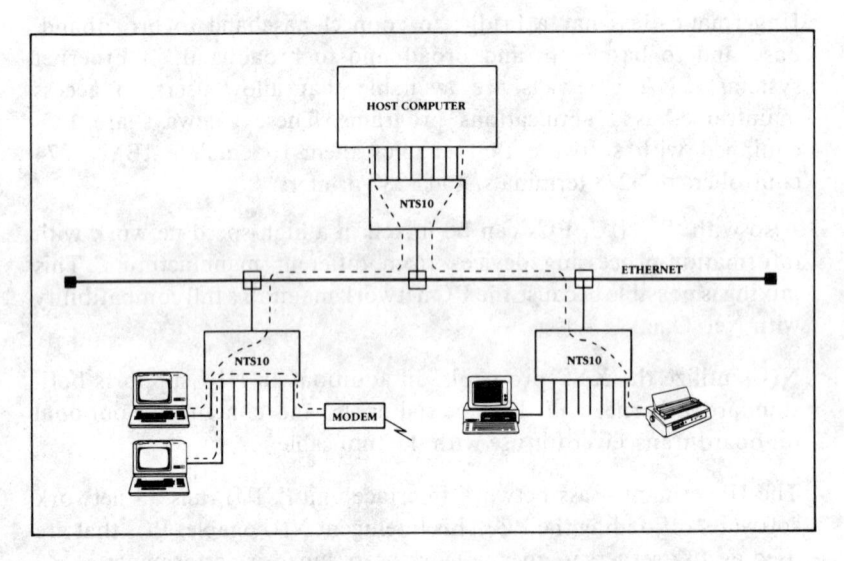

*Fig. 7.6. Interlan's NTS10 Terminal Server interconnects RS-232-C devices with virtual circuits. Reprinted by permission of Interlan, Inc.*

The controller boards are basically the physical and data-link layers of the Ethernet standard protocol. The high-level protocols are addressed with the Xerox Network Systems. These protocols support reliable virtual circuits between host computers. Interlan does not have file server capabilities. The network's primary use is to provide a low-cost interface to Ethernet and mainframe environments.

Net/Plus ties terminals and personal computers into the host computer environment. The NTS10 is an 8-port terminal concentrator onto the Ethernet. It provides a concentration of terminals, personal computers, printers, and modems connected onto 10Mbit/sec Ethernet. The environment permits host computers and all peripheral devices to connect transparently onto the Ethernet. A PC on the network can electronically connect and disconnect to any other devices on the network, including a PC, terminal, printer, modem, or host computer.

Interlan also provides multivendor personal computer networking software, which allows information sharing among dissimilar devices on the network: DEC to IBM, Data General to DEC, IBM PC to Rainbow PC, or PC to host computers. The software provides for terminal emulations and file transfers among devices that are connected on Ethernet. The transfer of both binary and ASCII data is transparently supported over the network.

With Interlan the user can either start by networking PCs together and then moving into the host area, or begin with the host and then gradually phase in the various personal computers. Both these approaches are made possible by a wide array of host-to-host support on Ethernet.

Interlan has an SNA gateway that permits the IBM PC to emulate a 3270 device going into the IBM environment. A virtual circuit capability is available for terminal or PC users to access the IBM 3270 applications program residing on the 370- or 4300-class machines. A baseband-to-baseband bridge is available to tie Ethernets together.

Nestar Systems, Inc.
2585 East Bayshore Road
Palo Alto, California 94303
(415) 493-2223

Nestar currently manufactures two networks. One, PLAN 4000, is a high-performance system designed for larger networks. The other, PLAN 2000, is a basic system for small offices and low-traffic conditions. Both these networks are based on ARCnet.

ARCnet is a token-passing technology and an established standard, IEEE-802.4. Its speed is 2.5Mbit/sec, and its topology is described as arbitrary. A common bus forms the backbone of the network. Coaxial junction boxes, called HUBs, are attached to the bus. HUBs are made in active or passive versions, each with between 3 and 16 ports.

Dedicated lines extend from the HUBs to the PC workstations. RG-62 coaxial cable is the transmission medium. When HUBs are used, the maximum distance between any two stations is 7,000 meters; the maximum distance from PC to HUB is 600 meters.

Nestar uses Xerox Network Systems (XNS) protocols for layers 3 and 4. Above these levels Nestar implements its own disk-sharing and printer-sharing protocols. A network interface card residing on the PC bus connects the cable with the network. This card contains 2K of RAM for buffers, 2K of RAM for programming, and 4K of PROM to support ARCnet.

PLAN 4000 uses a dedicated file server. Disks are available in 30M, 60M, and 137M versions, each supplied with 45M of streaming tape backup. A file server can handle three disks for a maximum of 548K of storage per server. Multiple servers are permitted on the network.

PLAN 2000 allows a number of users to share common disk storage on the IBM PC/XT by partitioning the hard disk into several areas. Each area can be either private or public. Password protection is provided. The shared disk station can also be used at the same time as a regular PC DOS workstation. Disk sharing goes on in the background while the user processes in the foreground.

Printer sharing in PLAN 2000 occurs through a lock scheme. The user requests control of a printer for a period of time and can then use that printer as though it were attached directly to the PC. When printing is finished, someone else can get in and allocate the same printer, then print a report. The printer may be attached to any PC on the network, and that PC runs a print sharing program in the background.

PLAN 4000 has print queuing. Neither network's print scheme prevents the PC to which a printer is attached from concurrently serving as a workstation while the printer is in use.

Text files on both networks can be shared on any supported operating system and among the various micros on the network. Workstations

## PLAN 4000

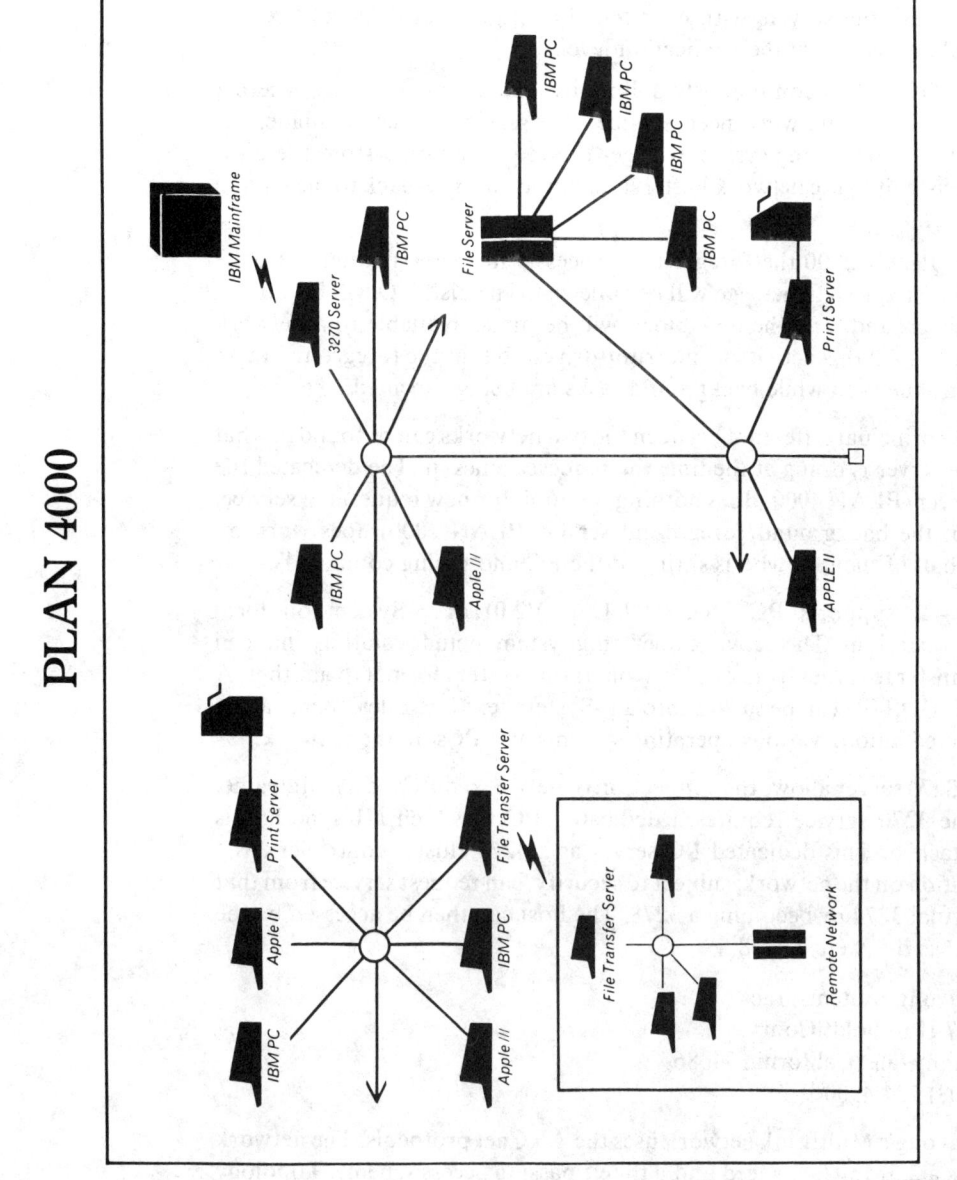

*Fig. 7.7. PLAN 4000. Reprinted by permission of Nestar Systems, Inc.*

can be reconfigured dynamically, allowing the sequential use of different file servers without manual configuration. File and record locking is done at the application level.

PLAN 4000 is continuously polling its incoming lines to see whether users on the network need service. If a service request is made, the network operating system will get the requested data from the disk, transfer it to the network buffer, and initiate a write-back to the station that made the request.

On PLAN 2000 the foreground process will be interrupted, and the entire requested message will be collected. The disk I/O will be done in background, and the disk block will be made available to a network buffer. All this activity is interrupt-driven so that the foreground tasks continue even while background tasks are being executed.

The principal difference between the two networks can be found in what the server is doing at the time the request comes in. The dedicated file server (PLAN 4000) does nothing but look for new requests to service. But the background/foreground server (PLAN 2000) does work on behalf of the user who is sitting at the PC and typing commands.

Nestar supports PC DOS (V1.1 or V2.0) or p-System on local workstations. The network operating system includes a utility that can transfer text files from one local operating system format to another. A PC DOS file can be turned into a p-System text file. Files, then, can be shared among various operating systems and PCs on the network.

A 3270 server allows the connection of networked PCs to a mainframe. The 3270 service requires a dedicated PC to which a bisync line is attached. This dedicated PC serves as a 3274 cluster controller. Any station on the network, subject to security, can request service from that virtual 3274 by becoming a 3278. The host can then be accessed by the PC as if it were a 3278.

Davong Systems, Inc.
217 Humboldt Court
Sunnyvale, California 94086
(408) 734-4900

Davong's MultiLink network uses the ARCnet protocols. The network has a 2.5Mbit/sec speed and a token-passing access scheme. Topology is arbitrary. (See the Nestar description for a more complete discussion of ARCnet.)

The system is built on the premise that every PC in the network can be both a file server and a network user at the same time. One hard disk in the network can be shared by everyone. A variation is also permitted in which a PC may be dedicated to server duties.

MultiLink is based on a disk cache. All the data going to or from disk must pass through a PC-resident RAM cache. This means that if a user is reading data in the cache, the data doesn't need to go out to disk. Data is first written into the cache and then written immediately into background out to the disk. In this way data flow is optimized through the network.

The network traffic is routed so that in a disk transfer several pieces of the process are done in parallel. The machine that is requesting data can work on generating the next request, while the machine that is producing data can work on shipping back the previous request and accessing the disk for the next request. All this activity is done in parallel. The process is called pipelining.

When a read from disk or a write to disk is issued, the request comes from the requesting station. This request is sent through the network to the server that will be processing the request. That server looks in the disk cache, finds the data if it is there, and sends it. If it is not in the cache, the server reads data from the disk into the cache, then sends the data from the cache to the user.

This transaction is done in the pipeline manner so that several requests are processed in parallel through the pipe, to get the best performance.

The write to disk is very similar. Data originating from the user station is sent over the network to the server. The data is then moved into the cache. From the cache the data is written out to disk as soon as the disk is free. Therefore, data is not left in the cache for any period of time. This process is basically a write through cache, done with pipelining so that the sending station can send additional pieces of data to the server in parallel, with the server moving data into the cache and writing the data out to the disk.

The network server has a multitasking kernel and interrupt-driven logic hidden behind the host operating system. These features let the user run CP/M, Concurrent CP/M, DOS, or Pascal at the server. In background, the system can be processing requests from any of these operating systems over the network.

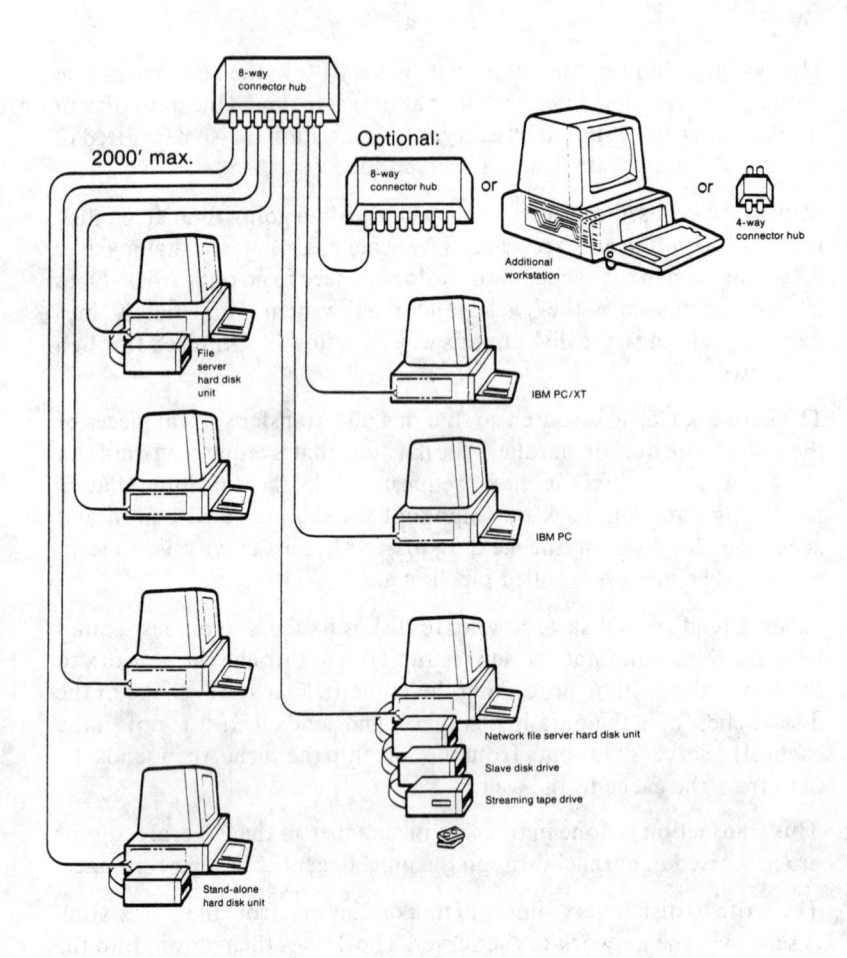

*Fig. 7.8. Setting up Davong's MultiLink. Reprinted by permission of Davong Systems.*

The server is a multitasking system. Internally, the server runs the disk management task, the network server task, the network data transfer task, and a background-resource-locate task that keeps track of who is on the network. At the same time, a server can also run a print spooling station, in which case each print spooler will run as a task.

Tools available to an applications developer are locks and pipes. Utilities are provided that let an applications developer examine locks which have been set, that clear or set locks manually, or that clear all the locks in a particular station of the network.

Also provided is a shared DOS mode. In this mode automatic locking is available for all file access done by the user program that is running. Locking is automatic for the directory, for the file allocation table, and for all use of the DOS directory and disk. Two people can share the same directory on disk through the server, Read/Write files, and delete files, without ruining the file allocation table. In the shared DOS mode, any user can treat the disk as if it were his own, and everything will work correctly.

The network operating system contains an inventory program to handle lock and unlock. Every time the user wants to read a record from the data base for an update, the program locks the record, then does the read. Consequently, a user who tries to access the same record will be told that the record is locked. The user must then wait until the record is unlocked. Only after the station that locked the record has finished its update, written it back out, and unlocked the record, can a user who has been waiting for the record pick it up and use it. The way this lock structure is implemented, when a record is locked, the type of use is specified by the user. As long as the use doesn't conflict with any other use, access to the record will be granted.

Orchid Technology
47790 Westinghouse Drive
Fremont, California 94539
(415) 490-8586

Orchid Technology's PCnet is widely used in small and medium businesses and institutions. Users can share files, disk volumes, and networked printers. PCnet runs at a speed of 1Mbit/sec. Access is contention-based CSMA-CD. A bus topology is used, with RG-59B/U coaxial cable, permitting cable runs up to 1,000 meters. Optionally, RG-11/U can be used, with runs up to 2,000 meters without repeaters.

On PCnet a server is any computer containing the shared data storage device. This device can be a hard disk drive, a floppy disk drive, or a RAM disk. All networked PCs, including those designated as servers, are equipped with the same network interface card. Multiple servers can be used on one network. Since servers cannot talk to each other, they can't share each other's hard disks. But any user on the system can share both hard disks and can therefore copy from one hard disk to another.

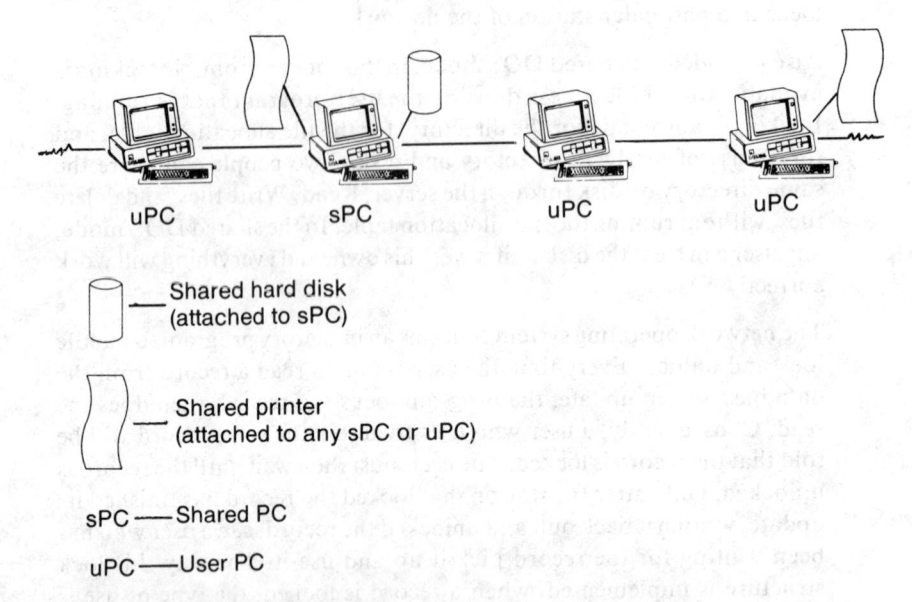

*Fig. 7.9. Orchid Technology's PCnet.*

The server does not need to be dedicated to network functions. It can be used in the foreground as a PC workstation while the network tasks run in the background. Foregrounding takes precedence on the server.

Using PCnet's remote command execution capability, any PC can send commands to the server PC. The command will be executed on the server as if it were directly entered on the keyboard. When commands are received at the time another command is being executed, the commands will be placed in a queue. Local commands take precedence over remote commands. A remote command must relate to a specified drive that is shared by both the server and the PC issuing the command. In a system where the shared PC is not undergoing heavy use, you can send a compile to the server and have it done there in background while you edit a subroutine.

PCnet has very flexible peripheral sharing. Only disk drives attached to the server can be shared. (Local drives are private.) However, any PC can become a server just by loading server software. Thus, if a server should fail, another PC can assume that role easily with no appreciable loss in system downtime.

The printer can be anywhere on the network, attached to either a server or any other networked PC. If the printer is attached to the server, it must have at least 192K of RAM; otherwise, without a printer attached, 128K is sufficient. Printer input can be spooled, which enhances the speed of a transfer. During printing, the print operation runs in background on the supporting PC so that any user operation in foreground can continue.

PCnet has both file and record locking. Record locking has to take place in an applications program. But a file can be locked at the command line level. In a standard office procedure in a PCnet office, when someone is using a program that doesn't have file locking, a user can lock a file from the command line and then go into a word-processing file and edit it. Unlike many networks PCnet has a lock utility that cannot be overridden.

When a command to lock the file is sent to the server, a prompt comes back indicating that the file is locked. If other users try to lock, they will get a message saying that the file is already in use. If a file is busy, a LOOPLOCK command can be issued. The LOOPLOCK utility will keep trying to lock until the file is available and the lock can be accomplished.

Drives can be given unique names on the network to identify each storage device and each file on that device. For each drive, a PC may have No Access, Read-Only Access, Write-Only Access, or Read/Write Access. In the installation phase, you can get a map of a PC's privileges.

A user PC directory tells what PCs are on the network and what permissions they have. If a user sits down at a PC that has been running for a while, typing NETDIR will produce a directory that shows to what drives the PC is mapped.

Orchid has a line of add-on modules for PCnet. With one, PCnetPLUS DISKLESS, the user can boot directly off the server. PCnetPLUS RAM has RAM disk logic and sockets for up to 256K of RAM disk memory. All these cards will offer cost savings by going to integrated functions. The cards also save expansion slot use in the PC. A multifunction card, called BLOSSOM, has disk caching, RAM disk, up to 384K of memory, and a daughterboard—configured network interface card.

Orchid services PCnet hardware at its manufacturing facility. In most cases repairs or replacements have a 24-hour turnaround.

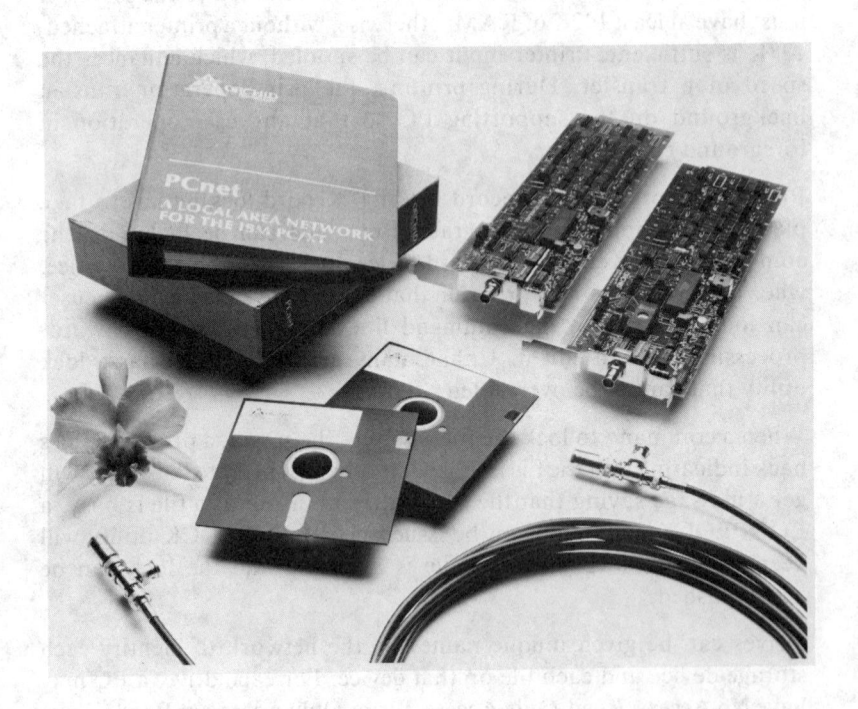

*Fig. 7.10. PCnet Starter Kit. Photograph courtesy of Orchid Technology.*

# 8
# Applications Software

Most network software used today is single-user, run by the "grace" of the operating system. Depending on the specific operating system and the application, this situation can cause considerable grief to the user.

Many new users who run applications on a network discover some surprises. Often the first thing a new network user wants to do is put a favorite application program on the hard disk and then share the program. Here the implicit assumption is that "the software works on a floppy, so it ought to work on a hard disk." Most of the time, however, this assumption is wrong because the program is usually on a copy-protected diskette. Equally wrong, but much more dangerous, is the assumption that single-user data base management software can be used in the shared environment of a local area network.

New multiuser software that addresses these issues has opened up a wide range of software functions not possible in the single-user world. In this chapter we'll examine the kinds of multiuser software now available, along with some of the applications this new software provides.

## Disk Sharing Only

Today probably 99 percent of all local area networks are used for simple disk sharing. Through software, network programmers have "fooled" the applications programs, making a remote shared hard disk look like a dedicated single-user device attached to the PC.

Program calls to the floppy drive are remapped out on the network to the shared disk. This process lets you put on the network your current floppy software and use it with a hard disk. On that hard disk you can store either a program or data. Because network programmers have made the network look like a single-user environment, less emphasis has been placed on the information sharing or communications capability of the network. People are generally unaware of the potential they are missing.

By the same token, people are using networks without understanding network problems. Users assume that when they use a network, sharing of communications and information is implicit. It isn't. The confusion is due partly to the hardware companies' telling us that we can share files and information. What companies really provide are tools for sharing. Good multiuser applications software is needed to put these tools to work.

In early multiuser systems, users often lost their data. The problem was attributed to the computer, the hard disk, or the software. Actually, all these elements were functioning properly, according to the set of rules they'd been designed to follow.

The problem was simple. Programs that had begun as single-user software were suddenly put on the network in a multiuser environment. Then people started to change data simultaneously, but the software wasn't written to handle simultaneous use. A single-user software program thinks it's using a private hard disk, and the network operating system may support that assumption. The user is therefore responsible for understanding how the system works and what protections are needed.

# Read-Only Applications Software

Not all software needs to have multiuser features to perform adequately on a network. Some applications are inherently single-user. They'll work properly whether they are run on a single PC or a network.

The following categories of software are available for personal computers:

1. Word processing
2. Graphics
3. Spreadsheet
4. Data base
5. Communications
6. Networking
7. Software tools

Word processing, graphics, spreadsheets, and communications software are single-user applications. There is little reason why you should let someone else modify a spreadsheet while you are modifying it. Communications refers to the modem-based, 300- to 1200-baud applications, not high-speed networking communications. Conferencing will make communications a shareable, multiuser application, but the applications software available today is still single-user.

Right now, the problems of concurrent access relate primarily to data bases and data base management systems (DBMS). A data base is any compilation of information, usually including lists, records, and short amounts of text. Most companies have only one data base for a category of information. In fact, only one data base should exist so that everyone updates and uses the same information.

A DBMS is applications software that lets the user manipulate and perform several useful operations with the data base. As a common resource, the data base should be fully available to everyone who needs to use it. The networked DBMS is responsible for making the data base available simultaneously to multiple users, while protecting it from the problems that result from multiple access. Single-user DBMS software can be run on a network but may invite disaster.

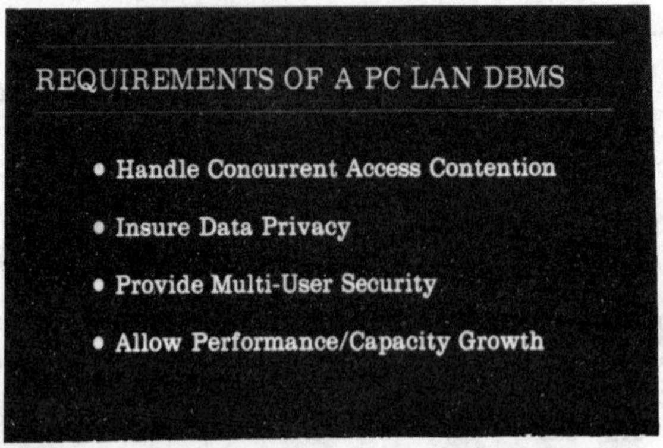

> **REQUIREMENTS OF A PC LAN DBMS**
>
> - Handle Concurrent Access Contention
> - Insure Data Privacy
> - Provide Multi-User Security
> - Allow Performance/Capacity Growth

*Fig. 8.1. A Data Base Management System in a shared multiuser environment must perform many functions not required of single-user software. Courtesy of Software Connections.*

# A Multiuser Approach

The operating system can protect single-user applications in several ways. If one user opens a file and a second user also attempts to open it, the network can automatically deny file access to the second user. In a sense, this approach is multiuser. When applications require that several people open and access the same file, the approach is inadequate. In the example that follows, consider what happens on a typical network if the DBMS has not been written to handle multiuser access.

Two users each load a copy of the data base manager software. One common characteristic of the DBMS is to make as few writes as possible because disk access slows the system down. When loaded, the DBMS is therefore held in memory. If user A wants to retrieve a record, the information on where it is and how to retrieve it is found in the memory of user A's PC, not in the disk server. Since the two PCs are not sharing each other's memory, they do not share the data, but only copies of the data.

As long as the data on the disk remains unchanged, no problem occurs. But let's suppose that user A deletes a record from a data base that user B is also using. User B should somehow be informed of the change.

Otherwise, both users have the potential of destroying one another's work.

A network operating system can provide locking down to the record level. But locking the record, deleting it, and unlocking it will not solve the problem outlined here. The information found in the memory of one PC does not match the information in the memory of the other PC. User B must somehow be told to reread the data, and user A must be told to write the update so that when user B reads it, the data will be accurate. A single-user DBMS does not perform this task because it isn't significant to a single-user environment.

How then is this problem solved? The only solution is to use a multiuser approach so that the multiuser software writes the file out to disk and updates it properly. With this procedure user B knows when a change has been made and when to reread the data. In this way, multiuser DBMSs, such as Dataflex (DataAccess), DataStore (Software Connections), and PC-Focus (Information Builders), manage multiple writes to disk. When a record is marked, the multiuser DBMS informs the file on the disk. User B looks at the file on the disk and sees that it has been modified. This procedure lets user B know that the information and index are invalid and that the file must be reread.

When user A opens up a data file, deletes a record, or modifies a record, a bit is set on the file on disk. This bit indicates that the file has been modified. Before user B does anything with that data, the application checks the bit and sees that the file has been modified. The program rereads the data out of the index file. Then the program retrieves the data and performs an update on the file in the memory of the PC. These two users appear to be sharing memory, but they are really sharing only the disk and synchronizing its use.

# Categories of Network Software

Three categories of network software are available. Although these will probably change over time, they are useful now in charting progress in software for local area networks. The software categories are the following:

1. Unnetworked
2. Networked
3. Multi-accessed networked

Software may be unnetworked because it abuses the operating system through some unorthodox scheme. Or the network may be poorly designed and therefore may not offer transparency. Today these problems are unusual. Most IBM PC software is written according to the "rules" and uses operating systems properly. And most networks adequately provide transparency. Generally, the reason why software is unnetworked is that it is either hard coded for floppy diskettes or copy protected and thus is unable to reside on a hard disk.

The second category, transparently networked software, contains single-user software that can be run in a network environment. (A network environment is not necessarily a multiuser environment for all software on the network, as indicated earlier in the discussion of applications software.) To run single-user software, the network creates the illusion of a single-user system. The software expects to "see" local disks and printers, so the network simulates them with virtual devices. When a single-user package is run on a networked PC, the package "thinks" it's making calls to a dedicated local device; the device is actually in a remote location shared by other users.

To fit into the networked category, software should be network-deliverable. This means that software can reside on a mass storage device and be delivered to users across the network. Software that is sold on copy-protected diskettes cannot be used in this way. The network manager, or whoever owns the network, buys the particular application for the network and makes it available to the PCs through the server, not from diskettes on a local drive. A good example of this kind of software is VisiCalc, offered along with VisiWord in a network-delivered version by 3Com. No change occurs in the basic software, only in the method of delivery.

The third category is the multiuser or multi-accessed network software. This applications software is aware of the multiuser environment, unlike software in the previous categories. In this software a number of techniques are used to allow data to be shared in an orderly way. Quick*NET accounting software (TCS Software) is an example of this kind of software. Quick*NET uses an underlying multiuser, multi-access distributed data base. With this software, multiple PCs can function over a shared data base as order entry or payables/receivables workstations across the network.

## Upgrading Single-User DBMS Software

Many existing DBMS vendors will be upgrading their products to function in a multiuser environment. Some hazards and deficiencies accompany any simple upgrade, however. The first thing most DBMS vendors will do is to add concurrent access in the form of lock and unlock commands for the data base. Whether file locking or record locking, or both, the commands must be explicitly given by the user.

Lock and unlock commands are usually satisfactory if only two people are using the network. But three or more multiple users can quickly be confronted with a deadlock, in which case each user has possession of a file needed by another user. Here is an occasion where people need the same files but are getting in each other's way, thus effectively deadlocking the data base. And with additional users, the problem gets even more complicated.

If software offers commands only for lock and unlock, problems can crop up. As a user, you must understand the consequences of concurrent access and work out some method to avoid conflict. In most cases you will require a noncomputer, person-to-person scheduling of accesses, sometimes referred to as a "verbal semaphore." Preferably, the DBMS software will provide enough sophistication so that the user doesn't have to be an expert in solving any of these problems.

## No Central Resource

Mainframe data base management programs are migrating to the PC. They bring with them a wealth of business applications along with the sophistication of the mainframe software. One example of this mainframe-to-PC migration is a DBMS called PC-Focus. Several large banking and insurance firms have used the mainframe version of this DBMS to develop powerful applications. Now that PC-Focus is available, these applications can be easily ported to the IBM PC.

Some of the DBMS applications that were developed in the mainframe world are single-user applications. Most DBMS applications, however, are designed for multiuser systems and include desirable multiuser features. For microcomputer users to benefit most from these mainframe applications, they should be run in the multiuser environment of a local area network.

In this environment the mainframe-to-PC migration encounters a new hurdle. Mainframe multiuser systems and microcomputer local area networks typically have a fundamental difference: the mainframe (or minicomputer) system has a central computing resource and central control over attached terminals. A local area network often has no centralized facility. Most networks use disk servers and distributed control.

Disk server networks support a number of PCs attached to the network. A disk server network is designed to make the hard disk, which is attached to the network, look like a local disk. That way, the off-the-shelf software will work on the network. When this software tries to write something to drive C, the software will be successful even if drive C is in a remote location. The request is simply routed from the machine over the network to the hard disk. Disk accesses are controlled by the requesting PC workstation without central coordination.

The most common way for a minicomputer or mainframe to coordinate access is to use a queue, or waiting line. At certain critical times, such as when data storage is being rearranged, other users should not be permitted to use the data base. A queue holds requests until they can be answered. The central computer analyzes the requests to protect data and resolve conflicts among the requests. These are then automatically answered in sequence.

On a disk server network, providing this sort of facility is awkward because of the lack of a central resource. Multiuser software must use alternatives to overcome this lack.

# Equal Access to Data

Queuing and monitoring on mainframe systems also handle the problem of fair access to resources. A local area network, too, needs some kind of queuing mechanism for the data base so that no one can monopolize it and lock out other users for long periods of time. One way to handle equitable distribution of resources is by emulating the CSMA-CD access scheme.

DataStore, a multiuser DBMS from Software Connections, uses the concept of collision detection and applies it to granting access to the data base. As with the transmission line CSMA-CD, when a second person tries to use the data base that is already in use, the application detects the use and backs off for a while.

Every network company provides a tool called a semaphore, which is a message to the program that signals a predefined condition. A semaphore is locked before the user gets into the data base and unlocked when the user exits. Semaphores are used for two reasons. One is to stipulate the critical time periods and prevent simultaneous access. The other reason is to signal that someone is waiting at another machine. The "user waiting" semaphore is useful in scheduling fair access to the data base. A prerequisite for fair access is knowing what the demand is. In other words, are others waiting to use the data base?

Let's say that a first PC locks the data base. Then a second PC tries to get into the same data base. Because of the lock already in place, the second PC is refused access. It backs off, and the user may try again later. Furthermore, suppose that the PC with the lock is running a program that goes back and forth between data base operations and other processing. This activity creates a time window in which other users could use the data base, but the window may be very small. Thus, the first machine can easily monopolize the resource and not let anyone else use it.

To prevent a monopoly from developing, semaphores are used to inform the PC with the lock that someone else is waiting to use the data base. A PC that is denied access sets a special "waiting" semaphore on the data base. When the PC with the lock finishes its work, it looks for that special semaphore. If the semaphore is found, the PC unlocks the data base so that the waiting PC can get in.

Now a further refinement can be added. A brief delay is imposed on the next PC's lock request. Since this delay is a random time period, the delay works for more than two users. If the time were constant, two people could get into synchronization, bouncing the data base between them and shutting out a third person. But with a random amount of time, within some reasonable range, this problem doesn't occur. Everyone can get access. The random time delay is used instead of the more traditional queuing mechanism used on mainframe and mini-computer systems.

# Keeping Track of File Activity

With single-user software packages, when a user writes to a file and then reads it back, the user can expect that the content will be the same. This assumption cannot be made in a local area network. You may write something, but then someone else can read it and write it. When you reread the file, its contents may be different. This problem is a serious one for data bases because most data base software expects a certain structure; that is, some things are expected to remain constant over a period of time.

This kind of problem occurs when a DBMS uses a B-Plus tree. A B-Plus tree is a hierarchical system for storing and retrieving data. Data is placed at particular locations on certain levels of the tree. A table is maintained as a map to the data wherever it is located on the tree.

Suppose that user A has a data base with B-Plus trees and a report writer program that is putting in a report of everyone, sorted in order by name. Report writing is a common function of data base managers. A report is generated, in sequential order, by doing an ordered search along the tree. The data base has the records in some random order; the records haven't been sorted. A key structure points to the records so that they can be retrieved in alphabetical order.

Now let's assume that program number one, a report writer, is printing a report. The program reaches a point in its search when user B requests to enter a new record in the data base. The program leaves a pointer, marking its position in the B-Plus tree, and lets the second PC add the new record.

Now with this new record, the data base must dynamically update the structure. After the updating, the tree looks nothing like the original structure. The question is, what happened to the pointer? Before the restructuring, it was pointing to a particular physical spot, but that spot now contains different data. For the report to be correct, user A must be aware of the reorganization. The file, in other words, is a moving target, and users cannot assume that things will stay the same.

This problem must be solved by coordinating pointer position with restructuring. As the second person is updating the trees, the pointers of other people who are using that same key tree will be modified. The first person then comes back and requests the next record. The position of the internal pointer was changed between the two calls but is still pointing at the same information. When the tree was restructured, the pointer position was changed to reflect that restructuring.

The user doesn't have to be aware of this restructuring at all but simply goes to the data base to create a report. It doesn't matter that another user may be using the data base. Even the operations performed by that person are irrelevant. When the report comes out, it will be correct. The user can run a program to get successive records, and these will be correct even if others are using the data base, adding keys, or deleting keys.

Multiuser software cannot make the same assumptions that a single-user package can. A multiuser program must maintain information to keep track of the activity. Designers of that mechanism had to decide first where to put that information. On a minicomputer or mainframe, the information is usually in a table located in the privileged or system area of memory. Only the data base management system can get access to the memory; users cannot. But most microcomputer local area networks don't have any central memory. The only place left for storage is on the disk, with the data base. The designers of DataStore put a table, called an open user table (OUT), on the disk. OUT keeps track of who has the data base open and what that user is doing.

As in an earlier example, when user B added the record, the table notes that user A is printing a report and, therefore, has a pointer to one of the keys. User A's pointer must be modified to reflect the new location of the data that the user is reading. A major function of the multiuser DBMS is to keep track of who is doing what. Of course, there is no equivalent on a single-user package.

Besides this dynamic updating feature, other multiuser features are helpful. At every disk block, a checksum is provided by some multiuser programs, which provides protection in two ways. First, if something happens to the data and the key structure is damaged, the error will be detected and repaired at that point. Second, if someone enters the data base and tampers with the data, the checksum notes the change.

On networks a tamper-detection mechanism is very important to protect the data base. For instance, no one can go in and use DEBUG to give himself a raise. The data, however, is sitting on a hard disk, and,

*Fig. 8.2. Sophisticated multiuser applications software often provides important security and accounting functions. These applications can restrict access to the data base and also record data base use. Courtesy of Software Connections.*

realistically, anybody can log on. Again, this kind of problem does not exist in single-user systems.

# Defining Users

Another useful feature for the multiuser data base is the capability of defining users. Definitions can be keyed to passwords that must be entered to access the data base. When you define users, you can define their attributes, so that users can have independent Read/Write, update, and delete access. This user-protection mechanism can define several classes of users. You may not want everyone to have all-powerful rights to the data base.

Most networks have the capability of defining users, but not at the data base level. For example, you may be able to authorize Read-Only, shared, or public access. With local area networks, at the data base level, you can build on capability. A user may have the authority to read the file and perhaps delete some records but not the ability to add records. Or access may be limited to the ability to add records but not to delete or change them in any way. This level of access rights can be built into the data base because only the data base knows the structure.

Other changes can be made at the data base level. When a user is defined, access privileges can be limited to specific fields in the data base. For instance, you can have a large integrated data base for personnel records. Performance evaluations will be part of the data base and accessible to the department head or some other appropriate person, but certainly not to the general office. Other users can access the data base, but they will never see this particular field. Thus, not only are privileges restricted by access rights, but limitations also exist regarding what fields people are permitted to see.

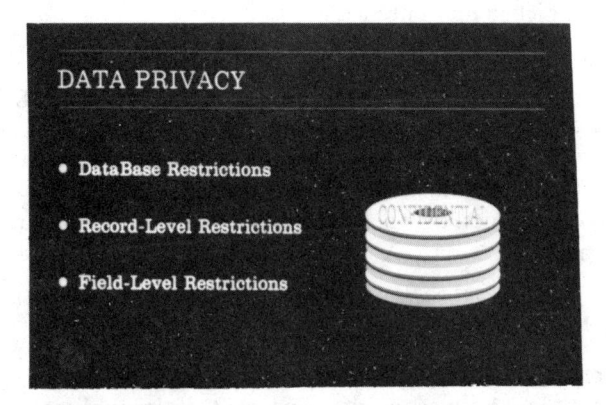

*Fig. 8.3. Multiuser applications software can limit access to the entire data base or to specific fields or records. Courtesy of Software Connections.*

The specific examples mentioned here suggest ways to overcome certain multiuser problems. Different multiuser software may solve these problems in different ways. Obviously, the important criterion for multiuser software is that the problems are addressed and solved, not how they are solved.

# Efficient Use of the Network

Certain software programs are better suited to networking than comparable programs in the same application. For instance, a program that runs mostly in memory is more efficient than one that accesses the disk frequently. Even in a single-user environment the number of disk accesses will slow down response time. In a network environment, disk-access requests must contend with requests of other users, so that a high number of requests may reduce performance to an unacceptable level.

Older software programs are often guilty of a flagrantly wasteful number of access requests, at least from a networking perspective. These programs were written at a time when 64K of RAM was considered standard. In order to deliver functionality but stay within the memory constraints, programmers left much of the applications on disk, to be picked up as needed.

Programs may be written under the assumption that they are supported by a very large and fast, dedicated hard disk. Instead of using disk time as a shared and limited resource, these programs waste disk time with random writes. Graphics applications and some data base managers are guilty of this wastefulness. Programs that use disk requests wastefully will look much worse on a network, compared to programs that run out of local memory.

## Software: Application or Tool?

Software may be classed as either an application or a tool. Some products fit into both categories. Generally, if the application must be created and the package supports that operation, the package is a tool. Multiuser dBASEII is an application. Even though it is a tool to create some application, dBASEII does not allow you to manipulate it except in its present state. COBOL and BASIC are tools.

It is important that both tools and applications be multiuser. Multiuser tools were designed to create programs that work with a network environment. Therefore, they automatically include multiuser features in the applications rather than require those features to be individually written.

## Languages on the Net

When you buy an IBM PC, Microsoft BASIC is the language that is built into ROM. Microsoft BASIC is not multiuser by design. Users who want to write multiuser applications with Microsoft BASIC are confronted with many difficulties.

Microsoft BASIC provides the user with two methods of accessing files: sequential and random. These access methods must create the algorithms that will retrieve the data either sequentially or randomly. Consider an application in which a person's last name is entered and a record containing that person's data is retrieved. The programmer must write this algorithm from scratch. Sort methods that sit on top of BASIC make this easy. All the programmer must do is pass a key to the program, and it returns the record number and perhaps even the record itself.

BASIC, however, has none of these features built into it. A programmer must make the multiuser algorithm to retrieve records, read records, write records, and maintain the data base. And many complex questions must be answered. For example, if you retrieve the record XXX, and I attempt to get it, what are you going to do? What do you tell me, even if you locked that record? Do you say to me, "Come back again later. Do you want to try again?" How long do I wait for you to update that record? How many times will I retry? Will I just hang around and wait until you release the record? What happens when you update the index that was given to retrieve the record? Do I lock the whole file? All these questions are the concerns of a programmer.

Consider for a moment that you are running a tennis court and taking reservations on a personal computer. You call up the computer to find the available courts and relay the information to someone who requests a reservation. At the same time, someone else is also making reservations. Does that person wait until you are done with your customer on the phone and until the records are released? A programmer must seek solutions to these kinds of problem.

The algorithms that access the files created in BASIC must also address multiuser problems. And the familiar microcomputer Microsoft BASIC is really very primitive. Of course, BASICs with multiuser support do exist. A number of minicomputers and mainframe computers have BASICs that have already addressed these issues.

Examples are Business BASIC 2 and Business BASIC 3, from Point-Four Systems, on a time-sharing minicomputer. These BASICs have a built-in retrieval method. The programmer hands a key to the BASIC, and it hands back the file or record. Anything written in BASIC 2 or BASIC 3 will automatically be multiuser. A version of these BASICs has been moved down to PC DOS as BI-286, which is available on Novell's NetWare.

# 9
# Administration

Personal computers encourage individual ways of doing things. If an office has six PCs, it undoubtedly has six ways to do everything: six formats for correspondence, six modifications of every application program, maybe even six totally different programs for the same application. When several marketing personnel are doing marketing analysis, you hope they're all using the same information. But they probably aren't. Once the marketing data base is put on a local floppy disk, the data base will be changed, and the resultant analyses will be based on somewhat different data.

Managers have dealt with this problem in one of two ways. They either ban PCs and use a host-based terminal network. Or they use PCs to generate batch files, collect the files at the end of the day, and merge them onto a central data base.

Other problems are a little more subtle and difficult to control. For instance, one employee may be creating and using excellent applications on the PC. Yet no one else is given access to the applications. While the employee stays with the company, all this creative potential is lost to the other users. And when the employee leaves, the applications are frequently lost.

Problems like these illustrate the need for every office to have a system for handling its information flow. Such a system is necessary whether the office uses typewriters, PCs, or networked PCs to generate information. But since a network is based on sharing and communicating, an organized plan must be a part of the network from the start.

# The Network Manager

The most practical approach to organizing the network is to appoint one person to manage it. Essentially, the manager's duties are to make sure that the network functions at its best and that data on the network is protected from loss or misuse. Much can be done in software to organize a network and protect networked data. For the most benefits from a network, though, a human being must be put in charge of network operations.

Marketing verbiage to the contrary, a good network is a very powerful and, therefore, complex system. One of the responsibilities of the network manager is to tailor the network for every user's needs and capabilities. Each user should "see" only as much of the network as is necessary. By the same token, users should be educated about how the network operates so that they don't try to override safeguards. User education is, thus, another duty that falls to the network manager.

This chapter begins a discussion of how to organize and implement a local area network. The goal is to offer the network manager a set of strategies for performing these managerial duties effectively.

# The Initial Planning

Most local area networks have some central data storage. The first thing to do is to decide how best to utilize that storage. To make this decision, you'll need to map out the areas connected by the network. For an example, let's consider a sales company with the following departments:

1. Administration
2. Accounting
3. Sales
4. Shipping and Receiving

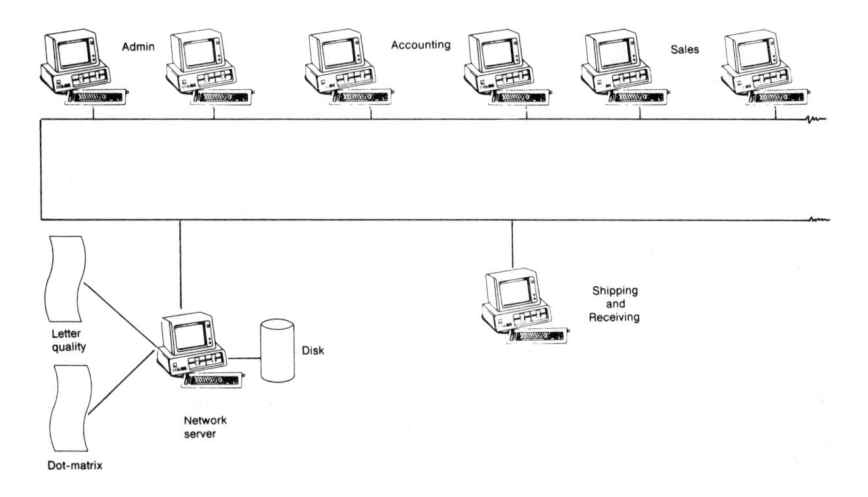

*Fig. 9.1. Typical office layout.*

In Administration there are three users: the owner, the manager, and the secretary. In Accounting there are two users: the accountant and the bookkeeper. Shipping and Receiving has one employee, a clerk, who is a network user. Sales is the largest department with six salespersons and two secretaries, all of whom are given user status on the network. The manager, listed in Administration, is designated as the network supervisor.

Included in the company's shared data files are the following:

1. A data base with customer records
2. A data base with sales orders
3. Contracts and proposals
4. Correspondence
5. Sales objectives
6. Individual sales records
7. Personnel records
8. Purchasing
9. Inventory
10. Accounts receivable
11. Insurance records
12. Tax records

Now that we've looked at the departments, the users, and the data files, the next element in planning out the network is the hardware. In this hypothetical company, there are one dedicated network server, one PC per user, one high-speed printer, and one letter-quality printer. Accounting, Sales, and Shipping and Receiving each have a dot-matrix printer, loaded with forms most often generated. Company data storage is on a single hard disk. Each of the PCs has two floppy disk drives as well.

# File Organization

With our files identified (admittedly an abbreviated list), let's next group them according to the department that usually generates the data contained in each file.

Personnel records, insurance records, and correspondence will come from Administration. Individual sales records are also maintained here. So we'll put an "Admin" after each of these files.

Accounting will create the accounts receivable and tax records. We'll add an "Acc't" after each of these.

Records of shipments to and from our company are created by Shipping and Receiving. In addition, this department has the task of stock control, so purchasing orders and inventory records are handled here. We'll put an "SR" after each of these.

Sales is responsible for generating the customer records and sales orders, the contracts and proposals, and the sales objectives. We'll label these files "Sales." Our list of files and their "owners" now looks like this:

    A data base with customer records—Sales
    A data base with sales orders—Sales
    Contracts and proposals—Sales
    Correspondence—Admin
    Sales objectives—Sales
    Individual sales records—Admin
    Personnel records—Admin
    Purchasing—SR
    Inventory—SR
    Shipments—SR

Accounts receivable—Acc't
Insurance records—Admin
Tax records—Acc't

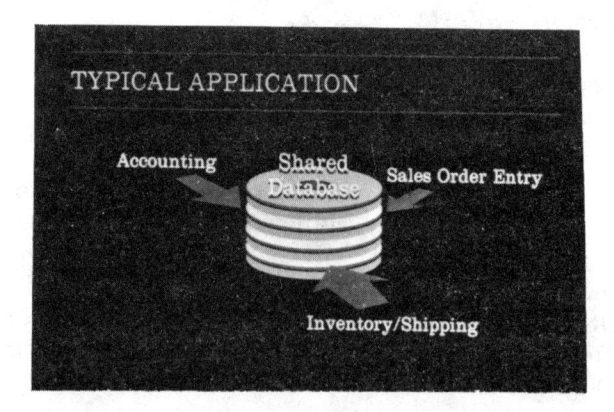

*Fig. 9.2. Organizing users and applications is the first task in setting up the network. Courtesy of Software Connections.*

# Assigning Users

Next, we need to identify who uses which files and what type of use is required. Such decisions will differ from company to company. The reason for setting up this exercise is only to illustrate the options. For brevity let's look only at four users.

1. Manager (M)
2. Accountant (A)
3. Shipping and Receiving clerk (Clerk)
4. Sales secretary (Sec)

The files that these users need to access would probably be the following:

A data base with customer records—Sales—M, Sec
A data base with sales orders—Sales—M, Sec
Contracts and proposals—Sales—M, Sec
Correspondence—Admin—M,

Sales objectives—Sales—M, Sec
Individual sales records—Admin—M, Sec
Personnel records—Admin—M
Purchasing—SR—M, Clerk
Inventory—SR—M, Clerk, Sec
Shipments—SR—M, Clerk
Accounts receivable—Acc't—M, A
Insurance records—Admin—M
Tax records—Acc't—M, A

Our users, of course, have different uses for the files. One user may need to be able to see a file, but will not be involved in updating the information it contains. This user would be given Read-Only (R-O) privileges. Another user who actively updates the same file would require Read/Write (R/W) privileges. Although some network operating systems offer many more privilege levels, these two should suffice for our illustration.

A data base with customer records—Sales—M (R-O), Sec (R/W)
A data base with sales orders—Sales—M (R-O), Sec (R/W)
Contracts and proposals—Sales—M (R-O), Sec (R/W)
Correspondence—Admin—M (R/W)
Sales objectives—Sales—M (R-O), Sec (R/W)
Individual sales records—Admin—M (R/W), Sec (R-O)
Personnel records—Admin—M (R/W)
Purchasing—SR—M (R/O), Clerk (R/W), A (R-O)
Inventory—SR—M (R-O), Clerk (R/W), Sec (R-O), A (R-O)
Shipments—SR—M (R-O), Clerk (R/W)
Accounts receivable—Acc't—M (R-O), A (R/W)
Insurance records—Admin—M (R/W)
Tax records—Acc't—M (R-O), A (R/W)

# Directories

Each user has an individualized directory. The likelihood is small that any two directories will be identical unless two users' duties are identical.

As supervisor of the network, the manager has the most extensive directory. The manager's main directory would probably include the following subdirectories: SUPERVISOR, SYSTEM, ADMINISTRA-

TION, ACCOUNTING, SHIPPING AND RECEIVING, and SALES. Even though the manager may be given only Read-Only privileges in some of these areas, having the status of network supervisor permits the manager to change these privileges at any time, as well as the privileges of any other user in the network.

The accountant's directory includes the SYSTEM directory, ACCOUNTING directory, and the SHIPPING AND RECEIVING directory. The version of this last directory will be limited to the two subdirectories assigned to the accountant: Purchasing and Inventory.

The remaining directories for all the network users would be set up in a similar manner. Each user is given a directory that reflects that user's particular needs and functions within the company.

One important point should be made about directory privileges. Although a great deal of data may be stored on the network in potentially shareable form, opening up all the data files to every user is not necessary or even desirable. A good network operating system provides considerable flexibility in structuring a user-access scheme. The network also is much easier to use when the clutter that each user must deal with is reduced. In addition, this kind of system improves data security.

The objective in organizing the network is to give each user only as much authority as is needed to fulfill a particular job. For example, the user in Shipping and Receiving doesn't use the accounting files, the sales report, or even DOS. These files should not be available, even on a directory, to the clerk in Shipping and Receiving.

## Files on the Network

To illustrate the organization of a typical system, we've made some general assumptions about the data that will go into the central storage. Actually, *what* goes on the central disk is as important as *how* that data is arranged—perhaps even more important.

The first decision that a manager must make is how to get applications software onto the network. Some software packages fill three or four floppy disks. If you use several packages in your normal activities, you must have a large storage box of floppies and spend much time swapping disks and searching for the right one. Putting all this software on a hard disk would not only clear off your desk, but also enable you to bring up the program you want simply by typing in a command.

If the software comes in a multiuser version and is not copy protected, it can be stored on the hard disk and shared by anyone on the network. (Certain limitations were discussed in Chapter 8.) The software should be listed in the directory of every user who may use the software. In most cases access to the software will be restricted to Read-Only. In this way the program can be used but not modified. The manager, of course, will have full Read/Write privileges to the program for maintenance. The manager can add utilities and make key assignments as needed. But the important thing to note is that user files are all created with the same software; therefore, all the files are compatible.

When your favorite software is copy protected and not available in a multiuser version, your options are more limited. In this case the applications software stays at the individual workstations. Only the data files, which are the end products of those applications, will be out on the hard disk.

The next decision concerns what data files should be stored on the central shared disk. In most instances users should not be permitted to create new files at will. Otherwise, the maintenance and control of disk space will become impossible. Furthermore, as you will see in Chapter 10, there are some performance issues that should be considered before new files go onto the shared facility.

Files that are permitted to be stored on the central disk should be classed as shared and nonshared. In the few cases in which someone finds an exception to these defined classes, the network manager should be contacted.

Numerous alternatives to storing on the central disk are normally available. Data might be stored locally on floppies or a department hard disk. Larger companies may have the additional option of storing data on a mainframe or minicomputer. The manager, though, makes the final decision about storage. Since the manager has the responsibility for data security and network efficiency, the manager must be involved in deciding where to hold the data and how to back it up.

Decisions concerning file-access privileges should be determined at the time the file is approved for storage. These decisions will cover the questions of who will have access to the file and what the level of access will be. In most data files—lists, analyses, reports, etc.—Read-Only privileges will be appropriate. This useful option permits information to be disseminated but not altered. If files are indiscriminately added to the central disk, such refinements are often forgotten.

## Naming Conventions

A data file can be something of an enigma to everyone but its creator. One of the easiest ways around this problem is to adopt common naming conventions for your files. If names are well chosen, a quick look at a directory can provide considerable information.

PC DOS allows an eight-character file name, followed by a three-character extension separated from the file name by a period. Certain characters and extensions are reserved by DOS, but essentially you are allowed a wide variety of characters—enough for considerable file identification.

You can start your naming scheme with the kind of information that would help identify the type of file. You can adopt some of the familiar file name extensions for this purpose and add extensions particular to your own office. Thus, .BAK will indicate a backup file, .DOC will be a document, .TBL will be a table, and so on.

In many cases you'll want to know who last updated a file. You can take three of the eight file name characters to make this identification—two characters for the initial, preceded by a hyphen.

Now you have five characters left for the particular file. If five isn't enough, consider assigning an available character, such as a percent sign or ampersand, to each file user who has Read/Write privileges. In this way you've raised your possible file name characters to seven.

The file names should be standardized for quick recognition. For instance, a typical file in the Sales Department may be simply a record of all the sales made for a given month. The file name might be SALEJAN%.DOC. This indicates to the directory scanner that the sales file for January was last updated by Fred (indicated by the percent sign) and that the file is the primary document. If this data is also saved in graph form, the file name might be SALEJAN%.GRF.

The time and date of the last update are often significant. You have the option of trying to squeeze this information into the file name.

However, many networks have a clock that labels the time and date of each write. This label becomes a useful adjunct to each file name.

Regardless of the naming conventions you use, each user should be required to get information on the file before updating it. For example, as part of the procedure for updating a spreadsheet, the user should find out who updated the spreadsheet most recently and when the update was performed. The user then has some basic information about how to proceed.

# Backup

The primary advantage of computers is the speed with which they can manipulate data. Magnetic media enable us to do all sorts of blink-of-the-eye operations, including letting us erase or scramble data. Crashed files and accidental deletions are going to occur. The only way to prevent them from being catastrophic is to have a reliable backup procedure.

Streaming tape is a dependable, proven technology that has become a standard backup medium. Other backup technologies, such as removable Winchester hard disk cartridges, have their own advantages. When removable Winchesters become readily available, they will be a feasible alternative.

For the present, most mass storage systems use a hard disk storage device for primary storage and a removable cartridge tape drive for backup. This approach puts the faster but more expensive hard disk drive into the performance-critical position, answering user requests for data. The less expensive and slower tape drive, as a backup device, is asked only to function reliably; speed is not critical.

Tape backup systems come in two types. One is a pure image recording that backs up a mirror image of the disk. The other type is file-by-file tape backup, which can back up and restore by specific file. Image backup has two advantages: it requires less overhead, and you can store about twice the data using image backup as you can with an identical tape using file-by-file backup. The latter has the advantage of permitting individual files to be restored. An image system requires the restoration of the entire disk before a particular file can be retrieved.

Some manufacturers now offer both file-by-file and image backup on the same tape backup system. Thus, data can be stored efficiently in image mode. Should some user accidentally wipe out a file (the most common reason for needing the backup), restoration of the single file can be done in the file-by-file mode.

Avoid backup systems that back up a mirror image of the disk, bad sectors and all. Good image backup systems skip over bad sectors and also verify the accuracy of the backup transfer. These intelligent tape backups check the new disk as part of the restore process. If the new disk has any bad sectors, the backup will skip over them. Without this intelligence, the restore could dump data into a bad sector and lose the data.

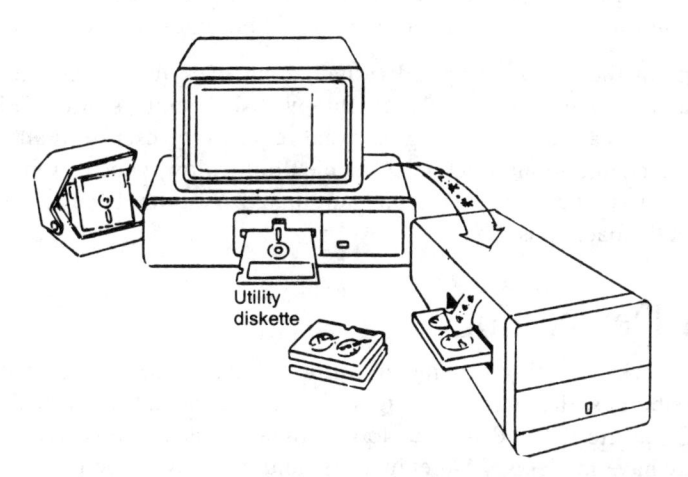

*Fig. 9.3. Davong uses streaming tape mode to transfer files from a hard disk to tape, thus reducing backup time and maintaining high tape data capacity. For restoring individual files, Davong uses a buffered start/stop mode. Reprinted by permission of Davong Systems.*

# Backup Procedure

The most common routine for hard disk backup is to rotate four tapes. Three of the tapes are used for daily backups; the fourth is a weekly backup. Store your data each day, taking the oldest tape out of the safe to use for the new backup. Normally, you will back up only those files that have been modified that day. These are identified by their file names.

Using three tapes, you will always have one full day's backup, yet you are never working with yesterday's backup. Once a week, you should take the fourth tape and put it into a safe deposit box for archival purposes. In this way, in-house backup protects three days' work. Last week's work is stored "off-campus," both to archive and to protect against a catastrophic occurrence, such as a fire.

Ideally, you should have a centralized backup facility, with a network supervisor assigned the task of backing up all the data. Such a facility is not only possible with networking but also one of its benefits. Although everyone acknowledges that backups are important, virtually all case studies show that the individual user will not back up files.

One of the reasons why individuals don't back up files is that local backup schemes often rely on floppy disk backup storage. Floppy backup is a time-consuming task that requires the user to sit and serve the machine, something most people don't enjoy. Tape or removable Winchester backups are fast and automated. You simply push a button, and the backup is done.

## A Device Log

Network operating systems are often written to permit considerable flexibility with regard to configuration and services. Outwardly, all the PCs, printers, and disks may look standard. Inside, however, the PCs may have modems, 3270 emulators, and gateways. The printers may have graphics or memory features. The hard disk may be reserved for a special function. These additions pertain to the network. But non-network additions will also be found in the machines, such as a color graphics card, a multifunction board, or an 8087 numeric coprocessor.

Whenever a new application is added to the machine or the network, machine configuration must be checked. If a software package doesn't run properly or if a malfunction occurs on the network, machine configuration should be considered as a possible cause.

One very useful item to the network manager is the device log, which should be made part of every networked device. If properly maintained, the log will eliminate the continual need to take the cover off the system unit and check circuit board manuals for specifications. (The device log can be combined with the maintenance log, discussed in Chapter 13.)

On the first page of the log, you can attach a printout of the PC diagnostics screen that shows configuration. On the next page, you can list every piece of hardware on the system that exceeds basic specifications. List the amount of memory. List DIP switch configurations. If there's an 8087 chip, list it. Local storage, such as a hard disk or floppy disk drive, should also be listed. With the drives, indicate the manufacturer, model, serial number, capacity, and where and when purchased. List warranty information, too.

Circuit boards should be listed with the same information as the drives. In addition, you should note any special features of the boards. Memory and I/O address assignments and service request interrupt numbers should be noted in the device log. This information can be obtained from the documentation supplied with each piece of hardware. Memory, I/O, and interrupt settings of your installed equipment should be checked every time that new equipment is added. Settings must be unique to each PC; otherwise, a conflict will cause the PC to fail.

Sometimes a problem may not show up immediately. For example, as long as two communications devices with identical I/O addresses are not activated at the same time, no problem will occur. But when the devices are used simultaneously, the resulting system failure may be hard to diagnose because everything had been performing properly up to that point. The log should help catch such conflicting settings during installation. If conflicts are missed at that time and a system failure does occur, the log will readily point out the cause of the problem.

Another section of the device log should describe any locally maintained software. And if any local hardware requires its own software program, that program should be indicated, along with its location. The manufacturer, the product name, a printout of the programs in the package, and any modifications should be included. If a user has written a program or utility, that person's name and the application should also be listed in the log. In many instances, the user may be asked to write a brief but sufficient description of how to use the application.

# 10
# Performance

Once you select a local area network, you will want to consider efficient ways to configure and use the network. Network performance, which includes speed and responsiveness, is greatly affected by several factors that the user can control, including the amount of traffic, storage strategy, and network component selection.

People become accustomed to speed; how much is enough will probably depend on what you get used to. When you first get a 300-baud modem and watch a transmission being sent, the speed is impressive. But after a while, 300 baud doesn't seem fast anymore, so you get a 1,200-baud modem. Later, if you have access to high-speed lines and a 9,600-baud modem, 1,200 baud will seem slow. Where computing is concerned, users probably won't be satisfied until all tasks can occur instantaneously.

## Reducing the Load

Networks, especially small ones with a single server and one central hard disk, tend to perform poorly in heavy traffic conditions. If many people are using the network for program transfer or are downloading a word processor or data base, the strain on the network will be noticeable. Network response time can drop below the speed of a local floppy drive.

Most people want fast response; they want to have that "personal computer feel." What they don't want is to turn their computing back into a time-sharing system.

If you are trying to improve the performance of your network, the very first thing you might consider is network utilization. Are you networking data that should be run locally? Even though you have a network, it doesn't need to be used for every file and application program. Using local drives and local storage reduces the load on the network and thereby helps improve network performance for those jobs that should run on the network.

Generally, company data should be stored on a common data base and available in a shared status. We've already discussed many examples of this kind of data, as well as the benefits derived from putting such data in a multiuser environment.

Personal files, however, should usually remain in local storage. They probably have no value in a shared system and, for many users, are quite appropriately stored on a floppy disk. Every user is going to create files that are local by nature. Memos, calendars, summaries of meetings, and similar files are more efficiently stored locally. Occasionally, when you want to send one of these files to somebody else, the network can provide the service. An appointment calendar is a good example of a file that would be improper to network, although you may share this file with your secretary. A secretary might actually keep your appointment calendar and send you daily calendars. But storage would be kept locally.

Another network utilization strategy is to download from the central hard disk and process locally. This strategy effectively permits the network and stand-alone modes to be used in combination. Such a situation occurs if you are doing computer-aided design (CAD) on a graphics station. When frequent references must be made to a large CAD file, you can work more efficiently from a local hard disk. Perhaps you want to make modifications to a certain part that is being designed. You can get the part drawings from a central storage and put them on your own local hard disk. Then you can manipulate them in the stand-alone mode on your own disk. When you're done, you check the modified drawings back into the library on the central disk via the network.

Hard disks are inexpensive enough to make this approach practical, even when network storage is available. Heavy users can be furnished with a dedicated 5M or 10M drive at their PC workstations, and they can use the network storage only when appropriate.

## Caching

For a local area network, speeds are commonly given as the rate of clear line, point-to-point movement of data across the network cable. This rate of movement is referred to as the "raw bit rate." Raw bit rate, however, is of limited value in gauging network performance because the cable is only one segment of the data path. From the point where the cable attaches to the PC to the actual user interface (display or keyboard), a series of bottlenecks reduces network performance.

An important concept to understand is that the amount of data moved is less a performance factor than the number of times it is moved. In other words, data is accessed in blocks. Moving several blocks at once is more efficient than moving the blocks one at a time. What slows down the network is a series of transfers.

A networked message moves from local memory to the local operating system, through a couple of other transfers, and onto the network card where the transmission is readied. After the message passes across the network at the raw bit rate, the same series of transfers occurs at the central server. If the message involves a request for data from the central hard disk, as is usually the case, the operating system must search the disk for the data and assemble it. Then the answer to the request proceeds back through the same process eventually to be displayed on the local PC.

If you count up all the data transfers and movements, the number is sizable. Network speed is reduced by each of these transfers and data searches. One likely possibility for speeding up networks is to eliminate as many of those data transfers as possible. They can be eliminated through a technique known as disk caching.

Most network operating systems have some form of disk cache, or electronic memory storage system. With caching, the buffer (memory) size is increased on the controller card. Information comes off the disk in 512-byte sectors. If you have a 2,000-byte buffer, you can retrieve two extra sectors per read instead of only one. Then when the next sector is called for, it will probably be in buffered memory and can be delivered quickly.

Let's explain the process in a slightly different way. The simplest caching is a read-ahead scheme. When a program requests data from a disk, the cache system picks up the requested data and any additional data that follows. Since the next read request to disk will probably be for that additional data (following what was originally requested), then the additional data will already be in electronic memory when the second request comes. In other words, if the next batch of information you request is already in the cache, the operating system won't have to go to disk. Electronic memory is much faster than disk accesses. And the caching technique serves to eliminate time-consuming data transfers.

When four or five people are working on a hard disk, disk accesses may run at about the same speed of floppies when you use your computer, depending on the application. But if each user can get a large block of data each time a transfer is made, then the network can handle perhaps two to three times as many people. By having the cache memory in the system, the number of "seeks" is reduced. A random seek from one region of the disk to another takes from 50 to 100 milliseconds. By caching, you can eliminate all the directory and file allocation seeks, beyond the initial acquisition.

The efficiency with which a network uses cache memory greatly affects the overall efficiency of the network. To enhance performance further, you can add optional memory boards and caching systems to network servers and PC workstations. These additions will optimize disk access by keeping more data in memory.

# File Structure

Access time can also be altered to improve overall performance. With a network many people will inevitably be using the mass storage hard disk

*Fig. 10.1. Orchid has PCnet products with several different performance enhancers. These include a RAM expansion with up to 256K of memory, a boot ROM for diskless operation, and an 80186 coprocessor board. Shown here is the PCnet BLOSSOM with RAM disk, disk caching, clock/calendar, and space for 384K of RAM. The daughter board is the PCnet network interface card, so the whole package requires only one expansion slot. Photograph courtesy of Orchid Technology.*

and creating files on the disk. If the users organize the file structure to its best advantage, they can reduce access times.

Not long ago, files were kept in a flat directory. After the introduction of PC DOS V2.0, tree-structured, or hierarchical directories came into being. This kind of structure nests, or subordinates files like branches on a tree. Each file in a main directory may have many files under it. Each of these files, in turn, may have many files under it, and so on.

Thus, you can optionally create many levels within the hard disk directory. A person who is new to the wonders of hierarchies often is inclined to create very elaborate paths and structures. The pleasure in this activity is usually reduced after a few files are lost in the labyrinth.

Another more serious problem with hierarchies is that they can degrade performance. Generally, the number of levels you create should be carefully limited.

To retrieve a file, the system must proceed through the tree in the same way that you would if you were searching manually. Nearer files are quickly retrieved; distant ones take more time. Even if you are 20 levels down from the root directory, you can work in that area, retrieving and storing files without noticing a speed degradation. But if you are 20 levels down on one path and you want to get information from a subdirectory on an entirely different path, which is also 20 levels down, then you will sacrifice considerable speed. The reason for limiting the size of a hierarchy thus becomes apparent.

To find a particular file, the operating system must look into each subdirectory, following the path that you've specified to the file. The operating system looks at the first directory you specify in the path, then moves the pointers to the next directory, and so on, through the path.

For the best organization, you should keep very horizontal hierarchies. You'll have a root directory as the base. Besides the common information that everyone uses, you might keep in that root directory one subdirectory for each user. Then each user could have one or two subdirectories below that. Very rarely will you need to go more than two or three levels deep in hierarchical directories.

If you think you need more levels, you can better maintain network access speed by opening up a new directory in the root to handle the new files. This approach has a side benefit of helping you to find files. Files that are nested very deep have a tendency to get lost, as was noted earlier.

# Multiple Servers

The single most significant and easily cured bottleneck on the network is the hard disk. A large amount of data is stored on this disk, and many users must have access to that data. But only one narrow route to the data is available, so narrow that no more than one person can use it at a time. Since the number of routes into the disk cannot be increased with present technology, the best solution is to add more disks and spread the data out among them.

On most local area networks a couple of options for adding hard disks are available. You can either connect a second hard disk to a single intelligent server (a computer that is running server software), or install a second server and connect the new hard disk to it. If you need more storage space, either of these options will work. But if you're trying to improve performance, installing a second server is a better option.

Most hard disks are single-user devices. The hardware is not set up for overlapping seeks and multiple drives. With a single server, data requests will therefore be answered one at a time, even though the data may be on two different disks. With two hard disks, each with its own server, you can open up the hard disk bottleneck because the system can effectively perform multiple seeks in parallel.

You also have some reliability assurances with two hard disks. If one of the servers or hard disks fails, the network can use the second server or hard disk as a backup. Of course, the data on every hard disk must be backed up on tape or other media and must also be restorable onto the second hard disk.

Multiple hard disks alleviate another speed constraint common to networking. When multiple users are accessing the same disk, they are requesting data from different spots on the disk. The users are not loading sequential data, but they are jumping around from one area to another. This activity slows down conventional disk access considerably. Having fewer users per disk reduces the problem. The question of how many people can be accommodated by a single server depends primarily on the application.

If 15 or 20 people are using the network for word processing and occasional data base runs, the performance of a single IBM PC/XT server and hard disk may be adequate. But if your network has intensive use—say, people on the phone doing order entry and others doing extensive data base searches—then you may want a file server and hard disk for every three or four users.

## Hard Disk Storage

Some vendors are finding ways to improve disk performance with software. The hard disk data transfer rate is listed at 5Mbit/sec. In reality the transfer rate is slower than 5Mbit/sec for two reasons: rotational latency and multiuser accesses. You never transfer continuously because data is sent from the hard disk in sectors. The operating system usually takes some time to work with each sector. When the operating system goes back to get more data, the system must wait for the disk to come around again with the desired sector. This condition is called rotational latency.

Interleaving, a process commonly used in hard disks, can remedy this problem to some extent. In interleaving schemes, data is stored on nonconsecutive sectors; in other words, a space is "interleaved" between the data.

Think about the disk rotating around. You read the first sector, then make a transfer from the controller buffer into memory. Note that once you get off the hard disk, some finite amount of time is needed to transfer the data to wherever you're going to put it in memory. The disk keeps rotating. You come back to pick up the second sector, and since you're already through the middle of it, you must wait for the next rotation to pick up the sector you want.

To improve performance, system designers might use a single-step interleaving scheme, which will store on every other sector, all the way around the disk. If you have an interleaf of one, you're probably very close to the beginning of that next sector when the operating system is ready to handle it. Thus, you can buy yourself time with interleaves.

Multiuser accesses create another delay. If a lot of people are accessing the disk at once, the head on the disk is jumping all over the place. One user gets a sector, then the head must jump somewhere else to get a sector for another user. The benefit of any interleaving scheme has been nullified. And with current technology, a designer of such a scheme simply cannot make it work for multiple users. For this reason, using several small hards disks may be more efficient than using one large disk and having everyone get all the data off that disk.

# Drive Technology

The heads on disk drives are positioned by one of two methods: stepper motor or voice coil positioning. All the 5 1/4-inch disks in the lower capacities are now using conventional, floppy disk, stepper motor technology. This method has a relatively slow seek time. Voice coil positioning has seek times that are two or three times faster, so a voice coil positioned drive will give significantly better performance.

Voice coil drives are more expensive, however, costing as much as 30 percent more than stepper motor drives. But if you're getting a 30M disk drive (or larger) to use on a network, the additional cost is probably justified by the decrease in access times. Voice coil drives, besides being more expensive, also draw more power. These drives cannot reside in a PC but are stand-alone units complete with their own power supply.

If you have a small network with under five users and only sporadic use of the network, you can probably get by with a standard 10M stepper motor hard disk as your main storage device. An IBM PC/XT-served network using the PC/XT's 10M hard disk for storage is the most common configuration for such a network.

Faster hard disk interfaces are coming out, some running twice the present 5Mbit/sec rate. These will not be used on small disk drives under 30M for some time, however. The hard disk interfaces will be implemented on the large, voice coil positioned drives that need to move large amounts of data quickly.

## Faster CPUs

Faster disk drives are only part of the solution. Even if you did have a faster interface available on a small disk for a single workstation, the operating system of the PC probably couldn't keep up with the faster data rate. In other words, although the disk may get data into its buffer quickly, the data must be read out. The answer is to increase the speed of the processor by going to an 80186, 68000, or other CPU that improves on the performance of the 8088.

The local area networks discussed in this book may use a server with an 8088 microprocessor, a Motorola 68000, an Intel 80186, all the way up to powerful DEC VAX computers. The IBM PC/XT, with its 8088 8-bit bus, is the slowest of the lot. If you use an 80186-based system, with its 16-bit bus, you'll see three or four times the throughput over an 8088-based system.

Some manufacturers, such as Gateway Communications and Orchid Technology, are offering circuit boards for the IBM PC or PC/XT that have an 80186 processor. In tests running PC DOS software, IBM PC/XTs with an 80186 working as coprocessors with the 8088 have shown as much as eight times the speed of the unmodified PC/XT.

When an application heavily depends on CPU cycle time (as with networking), these add-on boards may help.

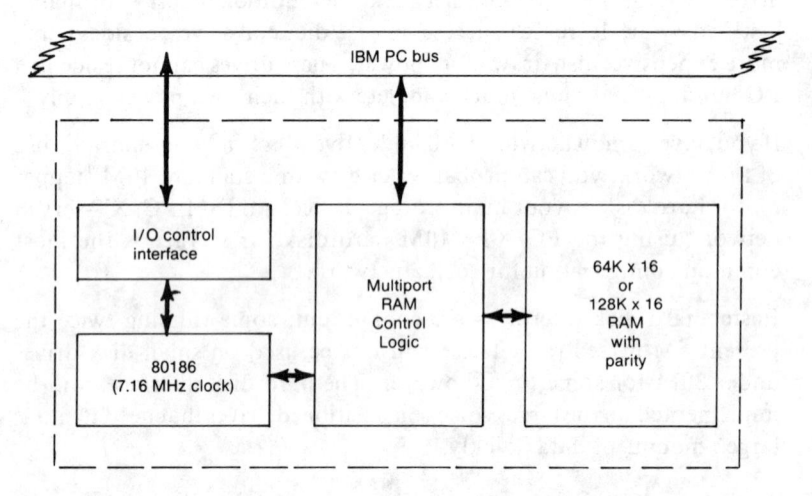

*Fig. 10.5. Coprocessor boards, equipped with an 80186 microprocessor chip, make use of the chip's 16-bit memory data bus to transfer data. The block diagram shows the data path of the Gateway Communications Supercharger board. Reprinted by permission of Gateway Communications.*

The local operating system is run on the PC's 8088 CPU. When an applications program is called up, the program is loaded onto the memory on the new board. The next time that a DOS call is made, it is redirected into the 80186 board's memory so that the 80186 executes the call rather than the 8088 on the system board. The server can thus give improved performance by utilizing the 80186 as a coprocessor.

# The Cable as a Bottleneck

Another possible bottleneck, especially on networks with multiple servers, is the cable. If a dozen people start exercising several disk servers simultaneously, the cable can become bottlenecked. A cable bottleneck should show up in collision and retry statistics.

The only way to alleviate a cable bottleneck is to reduce the amount of traffic on the cable. This can be done by evaluating how the network is

## Growing the Network

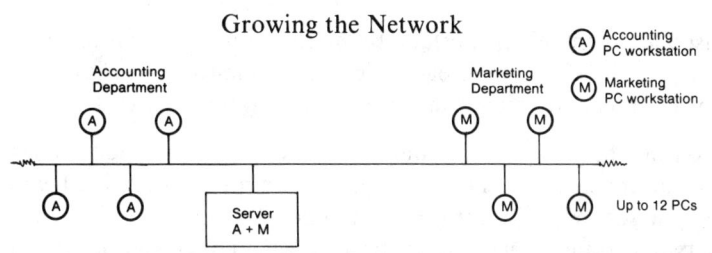

*Fig. 10.2. Small networks often start out with one server and hard disk, providing data storage for the entire network. Here the accounting department and the marketing department both have their files on the same disk and compete for server time.*

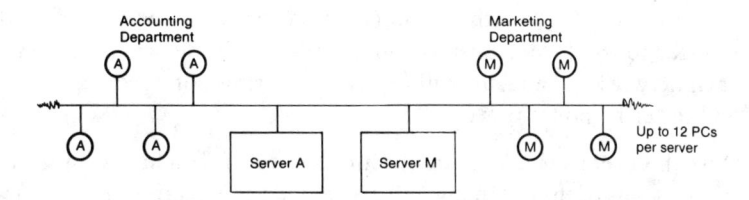

*Fig. 10.3. Large numbers of requests will slow hard disk performance and response time. As the network traffic grows, through more applications or more attached PCs, the single hard disk may become a bottleneck. Adding a second server and hard disk so that accounting and marketing each has its own storage system will reduce the load on the hard disks and speed up the network performance.*

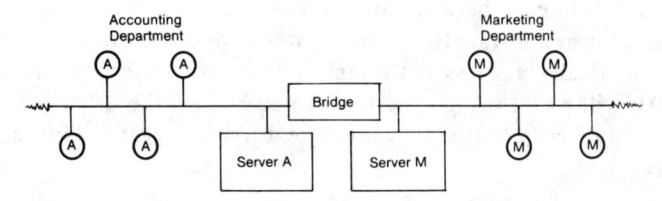

*Fig. 10.4. Even with two servers, each network message will travel the entire cable, regardless of the server or PC involved in the transmission. Very heavy traffic can clog the network cable. When this problem is indicated by high error/retry statistics, the single network can be split into two networks, one for accounting and one for marketing. In this way, either department's messages can remain intradepartmental. A bridge can be placed between the two networks to pass interdepartmental messages. Communications are maintained, and performance is maximized.*

used and, where appropriate, by pulling some applications back to a local mode. If you've already tried this maneuver and the cable is still overworked, you may want to establish multiple networks.

You should first examine your network applications and files. Usually, the intradepartmental file sharing and communications are heavy, and the interdepartmental traffic is minimal. You can therefore break the network connection between one department or cluster of departments and another department or cluster. The cable on each side of the break will need its own server and central hard disk and will become a self-sufficient network.

Before you divide the cable, every transmission sent by any device traverses the full length of the cable. Afterward, the traffic load is reduced to whatever transmissions are sent by the devices remaining on each network. The result will be fewer transmission errors and retries and faster response time.

With this break in network connection, however, you have now isolated two sections of the company and prevented these sections from sharing data and communicating over data lines. Remember that these activities are two of the reasons for networking in the first place. You can solve this problem by installing a *bridge*. Essentially, a bridge connects networks with identical protocols and permits internetwork traffic. With a bridge between your two networks, you can pass data back and forth and work virtually as if you still had a single network.

The main difference between an internet and a single network is that with an internet, intranetwork traffic does not cross the bridge. Only data specifically addressed to some person or device on the other network will pass through the bridge and run on the other network. Bridges have several other very useful features, as discussed in Chapter 14.

# High-Performance Peripherals

With a local area network, one option is to get high-performance peripherals, such as a high-speed printer. Another option is to buy several slower printers until their aggregate speed matches that of the high-speed device. We have seen that in many cases several small hard disks are preferable to a single, large hard disk. The issues are quite different, however, when you are considering printers.

With printers the primary issue is reliability. If you want to guard against a failure, two devices are usually better than one—that is, if the devices are equally reliable. Reliability is measured in MTBF hours (mean-time-between-failures hours). Most manufacturers can furnish this statistic. A heavy-duty printer, such as the Printronix MVP line printer, may have an MTBF of 5,000 hours for a given application.

Let's compare a network with one MVP and five users to a network with five small printers, one for each user. The reliability of these small printers may be 2,000 hours each. For a given 5,000 hours of printer use, the MVP network will be down once, but the network using small printers will have 2 1/2 device failures during the same period. This does not mean that the single large printer makes a more reliable system. The issue is somewhat more complex. When the single large printer goes down, all the printing on the network stops. But when one of the smaller printers goes down, the others on the network can be used while the faulty device is being repaired.

A second aspect of reliability concerns forms handling. Generally, the heavy-duty printer, which is built to move heavy forms quickly, has tractors with many pins engaging the paper. Because of the design of this printer, it usually does a much better job of forms handling. If your office uses multipart forms or has printers in a remote location, the heavy-duty printer is the obvious choice. You can't afford to have people spending their time in adjusting forms and rerunning jobs just because the forms jammed or came out of the tractors.

On the other hand, if your office uses a variety of light forms, it may be more cost effective to dedicate a small printer to each form. This approach will also reduce the amount of forms handling.

Reliability, then, is based on three component/system features: mean-time-between-failure, hardware backup, and functional design. Most networks should have at least two printers, with one providing backup for the other. Mean-time-between-failure, as a measure of reliability, should be based on the entire system rather than on individual components. The functional design of a printer, such as its forms-handling capability, should be adequate for the task.

After reliability, another important consideration is throughput. In our earlier example, we compared printer downtime on the basis of aggregate speed. As an actual test of throughput, this measurement is probably inaccurate since it implies that several users are printing at the same time.

In many offices most of the man-hours are spent in gathering and manipulating data, not in printing. For instance, if analysts are doing "what if" calculations on a spreadsheet, they'll be working mostly with the data. When they want a printout, they want it quickly. Unless the printer is shared by many users and the use is heavy, a high-speed printer will deliver hard copies faster than will dedicated small printers. Making a survey of office printer use will suggest your best choice of a printer for throughput.

Faster printer speed should be thought of in relation to PC compatibility and other features. You may be considering a 2,000-line-per-minute band printer, but will it do the job? As long as the network is IBM PC-based, you should probably concentrate on printers that are supported by PC software, unless you can justify doing some serious programming to get a bigger printer up and running. Should you decide to upgrade, you'll want to have the same character features that are on smaller dot-matrix printers: emphasis, boldface, superscript, subscript, and both raster and bit-image graphics.

The choice and distribution of printers are very much individual matters. Features such as print quality, throughput, forms handling, and MTBF must be weighed against use patterns and specific applications requirements. By letting you share printers and other peripherals, a local area network removes unit cost as the overriding factor in your decisions on printers, allowing you to focus more on satisfying the needs of your office.

# 11
# Security

Security for microcomputer local area networks is a new field. Most companies supplying encryption and other data security systems as yet have no specific products for use on PCs and local area networks. Nearly every company, however, indicates that such products will be forthcoming soon.

This expanding interest in security reflects two facts. One is that local area networks are rapidly growing in importance. The other is that users are becoming more aware of the value of the vast amounts of data they are accumulating and the need to protect this data.

Newspapers carry stories almost every week about some computer network being penetrated, either for financial gain or as a prank. Most of these break-ins involve large corporate networks and wide area networks. As local area networks proliferate and tap into national and international data communications systems, these local networks will also become targets.

Companies that do sensitive work, such as those with defense contracts, are often heavily involved in data security. Other companies may be aware only of the threat, but not of their own vulnerability. Most analysts agree that businesses and institutions, such as schools, will have to suffer a loss through theft or vandalism before they actually establish measures to protect their data.

## Networks and Security

All the features of electromagnetic media that are desirable to a user also make this media vulnerable to theft and damage. Information stored on disk is easily copied, easily altered, and easily erased. As larger amounts of critical data are stored in this way, the significance of the problem grows.

A stand-alone personal computer is easy to secure. You simply put your diskettes in a safe and store your computer in a locked closet. But when you hook up that computer to a network of computers, security becomes more complicated. Even a "local" network will probably spread out through several offices, with connecting cables running in ceilings and floors, and in halls and basements.

A thief or vandal can tap into any one of a dozen or more spots on the network, many secluded from normal observation. But tapping into the network from some secluded spot on the cable isn't usually necessary. A person can simply logon to a convenient PC and steal or damage data at will. Unfortunately, the easier a system is to use, the easier it is to misuse.

Like any other kind of insurance, data security involves trade-offs. You must weigh the cost of the potential loss against the cost of protection as well as any inconvenience the security measures may cause. The first thing to do in planning your data security program is to put a value on the data you're going to protect.

## Risk Analysis

Before you can realistically decide how much time and money to invest in data security, you must quantify the risk. Risk analysis has been elevated to a precise discipline. For our purposes, we won't need to examine formulas or other exact methods of quantifying every risk associated with networked data. But we can look briefly at some of the elements of risk analysis. These can help you to develop a preliminary description of your data's value and potential for loss.

First, you will want to determine two values, in dollars, for the information stored in your data system. One is the cost of re-creating the data; the other is the value of lost business if a competitor should gain access to your data.

These two figures should be easy to obtain or at least to estimate. Many smaller companies have never considered the potential loss of their stored data. If nothing else, such an appraisal should encourage the use of data backup and the insistence on serious password security procedures.

Next, you should identify any possible threats to your data. If your data has little or no monetary value to a competitor, then there is probably little risk of theft. On the other hand, the value of your data to a competitor may be quite great, with the risk of theft proportionally high.

The physical volume of valuable data is another element to consider. If the volume and diversity of the data are extensive, the chance of a total loss by theft is reduced. A related calculation is the frequency of potential thefts. This figure can be difficult to predict unless you have compiled a history of losses over some period of time. Law enforcement agencies and some trade associations keep extensive records of thefts, defined by type of business, kind of penetration, and value of loss. Contacting these groups may turn up sufficient data that allows you to make an intelligent prediction of risk. In addition, you should make a detailed study of any active attacks on your data so that you can estimate the cost of countering a similar attack.

Vandalism is another threat, possibly more serious than theft because the frequency of vandalism is often greater. A discontented employee may decide to "get even" by destroying or altering important files. Or an act of vandalism may be done simply as a prank or game, just to see if it can be done.

After you have calculated the value of your data and the types of risks, the final element in risk analysis is the vulnerability (or availability) of the data. If your local area network has remote access, the potential for loss increases. But if your network operating system has no means for hiding files from unauthorized users, an even greater potential exists for unauthorized access.

Making this kind of analysis will enable you to answer many questions about where risks are greatest and how much money and procedural inconveniences are necessary to thwart these threats. Next, let's consider steps to building a secure data network.

## Levels of Security

There is no such thing as 100 percent security. Any security measure can be defeated, given enough skill on the part of the perpetrator and enough time to complete the job.

Of the two security elements of skill and time, the most dependable protection is time. If you can make certain that a break-in will be a time-consuming project for a thief, you have gone a long way in protecting your data. Therefore, all serious security systems are layered with not one but several security measures. For a local area network the following strategies should be considered:

1. Physical security
2. Personal identification
3. Encryption
4. The diskless PC
5. Protection against cable radiation
6. Call-back security

### *Physical Security*

Data security can take many forms. The simplest is physical security, which may be a lock on the computer or a guard at the door. With physical security, a would-be thief must attack and defeat your security measures before becoming a threat to the data.

Locks can set up barriers anywhere from the back door to the office door to the computer itself. Key locks are now provided for IBM 3270-class terminals. The lock interrupts the power to the display and the keyboard, while still allowing the terminal to remain on-line. Turning the key powers up the user interfaces; the key cannot be removed while the system is on. This kind of physical security will soon be available for personal computers, especially networked PCs.

An alarm system works in partnership with your physical security measures. These measures, particularly locking devices, are designed to increase the time needed for penetration. Alarms put an effective limit on the amount of time available. Professional criminals don't run when they hear an alarm or when they think they've tripped a silent alarm. Most know precisely how much time they have before the police arrive. If they can't get through the security system's physical barriers in the time available, then they'll abandon the effort.

Locks and alarms can be part of effective security and provide excellent protection. But they may be of little value against employees.

## *Personal Identification*

A local area network presents some additional security problems because of its dispersed nature and because many people have access to the network. Remote access through modems and telephone lines is commonly available on host-to-terminal networks and will become widely used on microcomputer networks over the next few years.

Today on most local area networks the first line of security is personal identification. You physically recognize people who are authorized to be in your office, sitting at a PC. With remote access this kind of identification is impossible. Companies must rely on passwords and classified access schemes to protect their data.

Several techniques can be used to restrict access to authorized users. All these techniques are based on some kind of identification: personal, such as ID badge; key word, such as a login name and password; or key number.

Badges and personal recognition may not be successful in large companies where everyone is not personally known. In a company with many employees, a counterfeit badge may in fact be all that is necessary to penetrate a security system based solely on identification.

## Passwords

Password security adds no cost to the network and is potentially a useful security measure. After logging onto the network, the user must type in a password. Theoretically, if users must give a password, unauthorized access is prevented. But often the password system is misused and ineffective.

Passwords are usually chosen because they are easily remembered. This, however, also makes them easily guessed. Common assignments include first name for login name and last name or title for password. The value of passwords is further diluted when employees give their passwords to others in the organization. A password is often given out because another employee needs to read a particular file or needs to perform some task for an absent employee. Then, too, the computer is the perfect password breaker. A simple program can be run that attacks the network hundreds of times per second until the password is discovered.

Password protection can be improved through both systematized procedures and more sophisticated operating system password utilities. Passwords should be assigned by a network manager, not by the individual. This assignment method reduces the likelihood that someone will identify the password in half a dozen guesses. Many network operating systems have a password utility that allows authorized users to change their own passwords. Such a utility should be deleted from all users' directories and given only to the network supervisor.

Over time, passwords will become generally known, particularly within a small office or department. This decaying security can be stopped by periodically issuing new passwords, say, on a monthly basis. One additional advantage of changing passwords regularly is that employees will take more seriously both the password system and the subject of security.

## Security in Login

The network operating system should be designed to thwart attempts to break into the system. For one thing, the password should not be "echoed" back to the screen when the user types it in during login. The number of times that a password can be attempted should be limited to no more than three tries; after that, the login name should be temporarily invalidated, and the network supervisor notified of a failed login. An audit trail can also be provided to record the number of password attempts from a given user or station. The presence of the audit trail utility that monitors the password system is a deterrent in itself, especially to malicious or casual vandals.

A sophisticated thief, however, can collect login routines and passwords as they are entered, often simply by tapping into the network. The network operating system can be enhanced to make this activity more difficult for the thief. Passwords can be encrypted at the workstation and decrypted at the central processor so that the data on the cable is unusable through a tap.

As part of security planning and implementation, an independent analyst should evaluate the security measures, even to the extent of attempting to steal or corrupt a prearranged target file.

## *Encryption*

Encryption is the process of changing intelligible data into unintelligible data; decryption reverses the process. For most local area networks, data encryption is used only when the security threat is substantial.

Securing data in a network environment is more difficult than securing physical documents. In a network the data is typically held in a common storage facility. Anyone authorized to use the central storage can potentially access classified files. In a network the best remedy is to store the data in an encrypted form. Thus, any unauthorized person accessing the file will not be able to read its contents.

Encryption techniques cover a broad range, from simple encryption protecting against accidental disclosure to sophisticated methods that protect against all but the highly trained criminal with an in-depth knowledge of cryptanalysis and considerable deciphering equipment.

Most encryption schemes are based on mathematical operations that are "computationally infeasible." That is, they are based on prime numbers which are so large that even the computational power of a mainframe computer can't break the code within a practical time period.

There are two primary types of encryption: link and end-to-end. Link encryption is used to make data unreadable while it is on a point-to-point link, such as between two PCs. Link encryption prevents the casual reading of data but not the modification or deletion of data.

End-to-end encryption protects data anywhere on the system. This type of encryption corresponds to layer 4 (the transport layer) in the International Standards Organization Open Systems Interconnection (OSI) architecture. Because layer 4 is end-to-end, encryption at this layer can provide protection to any number of communications links or intermediate networks.

Norell Data Systems has a software program, called Crypt, that can be used for file encryption. The program begins an encrypted file with a heading that shows the version of the program being used for encryption. A random number generator is initialized in response to a user-provided keyword, and then each successive byte of the input file is altered by the next random number. Each random number depends on many of the earlier ones, so that finding one document in both open and encrypted form would not provide sufficient information to break the system.

The algorithm used by the Crypt program is stronger than that used in similar systems with a random number generator, but weaker than the National Bureau of Standards Data Encryption Standard (DES). Therefore, Crypt is not recommended for use in extremely sensitive applications, such as transfers of funds or national security.

## Encryption Keys

One encryption system that uses an encryption key is commonly found on dial-up networks and is now migrating onto local area networks. A key is essentially a formula for coding and decoding a message. Traditionally, keys have been carefully distributed to authorized users. In fact, the security of the distribution channel for keys often establishes the security level of a system.

Such a system of secret keys is very difficult and expensive to maintain, especially as the number of participants increases. To overcome these disadvantages, a new key called a "public key" was devised. Public keys may be published openly, and they permit virtually any individual to use a personal public key to code a message and send it to another person. To decode the message, however, the receiver must use a secret key. A secret key consists of two prime numbers that are not published.

One other application of public keys is authenticating messages. You can encrypt a message using your secret key and send it to a second person. That person will take your public key and use it to decode the message. If your public key does decode an encoded message presumably sent by you, then proof has been provided that you did indeed send the message. In other words, the public key is an electronic signature.

All keys are factorable and, therefore, limited in their level of security. Over the last few years, a debate has been going on about how complex a key should be. Generally, any encryption system will provide file privacy against casual perusal. Such encryption systems are quite inexpensive. Beyond this common benefit, the quality of encryption should depend on the probable competence of the intruder and on the value of the data.

## On-Line Coders

The easiest measure to take for local area network security is to attach an encryption device at either end of a communications link. Merritt Security makes such devices and will modify them for specific applications. After the devices are installed, the system is fully transparent to the user. With each person using an encryption box (Merritt's is called a Transcriptor), the message sent between parties will be encrypted while it's on the line.

Another way to set up a system is to place an encryption box between each PC and the network. Then all the data that goes out on the network and all data stored on the hard disk will be encrypted. Merritt uses a Z80 processor with 64K of memory, so the device can be modified and tuned to provide the speed and security needed. If necessary, a public key system can be built in also.

To show how a security system like Merritt's might work, let's suppose we have three groups on a network: administration (admin), accounting, and sales. All the data on the network can be encrypted. The administrator can read everything, but accounting and sales can read only their respective files. Each user encrypts the data on an optional basis. With each transmission the encryption device will ask the user whether to transmit in the clear or with encryption. The administrator's device will also ask of the administrator, "Which key do you want: admin, accounting, or sales?"

## *The Diskless PC*

The power of the PC itself is a potential security threat that should be considered. One of the advantages that the personal computer has over dumb terminals is its local storage capability. Information can be locally manipulated and stored on a PC's floppy diskettes, then transferred to the central storage. From central storage the information can be made available to other users and maintained and backed up properly.

With local storage devices, users can maintain their own backup system, independent of the central system. The degree of autonomy associated with a personal set of data diskettes is appealing to many users. At the same time, such autonomy creates two threats to data security.

One threat is unintentional. Because two copies of data exist, one on the central disk and one locally, the copies may be updated independently. Eventually, unique data on one version may be lost when the two "copies" are merged.

The other threat is that a local disk drive permits data theft. A person with access to the network and with a local disk drive can copy large amounts of data onto floppy disks in just minutes. The data, then, can be easily hidden and removed from even reasonably secure buildings.

Most network vendors now provide the capability of booting a local PC workstation from a central server so that diskless PCs can be used on the network. Such machines require full-time networking and permit no local storage. A common reason for using diskless PCs is cost. Because diskless PCs require no local floppy controller or disk drive, you save approximately $1,000 per machine. But equally important is the increased security offered by a diskless PC.

Take away the disk drive and you take away the means for stealing the data. But you also reduce the power of the PC. In many instances local storage is desirable. (See Chapter 10 for examples.) One answer is to exchange a local floppy drive for a local hard disk. Then not only would the user have all the benefits of local storage, but local speed and efficiency would improve also. No ready way, however, would be available to copy or remove data.

Diskless PCs have been hampered by software problems. Many applications programs are designed to run only from a local floppy disk drive. Diagnostics and the operating system itself have usually required at least one local drive.

Increasingly, though, software vendors are providing some mechanism for their applications packages to be stored on a hard disk and used in a multiuser environment. A company can then make its own decisions about how to configure PCs. Probably the answer will be a variety of configurations to fit particular circumstances.

## *Protection against Cable Radiation*

Anytime information is transmitted, even through cable, that information can potentially be intercepted by unauthorized persons. The possibility also exists that a vandal can tamper with data or destroy data files.

Several methods may be used for protecting data while it is on the cable. The first thing to do is to put the cable out of sight. This step should be taken anyway, to prevent damage to the cable and to meet building codes. Security is a secondary benefit. Install cables in protective raceways in areas where penetration is less likely.

A radio signal that is broadcast onto the air waves can easily be intercepted and the information stolen. Such emissions are not limited to broadcasted radio signals, however. A data cable also radiates intelligible signals, just as a transmitting antenna does. Simple intercept equipment located near the cable can pick up and record these transmissions. More sophisticated devices can intercept the signals a considerable distance from the cable.

The likelihood of signal interception can be eliminated by using a shielded cable, which is a cylinder of braided copper wire that encases the intelligence-carrying wires. If one shield doesn't reduce emissions to satisfactory levels, more shields can be added. Frequently, cable with the necessary electrical characteristics is available in only one version. If additional shielding is needed, special shielding conduit is available that meets government security standards.

Another way to eliminate the cable radiation problem entirely is by using fiber-optic cable. Fiber optics technology uses a glass fiber to carry a beam of light. Information is passed when the light is modulated. With fiber optics no signal is emitted outside the cable; thus, data cannot be intercepted. Because fiber-optic cable is also extremely difficult to tap into physically, it is ideal for security purposes.

## Call-Back Security

Remote workstations are becoming a significant aspect of local area networking. Today users can access networks remotely and execute batch transfers of data. Software will soon be available to let the remote user actually log into the network and use the system as if the user were local. Securing this type of access requires special measures.

Call-back security and user management are part of dial-up systems and can be used with remote PC-to-network traffic. With call-back security, when you want to access a computer, you can call into a different number instead of calling in directly. You indicate that you want to access the network, and the security device arranges for a call-back to your location. In other words, the system has embedded within battery-supported memory a complete listing for every allowed user. Included in this file is a seven-digit ID number that you must punch in when you want to access the file, a telephone number at which you can be reached, and the host systems to which you are allowed access.

The security device also keeps track of user priorities. If all available lines are busy, the device sets up a queue based on the priority of the user. The device will inform the caller regarding queue position. When a line becomes available, the device contacts the user. Therefore, the user never has to get busy signals. The device also keeps accounting information for traffic statistics and billbacks.

# 12
# Installation

Personal computer users tend to be blasé about PC installation and maintenance. This attitude may be justified because of the ease with which PCs can be repaired. When you install a network, however, the situation changes drastically.

A network is inherently more complex than a stand-alone computer. Unlike the single PC, a network is not movable. Many of its problems may be difficult to diagnose. Moreover, while downtime on a single PC won't seriously damage company operations, downtime of the network can bring business to a halt. How you handle the installation phase of networking will have an effect on the network's initial cost, reliability, maintenance, and expansion and reconfiguration.

As part of any network plan, building and electrical codes must be known. You'll want an assessment of the data security measures required by your company. You'll also need to know whether certain elements of the network, such as the cable, will be subjected to high heat, moisture, caustic fumes, or other conditions that might require special installation. Finally, no building layout is going to remain static indefinitely, but you should try to estimate the probable changes. With this basic knowledge, you can begin installation planning.

## The Installation Log

As you begin to install your network, you should maintain a record of the system. This record should include full details about what kinds of cable and connectors are used, how the connectors are installed, and the name of the cable supplier.

In the installation log, you should describe the limits of the network, including the number of nodes. You should describe the maximum length of cables and the minimum distance permitted between nodes. You'll also want to describe the various kinds of hardware used in expanding the network, such as taps, repeaters, and passive or active HUBs. Much of this information should already be in the user's manual or the technical manual supplied by the network vendor. Repeating the information in your log will ensure that these descriptions are readily available when work is done on the installation.

A schematic diagram of the cable system is essential, of course. Each PC, hard disk, printer, and any other device on the network should be physically numbered, with the corresponding number also marked on the diagram. Network addresses should be noted, too, especially if they differ from your equipment numbering system. If dedicated cables are used for any devices, you should tape an identification label to the end of each cable and also indicate in the diagram each cable's use.

Whenever the cables or nodes are moved or the system is expanded, the diagram should be updated. If you list and date every service/maintenance job in the log, each entry will serve as a reminder to update the diagram. The installation log should be kept in hard copy by the network supervisor. If you want the information stored on-line, this record should be kept only in addition to the hard copy log.

Faceplates and cross-connect panels should each be marked with a cable number and the location of the other end of the cable. With a faceplate the easiest way to do this is to write the information directly onto the back of the faceplate.

## Cable Distribution

Cable installation for a local area network is often just an afterthought. If you ask many network users about their cable, they'll point high on the wall to some exposed, stapled coax, snaking in and out of offices.

This simple method of installation has several advantages. It's inexpensive, fast, and easy to maintain and modify. Rearranging furniture and workstations poses little problem; just pull down the cable if necessary, and then tack it up to conform to the new layout.

One disadvantage of this open, informal cable installation is that it may not conform to some of the local building and fire codes. The exposed cables are also more likely to be subjected to physical abuse that could produce an intermittent short in the network. Another obvious disadvantage is the unsightliness of the exposed cables. Coax on the walls may be appropriate for a factory but not for many office decors. The trick is to install the cable so that it is hidden and protected, meets local codes, yet is accessible and easily adapted to new office arrangements.

The most commonly used methods of cable distribution are to route cables through one of the following:

1. Surface raceway
2. Conduit
3. Over-ceiling cable tray
4. Under-floor duct

Often you'll have to use several of these methods to complete one network system.

Surface raceways are covered metal channels that can be attached to walls and routed wherever necessary. This method of installation is simple, protects the cable, and is easy to maintain and modify. By using

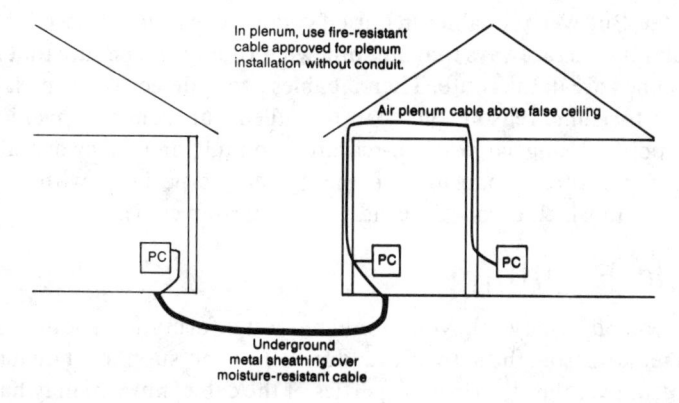

*Fig. 12.1. Additional cable protection. Courtesy of Anixter.*

surface raceways, you avoid the expense of going inside existing walls, ceilings, or floors.

Conduit is a metal pipe used to shield cable. Many local codes permit conduit-shielded cable to be run on the surface, as with surface raceways or through walls and ceilings.

An under-floor cable installation is the most secure from tampering but may be impractical unless the cable has been installed during building construction. Relocating workstations later on can be difficult with under-floor cables.

Use of over-ceiling cable trays is ideal, provided the over-ceiling space is accessible. Offices with drop ceilings frequently use this method of cable distribution. Cables are brought down to PC level through the wall partitions. Depending on the code, you may be able to omit the cable tray and simply route the cable through the ceiling. New kinds of cable meet fire safety codes by requiring the use of trays and other metal armor. Over-ceiling routing of nonconduit cable runs is often the most practical and inexpensive solution, particularly in small installations.

## Planning Ahead

Before you begin a network installation, you should plan for future modifications, growth, and periodic repair. This planning is especially important for the cable distribution phase of installation.

Unless you use surface raceways, some cables will be buried in floors, ceilings, and walls. The more you can minimize the burying of cables, the better. But even the cables in buried systems can be made accessible. Use conduit and raceways that are somewhat roomy and be sure that no sharp bends are in the route. Then if cables prove defective or must be changed for some reason, they can be pulled out from a convenient access point. Using larger-than-required conduit and raceways also allows for future expansion of the system, especially with Star topologies in which each PC has its own dedicated cable.

## Cable Handling

Before you buy a network, you should request information about cable characteristics from the network vendor or the cable supplier. You have no control over the electrical properties of the cable, but you may have three or four choices of cable that meet electrical specifications and also offer additional features. Any cable supplier should be able to show you the options.

A standard coaxial cable has a center conductor and a shield. Cable with a second shield is called triax. Twinax is cable with two conductors and a shield. Generally, you cannot substitute cables, such as using triax for coax, without making modifications. If the manufacturer puts a coaxial cable connector on the network interface card, you should connect coax to that card. Adapters are available that let you connect, say, twinax into a coaxial cable connector. Then if your installation were subjected to high levels of interference, twinax would enable both signals to be carried on inner conductors that are protected by the outer shield. You should check with a cable supplier for the feasibility of such an arrangement for your particular network.

Cable information from a vendor or supplier will include handling procedures for the cable. Improper cable handling can cause intermittent transmission problems to plague the network, which may force you to rewire the entire network. Severe damage can result from seemingly harmless actions. Small amounts of damage are magnified in longer runs of cable, so the longer the run, the more care you should exercise in cable handling.

If you kink cable, especially coax, you're inviting problems. Twisted-pair cable is less susceptible to kinking because the dielectric is not likely to be cramped as long as the kinking doesn't physically cut through the cable. Coax cable is different. Coax is a tube with a helical spiral that holds the tube around the center conductor. If you kink a coax cable, you change the distance between the center conductor and the shield, which will alter the impedance and the capacitance at that point. The result of a kink, therefore, is a damaged spot on the cable, which can block transmission.

The difference between kinking and bending is a matter of degree. Cables are meant to be flexible, up to a point. If a flexible cable is to be installed in a fixed, bent configuration, the minimum bend radius recommended is five times the cable's diameter. (This rule is only a general one, and it should be checked for each particular cable.) A greater bend creates a kink.

A cable is not designed to support weight, not even its own. If cable is run in the open instead of through conduit or trays, the cable should be

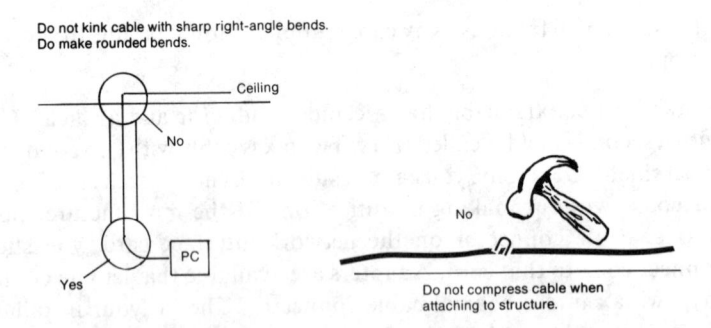

*Fig. 12.2. Cable handling. Courtesy of Anixter.*

attached with proper cable clamps at least every 10 to 15 feet. Transceivers, line interface devices, and other cable hardware should be attached to solid supports, either part of the building or specially constructed additions.

Attaching a cable to a wall can produce a problem like kinking. If you put over the cable a metal staple and pound it into the wall, the staple can crimp the cable just as if the cable were kinked. The cable should be attached with special cable mounts. These have a metal band that snugly fits the cable's circumference, and a tab that extends from the band and may be nailed into the wall.

In most installations, at some point you will have to pull the cable through a narrow opening. Too much force will stretch the braid and crimp the dielectric. Severe pulling can stretch or break the center conductor.

Moisture can also create problems for a network. For example, if moisture gets into the end of coax cable, the moisture changes the electrical characteristics of the cable and will eventually cause corrosion and signal degradation. The best protection from moisture is to keep the cable capped. But when cable is stored inside a building in a dry climate, the cable doesn't need capping. If cable is going to be in a wet location or shipped to a wet climate, the cable should definitely be capped. Generally, water is a problem, but humidity is not. Of course, in very adverse conditions, such as 100 percent humidity, corrosion of uncapped cable is likely.

Underground installations usually have moisture problems. Moisture may enter flexible cables through pinholes in the jacket or through the ends of the cable. The combination of moisture and large fluctuations in temperature can cause condensation in the cables. At low spots in a cable length, the moisture will collect and may cause corrosion or shorting of a connector. In addition, underground moisture has a rapid corrosive effect on buried cables. Special cables that are highly impervious to moisture are available for underground use. Underground cable should also be encased in a metal sheathing to protect against damage caused by rodents.

## Cable Connectors

You can purchase cables already assembled to your specifications, or you can make up your own cables from bulk cable and connectors. BNC connectors with two-lug bayonet attachments are commonly used on local area networks. These quick disconnect devices add very little resistance to the line. No special training is needed to learn how to install them.

There are two basic types of connectors for building your cables. One is the wrench-crimp type, and the other is the tool-crimp type. The wrench crimp is reusable and has a connection that must be soldered. Care must be taken to heat both the connector and the cable wire in order to avoid a cold solder joint. The tool-crimp connector needs no soldering but does require a special crimping tool. This tool must be properly adjusted for it to make a good connection.

These two types of connectors are identical in performance and strength. The only difference is that the wrench-crimp connector takes a longer time to install. However, for a person installing not more than 20 or 30 connectors, the wrench-crimp connector is the better choice since the tool-crimp connector requires the purchase of a crimping tool.

All cable hardware is being improved. One innovation is a single-piece BNC connector for RG-62. Because the connector is a single piece, it terminates more reliably and is mechanically stronger and simpler. Using just a stripper, you can install this connector in almost one-third the time that it takes to install other connectors. Installation takes only about 30 seconds per connection and requires no soldering or crimping.

**Stub Connection**

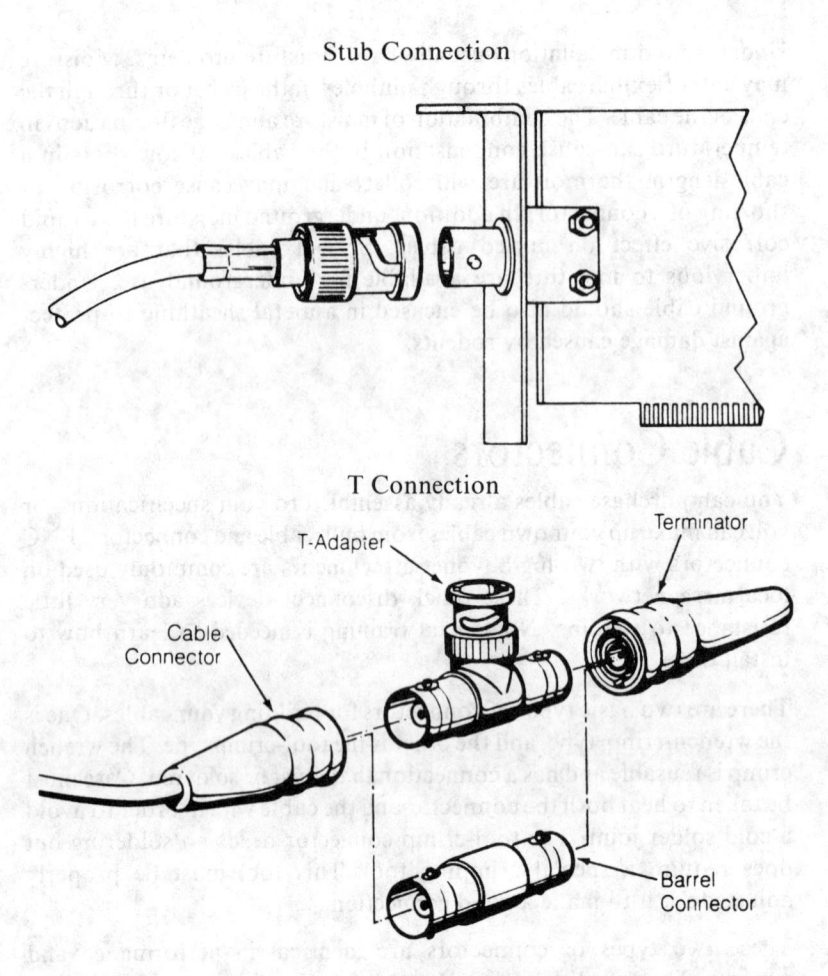

**T Connection**
- T-Adapter
- Terminator
- Cable Connector
- Barrel Connector

*Fig. 12.3. A distributed bus. Some bus networks permit a short stub (under six feet) on the main cable to connect PCs. Others connect the bus directly to the PC through a T connector. Stub connection reprinted by permission of Gateway Communications. T connection reprinted by permission of 3Com Corp.*

Wall plates that will fit on a standard electrical box are available from any electrical supply house. These plates are drilled with one, two, or four holes to hold BNC bulkhead connectors. The cable can be brought through the wall; then the BNC connector can be installed. Twisted-pair cable can be terminated with a modular phone jack for which a variety

*Fig. 12.4. A wrench-crimp connector. Reprinted by permission of Trompeter Electronics, Inc.*

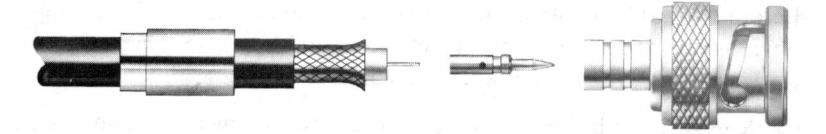

*Fig. 12.5. A tool-crimp connector. Reprinted by permission of Trompeter Electronics, Inc.*

of wall plates and other accessories are available. Phone lines and network cables can conveniently be run to the same wall plate. This can be done with appropriate plates, and no interference should be experienced.

A tremendous amount of new hardware is designed for twisted pair telephone use. Most of this hardware works fine for data network applications. You can get modular panels that support the little square connectors that you see on telephone cords. And both six-and eight-position modular jacks are available for use with data. Some of these are shielded.

## Fire-Retardant Cable

The plastic jacket on cables will burn much like a fuse. A flame will start at one end of the cable and move quickly down its length. This spreading of fire is commonly referred to as the wicking effect. When the jacket burns, it produces a very toxic gas. Fire codes increasingly reflect this danger, making some fire shield or other safety device mandatory for new installations.

Often the best way to meet the fire codes is to use plenum cable. Plenum cable versions of RG coaxial cable are fire retardant. The jacket of plenum cable is made with fluorocarbon insulations. The jacket will burn, but with low smoke and low flame. Plenum cable can be installed in false ceilings without conduit.

Plenum cable is more expensive than standard cable but less expensive than standard cable with code-required conduit. Plenum cable also is stiffer than RG cable and difficult to manipulate. However, since plenum cable doesn't require conduit, the installation is easier.

## Cable Testing

Before the cable is installed, you should visually inspect it for any obvious cuts or damage to the jacket. Look for kinks, too. Then test the electrical soundness of the cable and connections.

Cable testing can be an expensive process. But in most cases, you can run a DC test on the cable and connectors. Take an ohm meter and check for a certain number of ohms resistance in the line. Don't confuse the ohms of impedance, which are a cable specification, with the ohms of resistance, for a given length of cable. A DC test is based on the ohms of resistance, which are documented for every type of cable at specified lengths. If you've made a good connection and the cable is in good condition, the DC resistance should be very close to the resistance specified by the cable manufacturer for the length of cable.

To check resistance, place the ohm meter probes on the center conductor at each end of the cable. Then test the shield by holding the probes on the outer shells of the connectors. Finally, place a probe at one end of the cable on the center conductor and the probe at the other end of the cable on the shield. The resistance should be infinite, indicating that the conductor and shield are properly isolated from each other.

## Fault Tolerance

As you plan for network installation, you should consider fault tolerance, which is a design concept that reduces the likelihood of system failure. Ideally, any component on the network that constitutes a single point of failure should be duplicated. Then if the component fails, its redundant counterpart can fill in while the repair is being made.

Obviously, fault tolerance can be very expensive insurance. The single points of failure on a local area network are a dedicated disk server, a hard disk, a printer, and the network cable. Duplicating each of these, just for the sake of protection, might be unjustified on a typical network. On the other hand, we've already seen that the performance of multiple small hard disks may be preferable to that of a single large hard disk. And on most networks you can usually justify at least two printers for normal operations.

Depending on the network's architecture, the server may be any PC that is designated a server by application. If you have more than one PC on the network, redundancy is built in. But if the network requires a special computer dedicated to server duties, then redundancy will require a significant cost. If the dedicated device is an IBM PC/XT, you can use a second PC/XT in the network as a workstation. Then, should the server PC/XT fail, the workstation PC/XT will be available to act as server. Small PC/XT-compatible hard disks are available, such as one from Mountain Computer, that make a PC function identically to a PC/XT. With a PC/XT-compatible disk, you'd have both a redundant disk and, in the PC, a redundant server when you need one.

If your network uses a dedicated 68000-based server or a larger machine, you may not want to buy a second redundant server. Most network companies, however, offer 24-hour turnaround on repairs. Two days' downtime may be a reasonable risk compared to the cost of another server, especially if your backup tapes can be offloaded to an available hard disk and files can be processed in a stand-alone mode.

The final single point of failure is the cable. Ideally, you should have another cable that will permit you to jump across a link in the event that it fails. If your system is reasonably accessible, you might accomplish this new link simply by having a couple of cables made up and stored somewhere, ready to use as jumpers. However, if your system runs underground or is difficult to access, you should run two cables for each link and use one as a standby.

In the purest sense, fault tolerance means that the system will continue uninterrupted if one component fails. The solutions suggested here will involve some downtime. With current technology true fault tolerance is prohibitively expensive, except on very large networks.

# Interference

As you plan your network, one of your aims is to reduce electrical interference in the system. Interference is generated both internally and externally. Longer cable runs and higher data rates result in increased interference. This kind of interference is difficult to regulate. Some interference, however, is caused by the radiated fields of nearby electrical equipment; this interference can be reduced or eliminated by avoiding the source.

A signal in one system can produce electrical interference in an adjacent system; even circuits within the same system can cause one another interference. Network cables can radiate, or "cross talk," a signal into nearby cables. Cross talk is the passage of two signals through the same circuit. One signal is the intended signal, and the other is an unwanted signal that may be caused by outside sources or by the cable itself.

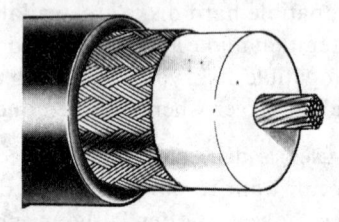

*Fig. 12.6. Coaxial cable has a center conductor surrounded by a dielectric. A shield of wire braid (also a conductor) goes outside the dielectric, and a plastic jacket covers the shield. Reprinted by permission of Trompeter Electronics, Inc.*

Using a good quality of cable and having tight connections properly affixed to the cable will reduce the likelihood of interference, which corrupts data. No transmission cable, either shielded twisted pair or baseband coax, should be routed next to power cables. If possible, anything electrical should be avoided, such as an electrical motor, which will generate static. An elevator switch room will almost always generate interference. Fluorescent lights and air conditioners generate interference because they are high voltage transformers.

Any of these sources of interference can create problems. Unfortunately, there is no hard and fast guideline to tell you what you can and cannot do. Appropriate measures will vary from cable to cable and from installation to installation. The measures you select will also depend on the type of cable and its use. In the real world, sources of interference may be impossible to avoid without considerable effort and expense.

Sometimes cables can be laid directly on top of fluorescent light fixtures with no problem. If your cable must go under a runway and you have only one conduit, or under a street and you have to put your signal cable in with electrical cables, then try it out. You have no other choice. But anytime you can avoid getting near a power cable, you'd be better off to do so.

If the cable is well shielded and the demands on your signal cable are low, outside interference probably won't affect network operation. This is particularly true if you're making short runs of 50 feet or less. If you're not using the network for anything that is especially data-intensive, such as CAD/CAM requiring heavy data rates, you're less likely to have trouble. Simple order entry traffic with low data rates may be fine, even in close proximity to a source of interference. High data rates tend to intensify an existing interference problem.

Sometimes a problem of interference will be intermittent. For instance, it may appear only when an air conditioner motor starts up. The motor throws a large pulse down the ground wire, and somehow the pulse is picked up on the ground of the network. This problem is best cured by putting a bypass or filter directly on the motor, instead of altering the network wiring. You should probably filter the line where it plugs into the wall.

When you are forced to run data cables through fields of interference, such as in a cable tray with high voltage power lines, you can use fiber-optic cable. This kind of cable is completely immune to electromagnetic interference. Fiber-optic cable is just now becoming readily available as a standard item.

# Grounding

Another important element in proper network installation is grounding, but it can create more problems than it solves. For one thing a ground can be a source of interference.

A ground is a path that lets an electrical system dump high voltages that may damage the system and its components. With coaxial cable, that path is usually a connection to the shield that is routed to an earth ground. A spike of high voltage electricity is shunted off onto this ground system and dispersed into the earth.

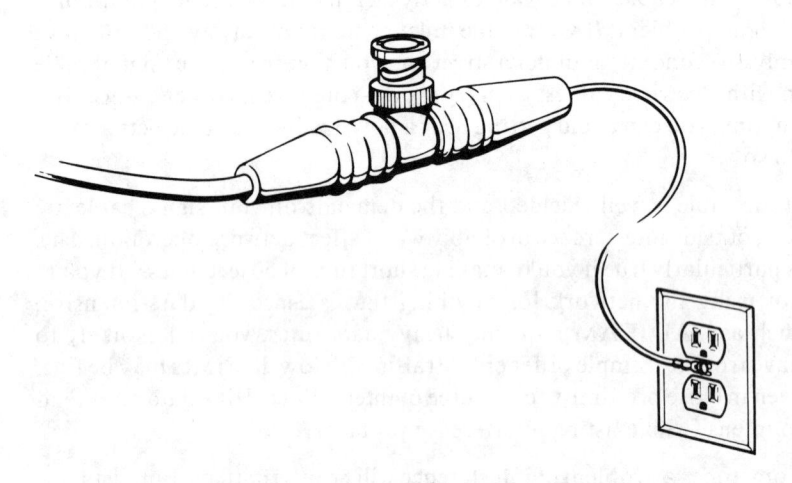

*Fig. 12.7. Grounding a terminator. Reprinted by permission of 3Com Corp.*

Problems arise when the ground system is attached in more than one place. A "ground loop" may develop, which is external interference riding the ground and staying on the shield without being shunted off. This ground loop can damage the desired signal. Unfortunately, ground loops cannot be avoided in any practical way because a network usually has many grounding points. Adding another ground to those already present simply increases the number of possible ground loops.

Most small local area networks have sufficient grounding in their hardware design. The shield is connected to the chassis of each device, which is connected to a ground wire on the AC plug. Usually, you can install the network with no additional ground, and you can depend on the chassis to provide the ground. If a problem shows up, such as noise on the network cable or a large number of message retransmissions, the system ground is not functioning properly. In this case, you should ask for some advice on additional grounds from your network vendor.

Some larger installations, however, will definitely need special grounding. Ground potential in the same building can vary. One circuit in the lab may have its own transformer, and a circuit in accounting may also have its own transformer. The result is a sizable potential in ground level; you can get many 100s of volts of static discharge on the cable.

Every AC circuit that network devices are plugged into should be on the same transformer. If these circuits are on different transformers, then you should ground the cable. Otherwise, you shouldn't have to worry about the circuits because they ground through the connector, back through the AC line into the outlet. But on a long cable run, you don't want the cable to ground through the chassis. You want it quickly grounded to earth. As a general rule, if the network cable has a span of 200 feet or more, without any PC or peripheral device connected to the cable, an extra ground connection will be necessary.

# 13
## Maintenance and Diagnostics

Local area networks pride themselves on their simplicity, economy, and responsiveness. And they should. These attributes are very desirable in a small shop of from 4 to 12 workstations, where the local area PC network is most often found.

Yet even though we acknowledge the advantages of the small system approach, we still seem to want more—more speed, more capacity, more features. Diagnostics and network monitors come under the category of "more advantages," those that may or may not be relevant to the local area network user.

Diagnostics are mandatory for very large networks. On very small networks, with a couple of PCs sharing a hard disk and a printer, diagnostics are an unnecessary overhead. But as a network grows, so does the need for monitoring the network and diagnosing its problems.

To see what diagnostics can do and where they fit into a local area network, let's first look at the upper end of the diagnostic scheme: the NCC.

## Network Control Center

Local broadband networks have within themselves sophisticated dedicated systems with the dual purposes of monitoring and diagnostics. The Network Control Center (NCC) is a passive monitoring device that gathers and records every imaginable network statistic. These figures are analyzed by NCC software and used by the network manager to keep the network running at optimum efficiency.

The NCC gathers data on network traffic, performance, and malfunctions. Traffic data tells who uses the network and when and how it's used. This information can then be used for more efficient distribution of the traffic load. Traffic data can also be used for that all-important accounting feature, billback, where the cost of the network is apportioned according to its use. And if someone is trying to access files for theft or vandalism, the traffic data provides a record of that activity, too.

Performance is measured in throughput and error rates. Throughput data, together with traffic statistics, helps managers in configuring and expanding their networks. Malfunctions, collected as network error statistics, point to intermittent problems but may also substantiate network overload.

Thus, the NCC is a very powerful and useful network feature. Its primary drawback is that it costs tens of thousands of dollars. However, as with so many other functions, ways are being found to bring large-system functionality down to the local area network.

## Local Area Network Diagnostics

Most networks have low-level, self-test procedures that should be run when the network is powered up. These tests usually cover the cable and hardware configuration, particularly the network interface card. If a new PC has just been added to the network, a self-test may show that both the network interface card and another circuit board in the PC are using the same set of interrupts or memory addresses. This discovery will require going back to the documentation and making the appropriate changes.

Self-tests may have the ability to perform loop-backs by electrically isolating the network interface card from the rest of the network. A signal is transmitted and "looped back" to the same card for testing. Another self-test may be used for specific links within the network to verify whether attached devices can communicate with each other.

Error codes are displayed when a problem is encountered. The intention is that the user will call the network user-support center and report the error condition. The user will then either be told which part is malfunctioning or be talked through more advanced diagnostics that are contained in the software but not documented.

Beyond this initial checkout, a great variety of network diagnostic support is available. Maintaining performance and managing and expanding a local area network require information. Network performance monitoring and diagnostics systems can provide much of the necessary information.

Generally, the needed information covers status, utilization, and performance data. Status and performance indicators include response times, traffic volumes, error rates, time-outs, and equipment failure. The central monitor, referred to as "tech support equipment," can record the activity of any individual user. The monitor shows the percent of the server's utilization, and this information is recorded in a statistics log.

One version of traffic monitoring is transaction counting. Many networks provide a primitive method of load measurement by displaying the number of transactions per second. Even though software may not be included to compile and save this information, the single reading can be useful for predicting when you need a second disk server.

An audit trail is a record of who used the network, how long it was used, and what file was accessed. This information can be used for billbacks and network security. Audit trails are presently implemented in one of three ways: in the network operating system, using existing hardware; in a special device attached to the network; or in the applications software.

Network status information is probably the most necessary of the diagnostics services. A status report from the disk server should include a list of files currently being accessed, the user's location, and whether a file is locked or available to others. If the network operating system permits queuing for files, the manager should be able to see the queue. The manager should be able not only to check the queue, but also to alter the order, delete requests, and redirect requests to other printers. Most print servers permit queuing.

Some networks keep a status directory of every device that is connected and logged on. Then if a connection fails, the failure is posted in the directory. Every PC has immediate access to the status directory, which lets the user know who is still active on the network. By doing a read/status request to the board, any user can find out what devices are active and what other nodes have been talking.

A failure may take place that can go unnoticed. If a workstation never transmits, the only way you'll know it has failed is that the workstation does not respond to a message or that the station sends a disconnect message. An extension of the diagnostics service is the periodic sending of status checking messages. These messages immediately report any failed device, but they also place additional overhead on the network cable.

Status checking also helps in planning the network. For instance, 200 devices may be on the cable, but the manager plans for only 10 to be active at any given time. Periodically, the manager does a status check to see how many devices are actually active. The manager may be surprised to find 20 or 30 active devices, in which case another server may be needed.

If the network itself does not support adequate diagnostics, then third-party products are available to attach to the network. For instance, a bit error rate tester makes test transmissions and loops them back, calculating the number of bits transmitted and the number of bits in error.

# NetWare Diagnostics

Currently, one of the more advanced local area network diagnostic systems is on Novell's NetWare. NetWare uses a central processor and monitor, which together act as a small version of the network control center common to broadband networks.

NetWare operates with acknowledged protocols and automatic retries. The network monitor displays a grid with cells for each workstation on the network. As more workstations are added, the screen can be scrolled to show additional cells.

The principal function of the cell is to indicate the activity of each workstation. The name of each file in use by the station is shown, along with the type of access—shareable, locked, etc. In addition, the cells display diagnostic data and error indicators for monitoring the health of the network.

A number at the bottom of each station's cell shows how many times the network processor has received a duplicate request from a workstation, after receiving the initial request. An incrementing number indicates that the network received a packet from the workstation, but the workstation never received acknowledgment that the packet was received by the network processor. This problem occurs occasionally in normal operation; but when the problem happens frequently, it suggests that the link between the workstation and the network may be faulty.

On NetWare, information is kept on the number of times that the network detects a nonsequential request from the workstation. A nonsequential request error means that an internal failure has occurred in the central processor.

Sometimes the network will receive a new packet from a workstation while the last request is still being processed. If this occurrence is not the result of a user's rebooting the system, an error message will be displayed at the monitor within the particular station's cell. The error is an indication that either the application program crashed or the workstation had a hardware failure.

Information is also kept on the number of times an internal network synchronization error has been detected. NetWare is a multiprocessed system, and a synchronization error means that some network process is responding to a packet other than the one the process should be working on. This condition can occur when a PC user resets the PC, causing a packet to be sent to the network while an earlier packet is still being processed. The network will handle this problem. But the same error will also occur when the data in a packet has been corrupted during internal processing. In this case a hardware error indicates a problem in the central processor.

In addition, a disk error can occur while a read or write to disk is being attempted. A disk I/O error message will be displayed to the immediate right of the disk I/O pending message. The error message will indicate the number of errors that have occurred. A disk error means a problem in either the disk interface or the drive. When such an error occurs, the hard disk should be taken off-line to minimize the loss of data.

Time-out errors are counted and displayed to note the number of times that the network attempted to send a packet and the number of times that the addressed PC failed to acknowledge. A time-out error occurs when a user reboots or shuts down the PC while a program is running. If neither of these activities has occurred, the failure is probably in the link between the PC and the central processor or in the PC itself.

Most networks do a certain amount of cache buffering to improve disk throughput and make the network operate more efficiently, as was discussed in Chapter 10. Thus, anytime the network is operating, some data is usually in a buffer. Modified disk buffers are written to disk during processor idle time or when more buffer space is required. If the network were to be shut down at one of these times, data would be lost and the entire file might be destroyed. On any network using cache buffers, all the buffered data must be written to disk before shutting down the network; commands are available to clear buffers. On the Novell network the monitor displays the number of disk cache buffers that have been changed in memory but have not yet been written to disk.

## Diagnostics in Hardware

Efficient coprocessors that incorporate diagnostics are starting to appear in network hardware. The Intel 82586 chip, designed for CSMA-CD networks, has built-in diagnostics and management. This controller chip sends status information on every message back to the CPU. The number of collisions and message errors is collected and reported. Such information is a good indicator of the overall condition of the network. For example, a high percentage of CRC (message error) messages suggests a hardware problem.

The 82586 can implement systematic diagnostics for the individual workstation and the rest of the network as well. A network user can put the chip in a loop-back mode in which a send and receive cycle is implemented within the single workstation. When a check shows that messages are properly transmitted and received at the workstation, the problem is usually outside the workstation. The chip also has external loop-back capability for isolating problems between PCs.

A break, or short, in the network can be found using the 82586. First, the chip not only diagnoses the short, but also estimates the distance of the short from the workstation. A diagnose command in the 82586 is available to perform a self-test routine for checking the main CPU.

The 82586 has hardware indicators that supply the software with routine information about the health of the network. These indicators record how many collisions are experienced before the message gets through and how many packets are received with errors. Statistics are kept on individual packets, and the chip keeps in memory a running tally of three or four key parameters. On a statistical basis these represent the health of the network. If many errors occur, the terminator has probably been removed from the end of one of the cables, causing reflection on the cable.

## The Role of the Network Manager

A local area network comes with the tools to tailor each user's environment to particular capabilities and needs. Stations can be set up to run a single application; this kind of setup requires the user to know very little about the network. Or stations can be set up to give the user considerable flexibility and power over the network's resources.

To manipulate these options, each network should have at least one knowledgeable user as manager. For most networks and most applications, the manager does not need to be a programmer. But the manager should be familiar with the network, the operating system, and the utilities.

The manager is responsible for setting up workstations, maintaining network applications, backing up files, and performing other administrative chores. Network security is also the manager's responsibility, which includes assigning passwords and access privileges.

An astute manager is an integral part of network diagnostics. This manager develops a feel for the way the network should function and is usually quick to note slower response times and higher error rates. The less sophisticated the built-in diagnostics, the more important becomes the manager's intuitive understanding of the network.

## Network Monitoring

Part of the manager's job is the periodic monitoring of the network (including percent of utilization, number of retries, etc.) to see how efficiently the network is working. One figure that is helpful is the number of transactions completed over a period of time. Records should be kept by hour, day, and month. Such records will show peak hours, days, and months when the cable is heavily used. Then these peak times can be managed more efficiently, conceivably enabling a system to last another year without additional hardware, simply by shifting use and distributing the work load.

Utilization figures also help to determine exactly where a bottleneck is developing, whether in the cable, the disk drive, the printer, or the server. Typically, these devices can slow down or bottleneck a network when you are trying to share central resources and manage peripherals.

Some good visual signals can suggest areas of bottlenecking. If the red light on the hard disk is on most or all the time, the hard disk is being overused. The system needs a faster hard disk, a second hard disk, or both.

Networks are seldom static systems. They grow, and planning for that growth is mandatory. Performance measurement helps with this planning, ideally with diagnostics that show performance degradation. A manager should to be able to anticipate a need for expansion so that the next phase of growth can be planned.

Network performance is usually defined as fast response and ready availability. Response time data should be maintained for each networked PC and for the network as a whole. Such data can be used to indicate the performance of network configuration and software. The performance of various applications software packages can also be monitored and compared.

Performance information can be used in cost control. One of the problems with networks, and with computing in general, is that use is not evenly distributed. Overall use of the network may be well within the range that permits good performance. But if 80 percent of the network use occurs in 10 percent of the work day, the network may need more equipment.

Applications monitoring can play a special role in both evaluating services and planning improvements. Basic performance indicators show how well the network is working. Applications monitoring indicates how well the network handles each separate application, how each application affects response time, and how each one ties up the mainframe. This monitoring also provides detailed productivity analysis of each workstation by showing exactly how much of each kind of work has been done at each station.

## Looking Ahead

Network diagnostics for local area networks are still primitive. But managers who gain experience with networks are going to want more sophisticated diagnostics, and their needs are likely to be answered by the network industry.

Office automation equipment is increasingly aimed at local area network compatibility. Thus, networks are growing rapidly in numbers of users, applications, and attached devices. All this growth will necessitate accurate monitoring systems.

# 14
## Internetting

Some interesting brushfires have burned sporadically on the networking scene. One short-lived debate concerned broadband versus baseband versus PBX. This argument was settled when we realized that "peaceful coexistence" was the best answer.

Our emerging understanding of networking includes a commitment to a hierarchical approach. One network can't solve all network problems. Of the many kinds of networks, including baseband, broadband, and PBX, none can be cross-optimized. The best balance of capacity, performance, and cost is achieved with a combination of systems.

A widely used analogy for this approach to networking is the highway system. Nobody would propose bringing an eight-lane expressway right up to your door. Instead, local streets are funneled into four-lane roads that eventually go into the interstate system. The interstate system carries the high-speed, heavy traffic that goes long distances, and the local streets carry the local traffic. If you're starting out on a long trip, you still start out on local streets.

This analogy is also applicable to data communications. A cluster is formed by the department manager who buys three or four PCs. Soon he realizes he doesn't really want to purchase three or four printers or three or four hard disks. He wants to buy one of each. Then after he buys the PCs, he gets a local area network. This decision making might be called a bottom-up approach.

The top-down approach is much less common. The vice president of computer information systems makes a decision, and one network is adopted company-wide.

Those who are concerned about continuity may argue for the top-down approach. But most companies, even large ones, are acquiring local area networks one department at a time, according to each department's needs. Thus, low-level clustered networks are beginning to spring up throughout a corporation: video and voice networks for certain applications; token-passing networks in high-traffic areas; and contention networks in low-traffic areas where a network's fast response time can be optimized.

Because clustered networks often produce problems of continuity and communications, a way is needed to tie all these communications links together. The solution is to have a broadband spine running throughout the organization. Clustered local networks and wide area networks will tie into this broadband network. The key to making this kind of arrangement work is a technology known as internetting.

*Internetting* is the process of connecting networks. It permits data to move freely among large numbers of networks and populations. Local area networks are attached to other local networks, to remote sites and individuals, and to wide area networks.

## Internet Hardware

The devices used for internetting will depend on the degree of compatibility between the networks. A *bridge* is a device that links local networks using identical protocols. Dissimilar networks are connected through *gateways*. Anytime that protocol conversion is required to connect networks, as it is between a local area network and an SNA or X.25 network, the connecting device must be a gateway.

### *Bridges*

A bridge is attached to a network much as any other node is connected. The bridge reads every packet (message unit) on the network and passes

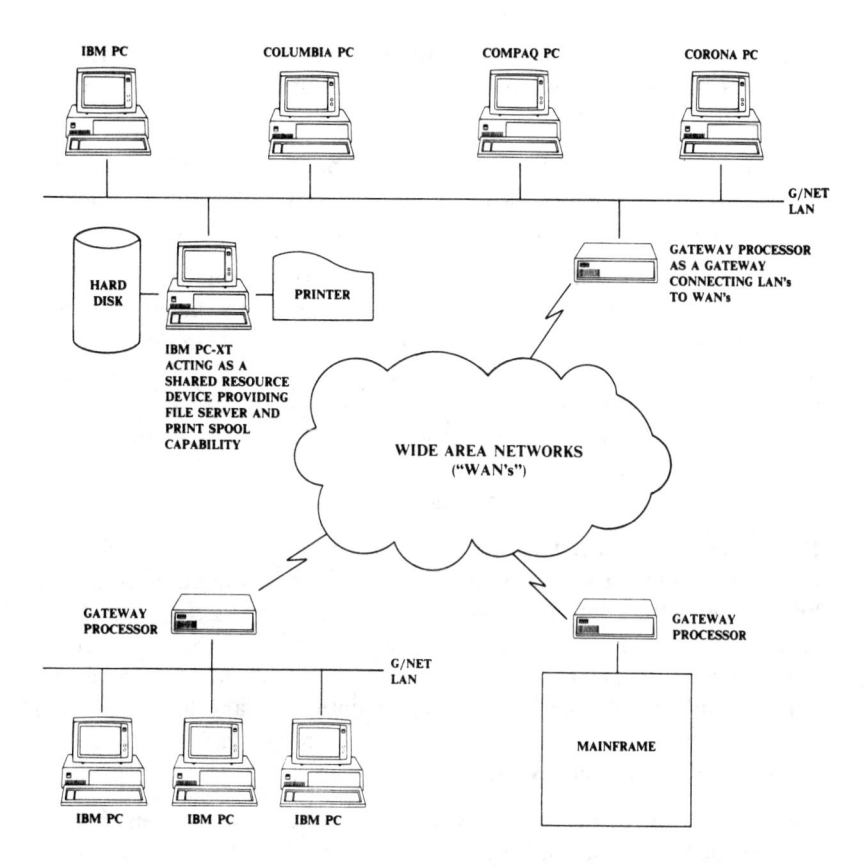

*Fig. 14.1. Wide area networks commonly use X.25 protocol and telephone lines as carriers. Gateway processors connect mainframes and local area networks to the X.25 "cloud," which represents the worldwide telephone and data communications system. Reprinted by permission of Gateway Communications.*

internet traffic onto another network. The packets passed between networks via a bridge are not altered but merely retransmitted by the bridge in each packet's original form.

A bridge, however, is not identical to a repeater. A repeater can be defined as a baseband device similar to a broadband amplifier. A repeater simply regenerates and repeats a signal, usually after the signal has traversed a long cable section and suffered attenuation. A bridge performs store-and-forward services in addition to retransmission of the signal.

The value of a bridge may not be readily apparent from the definition given here. If the protocols are identical, why not simply connect everything into one large network instead of two smaller ones?

Compared to one giant local area network, a series of smaller networks connected by bridges offers some highly desirable benefits. The foremost of these is security. Local area networks operate in a broadcast mode. If you have information to retrieve or transmit, it goes onto the network—everywhere. Only the station specifically addressed actually reads the data, but the data is physically presented to each station. A person wishing to thwart the addressing scheme and receive unauthorized transmissions has an open invitation to do so.

Partitioning the data system into small self-contained networks reduces this vulnerability. Even though the networks are interconnected by bridges permitting internet communications, normal network traffic remains local. For example, when your accounting system is on a separate network, accounting data will not be transmitted beyond that network unless you specifically send the data onto another network. You can download and upload files all day to accounting's central disk, without the data traversing other network cables.

Another benefit of bridges is reliability. If one network goes down because the server stopped functioning or because of a fault in the cable, other networks and the departments they serve will not be affected. Such a problem is entirely isolated when you use internetting bridges. The unaffected networks, though connected, will experience no work stoppage or data loss.

A third benefit of using bridged, multiple networks is performance enhancement within the individual network. Each network has its own server and hard disk, so fewer PCs make demands on network resources, compared to the single, large network environment. In addition, relatively shorter cable runs tend to improve performance and reduce cable noise and transmission errors.

A final benefit of bridge design is a greater networking range. In some networks, for example, cable length cannot exceed 1,000 meters. A bridge effectively nullifies this limitation by performing the function of a repeater and reconstituting the signal. Physical range can be whatever is required by the particular installation, provided a bridge is installed before the maximum cable range is exceeded.

## *Gateways*

Considering the diversity of networks, even within the same company, most connections will be between dissimilar networks. Internetting will then require a gateway.

The gateway receives data transmissions from one network and recreates them in the format used by the network of the addressed PC. This process probably means repacketizing the message to conform to size differences and adjusting to different access and routing schemes. The speeds of the two networks will most likely be different, which will require the gateway to hold (buffer) the messages and retransmit them at the appropriate speed.

Reporting the status of files, such as whether a certain file is locked, is a critical function of a local area network server. Yet with internetting, the server on one network will not be able to read directly the status of files on another network. Status must be read and correctly interpreted by the gateway.

Perhaps the most difficult service to be performed by the gateway is addressing. The gateway must store addresses for every device on both networks and then interpret and properly readdress internet traffic.

# Internet Protocol

Gateways may be developed using a special gateway protocol. Such a protocol, called internet protocol (IP), has been promoted and is now a recognized standard.

In IP, local area and wide area networks use the same protocol for internet traffic. A PC wishing to send an internet message creates the local packet, adhering to the IP format. The packet is sent to a gateway that alters the speed of the transmission to conform to the slower data rate of the wide area network. The packet format, however, remains unchanged. At the other end of the wide area network link, the packet is received by another gateway and changed to the local network protocol.

Because of the considerable differences between local and wide area networks, gateway design is critical. The local PC network has a raw bit rate between 1Mbit/sec and 10Mbit/sec. The wide area network is much slower, under 56Kbit/sec. When the faster local network sends data to the wide area network, a bottleneck occurs. Packets pile up while the gateway doles them out to the wide area network at the slower rate. One possible solution to the problem of speed incompatibility is to use a gateway with multiple transmission lines onto the wide area network.

# X.25 for Wide Areas

Beyond the local site, out in the world of communications, public X.25 networks are becoming the most common way to get from location A to location B. As data networks were being used in the early 1970s, the need arose for a common protocol that would make public data networks compatible. In 1976 the Consultative Committee for International Telegraph and Telephone (CCITT) adopted Recommendation X.25. It has since become the most widely used interface to public networks.

In the U.S. three different kinds of X.25 networks are available to the public on a leased basis: Tymnet, Telenet, and AT&T. Only very large companies use other systems for wide area networking, usually with a private X.25 network or with IBM's Systems Network Architecture (SNA) protocol.

SNA is common in PC-to-mainframe communications. To talk SNA, you need a dedicated network because SNA can't be used over public packet networks. SNA will support switched lines and dial-up ports, but the background links typically expect high speeds and are expensive to implement. SNA is primarily a master-slave protocol not suitable for internetting.

Significant services, such as business support systems, are best accessed through an X.25 network. These services are proliferating rapidly. Thus, the ability to gateway into X.25 networks is an important network feature, greatly expanding the range of network applications. Most local area networks discussed in this book have X.25 gateways in development, and a few of them are in production.

X.25 networks can be used in many ways. A business may use one to integrate dispersed branches or to access remote on-line data bases. One tax accounting company has put together a huge computer network to service some 7,000 clients located around the country. The company furnishes PCs to big and small accounting firms and then gateways them into an X.25 network. This arrangement allows everyone to communicate. If one center is busy processing tax returns, a request for processing can be relayed to another center. In this way, the load is balanced.

## X.25 Options

When you're planning to install a gateway, you must consider the amount of traffic that will go through the gateway. If the connection is solely for some low-volume administrative function, then a public network may be justified. You can get into public networks in two ways. Either you can install a gateway that is public network interface-compatible, allowing you to talk X.25 protocol. Or you can use a modem and connect into the public network strictly as an asynchronous (async) terminal.

An async modem and dial-up line are appropriate for very low traffic loads. To access the network, you pick up the phone and dial a number, then hear a tone and put the phone on an acoustic coupler. This inexpensive method enables many remote sites to get into the local area network or the mainframe center. The method even works with an electronic mail system in which the mail is collected at some regional point, and remote users dial in to pick up and send mail.

With heavier traffic this method is slow and inefficient. A dial-up port on a voice circuit can support only up to 1,200 baud. This speed is relatively slow and time-consuming, and can result in long periods of line use, making costs prohibitive. The solution is higher speed lines that can send messages quickly and cost less per mile than voice grade lines.

You can choose between a dedicated leased line or a public data network. Public data networks, such as Tymnet and Telenet, are more economical unless you have extremely high traffic, in which case the dedicated leased line may be the best choice. The cost of using an X.25 link on a public data network is inexpensive compared to paying the telephone bill for six or more PCs talking X.25 and using voice grade lines.

You may now be at the point where you must make a decision between going directly into an X.25 network or using an asynchronous device. This decision is very complicated, a subject beyond the scope of this book. Many variables must be considered, such as the type of communications (async dial-up, async dedicated, synchronous, etc.), reliability, growth plans, and cost.

# An X.25 Gateway Processor

One of the companies making X.25 gateways for local area networks is Gateway Communications. Gateway offers two solutions to X.25 gatewaying: a stand-alone gateway processor and a gateway card called a wide area network interface module (WNIM). The Gateway processor consists of a cabinet, a power supply, a board containing a microprocessor and memory, and eight adapter slots for a network interface card, a disk controller, and communications boards. The Gateway processor will support up to four flexible or hard disks.

For the WNIM card the company redesigned the board in its gateway processor so that the board is now compatible with the IBM PC bus. Essentially, the WNIM is the same as the PC network interface card that supports G/NET. The only difference is that the WNIM board has a different transceiver on it. The transceiver supports RS-232, RS-422, and B-35 interfaces instead of the coax cable supported by the network interface card. The Gateway card has its own microprocessor and 64K of memory, and supports a full X.25 protocol or the full SNA-plus software package offered by Gateway.

Connections can be made between networks or devices with different protocols, data transfer rates, and character sizes. Depending on the software used, the Gateway processor will support either X.25 or SNA protocol. A stand-alone X.25 gateway card can be attached to a remote PC and to an async modem to access the local area network. The capability will be the same as that of the locally attached PC, except the performance will be slower. A user may download a file and work on it, make an inquiry, or update a file.

The software is written so that PCs on two different networks can talk to each other over an X.25 communications link. For instance, a PC on

3Com's Ethernet in New York can talk to a PC on Gateway Communication's G/NET (its local area network) in Spokane, just as if the PCs were on the same network—provided both networks are using this gateway.

# Baseband-to-Broadband Bridging

Ungermann-Bass supplies a number of products for internetting, among them, bridges for baseband-to-baseband, broadband-to-broadband, and baseband-to-broadband, in either local or remote mode. In the baseband-to-broadband system, U-B's Net/One Ethernet baseband channel is run on a broadband channel. The software protocol is basically Net/One on both sides of the bridge.

The bridge is constructed with two sections. On one side is a transmit, receive, and processor capability for baseband. On the other side is a transmit, receive, and processor capability for broadband. When a broadband signal arrives at the bridge, it is buffered (stored), and some processing is done on the broadband side. Then the message is passed over to the baseband side of the bridge and transmitted onto the baseband network.

Networks may have several bridges on them, providing links to as many networks as needed. The bridge may receive a message addressed to another network. In this case the bridge is smart enough to know how to transfer the message to the appropriate bridge so that the message is routed to its destination.

In bridge design you have two choices. First, you can make every network interface unit understand all the bridges. (Network interface unit, abbreviated NIU, is Ungermann-Bass terminology for the circuit board that connects the PC to the network.) The overhead associated with this type of bridge implementation is so great that network performance is impaired.

Second, you can have bridges understand other bridges. This second type of bridge is used by Ungermann-Bass. When a message gets picked up by the wrong bridge, that bridge is intelligent enough to relay the message to another bridge so that the message can be sent properly. The time delay associated with the relay is negligible, and network performance is not degraded.

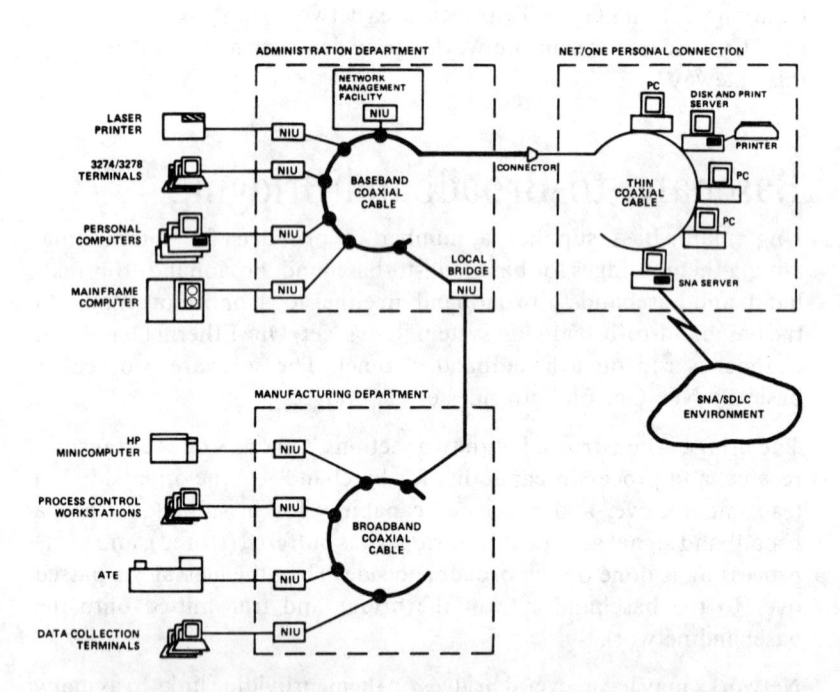

*Fig. 14.2. Ungermann-Bass' representation of network implementation and internetting. All that is needed to connect thin Ethernet coaxial cable to thick cable is the appropriate connection adapter. To go from a baseband Ethernet to a broadband network requires a bridge. The device labeled "SNA SERVER" is a gateway device that performs protocol conversions from the XNS/Ethernet local area network to the SNA/SDLC mainframe environment. Reprinted by permission of Ungermann-Bass, Inc.*

Bridges can also do routing. If one bridge link goes down, bridges are smart enough to retransmit messages to another route. Bridges know enough to be able to reroute a message a longer distance to avoid a bad link. Rerouting capability is important because it provides total redundancy in the system.

In addition, bridges can be made to handle load balancing. If for some reason the traffic load on one link becomes too heavy, bridges can shift some of the load to other bridges and links, to balance the message load going across them. The balancing algorithm is based on the percentage of bandwidth being used. When the bridge sees that the percentage is reached, the bridge implements alternate routing.

Current load-balancing schemes are not perfect. Focusing simply on a maximum percentage of use can still mean that a particular bridge is overworked, relative to the entire internet system. A new balancing technique now in development will not only look at a maximum utilization, but also be able to see an overview of the entire internet and thus balance the traffic on all bridges for maximum performance.

# Internet Addressing

To send a message from one network to another, users can be supplied with what could be called a data address book. A user just looks up the address of the person and keys that address in with the message. Internetting has not reached this level of homogeneity yet, especially when a message must go to a network that uses an entirely different set of protocols.

Addressing is possibly the most difficult problem to solve for reliable internetting. How does a person tell a machine to find a recipient on another network when the recipient's address is unknown? What is worse, suppose that the two networks in question use different message formats. In this case the format must be converted at a gateway in order for the message to be delivered successfully.

Staying within the same network "family" helps, of course. The packet, or message unit format is defined at the hardware level (data-link layer 2). Therefore, going from one Ethernet to another or from one ARCnet to another requires no packet format change. The Ethernet standard takes this process one step further. Every network interface card is fixed with a unique hard address when it is assembled. A message sent to an Ethernet user across an internet will have an address belonging only to that user's machine.

The actual switching and routing of messages between networks is done at the network layer (layer 3). This layer appends a second address to internet messages. For example, as long as the message stays within the Xerox Network Systems (XNS), compatibility is assured. But going to another standard may cause a problem. The IEEE is now working to develop a standard method of internetting between dissimilar networks.

## Selecting a Bridge or Gateway

Bridges and gateways are servers, much like the network's central server. Because these devices perform intelligent tasks, they must have an efficient coprocessor as part of their design. The throughput rate of the coprocessor must match the throughput of the network; otherwise, internet traffic will be severely impeded. In a corporate environment with diverse clusters of local networks connected to a general broadband network, the gateway must provide the interconnect capability.

Baseband-to-broadband gateways operate similarly to local-to-wide-area gateways. An internet transmission is received by the gateway and translated into the appropriate format. Baseband-to-broadband gateways, however, must operate at the applications level, resulting in an increased reliability burden.

Operation at the applications level requires that the gateway be capable of translating requests from one network into requests that are functionally identical on another network. As a practical matter, however, only a subset of the original requests is passed because of functional differences among the various systems. Part of the evaluation process of shopping for gateways is to identify the percent of functionality retained by internet traffic.

## Remote Connections and Communications

Very few PC networks even support shared modems. Those that run at 300 or 1,200 baud are so slow that any kind of serious, heavy use can produce unacceptably long queues. Then, too, the cost of the modems, like that of small dot-matrix printers, is low enough to warrant dedicating a modem to any PC that needs one. Usually, only one or two PCs on the whole network have a modem. If data must be accessed, say, from a public data base, the data can be pulled down by any of the modem-equipped PCs and made shareable among all the other users.

This situation will change as high-speed, high-cost modems come into general use. High-speed modems, such as the 9,600-baud versions, do more than reduce your waiting time for data; they also reduce the time-sharing cost incurred both at the mainframe data base and on the telephone lines. Thus, as the technology arrives, you will want to upgrade your modem power. And sharing these devices will spread their costs among as many users as possible.

Internetting with PC networks is still in its infancy. Although network vendors are actively building gateways between their networks and widely used protocols, such as X.25 and SNA, these vendors are reluctant to support a possible competitor. For instance, no one yet has a gateway for use between a CSMA-CD network and a token-passing network. As standards for local networks become accepted and the installed base grows, all kinds of gateways will be available to support any interconnection requirement.

# 15
# The Mainframe Connection

As we've already seen, a major benefit of networking is that microcomputers and the work performed on them are no longer isolated. Information can be passed from one computer to another and read and updated as needed. Linking PCs and combining their capabilities create a flexible new computing resource. In the corporate environment the next step is to link this new resource with an established one: the mainframe computer.

The IBM PC first entered the corporate world by the back door. The PC was quietly brought in on purchasing orders for typewriters. And when it arrived, most of the work it was given could probably have been done with typewriters, calculators, and pencils and paper.

Quickly, the PC began to achieve respectability. First-rate applications programs came along for word processing and spreadsheets. These programs were easy to learn and use. Often they were a distinct improvement over comparable mainframe programs. But the PC remained isolated from the mainframe, unable to do any of the "serious" work that was still the province of mainframes.

Then devices began to appear that let the PC communicate with the mainframe and manipulate mainframe data. PC-to-mainframe communications was a prerequisite to making the PC part of large-system computing. Now that the PC is established, the door is open to explore fully the other applications of an intelligent desktop workstation in a mainframe world.

Table 15.1
PC Local Area Network in the Mainframe World

Advantages:

- Responsive local processing
- Reduced mainframe processing demand
- Friendly microcomputer software
- Simple file format conversion
- Improved system dependability
- Fast file transfer

Disadvantages:

- Higher cost compared to terminal network
- Cost of replacing installed terminal base
- More difficult to control

In this chapter we'll first examine the alternative ways that the PC and the mainframe can communicate. Then we'll see how to get the most out of the new connection.

# 3270 Emulation

The most common way for a PC to communicate with a host mainframe is by emulating a dumb terminal, one of IBM's 3270 series machines. The 3270s are time-sharing terminals, which can be clustered locally or remotely to provide access to the mainframe. These highly functional terminals support such features as insertion and deletion of text, automatic cursor movement, and data compaction. But the 3270s are still terminals; all their processing and storage ability must be tapped from the mainframe.

On the other hand, an emulator-equipped PC is an intelligent terminal. In addition to acting as a 3270 device, the PC can receive and store data from the host computer, modify or reformat display data, run local applications programs, and send the output to the host.

The host can be an IBM System/370, IBM 308X, or 43XX processor. The PC can be connected via coaxial cable to a channel-attached IBM 3274 or 3276 cluster controller, or remotely to a BSC or SNA/SDLC 3274 cluster controller.

A 3270 emulator is basically an SNA gateway. Virtual circuits are established between host and terminal devices through this gateway and go to an SNA packet network and an IBM mainframe computer. The emulation package includes a circuit board, which supports the physical connection between the PC and the mainframe system. Also included is software, which runs on the PC and gives the PC its 3270 functionality.

Emulators are available to make the PC look like either the 3278 or 3279 terminals, although accommodations must be made for some models. The 3278 Model 2 display is PC-compatible with 24 lines by 80 characters. However, Model 3 has a 33-line display, and Model 4 has a 43-line display. You can't put more than the standard 24 lines on the PC screen, so to handle large displays, the emulators scroll the screen, with the PC's PgUp and PgDn keys.

The 3279s are color terminals. Again, emulation is not perfect because the 3279 resolution is higher than the resolution of the PC color monitor. The alternatives are either to use only the text mode of the 3279 and forgo the graphics, or to purchase a graphics monitor.

The IBM PC keyboard provides all the special functions of the 3270-series keyboard, although some adaptation is needed because the numbers and positions of the keys are not the same. Many companies, including IBM, DCA, CXI, Gateway Communications, AST Research, and Interlan, provide 3270 emulation packages.

# Evaluating an Emulator

The first step in evaluating a 3270 emulator is to check that it is both hardware- and feature-compatible with your system, beginning with the PC. All emulators will not work with all IBM PC compatibles. The emulator board should fit any slot and be used like any other circuit

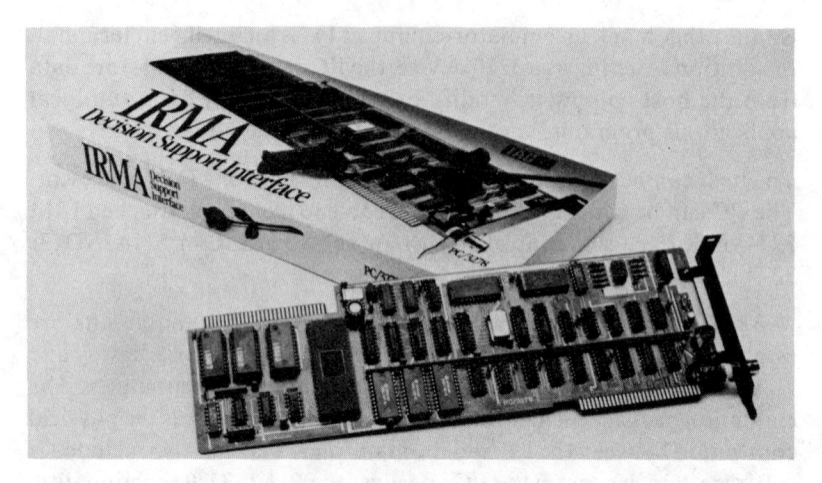

*Fig. 15.1. The IRMA 3278 emulator from Digital Communications Associates, Inc., fits into an expansion slot on the IBM PC and allows the PC to perform either as a 3278 terminal or a personal computer. Photograph courtesy of Digital Communications Associates, Inc. (DCA).*

board. Other parts of your existing system, such as cluster controllers, may be "IBM compatible" but not compatible enough to support a particular emulator without some modification.

After you check compatibility, the next step is to look at the quality of the emulation and how it is achieved. All emulator designers make accommodations for the screen and the keyboard, but these designers tend to follow their own rules. Which designer's scheme is best is a matter of personal preference. As you evaluate the emulator, test each key of the emulator-equipped PC. You may notice considerable variation in what a key actually does, what the documentation says it will do, and what the comparable key on a 3270 does.

A third step is to evaluate the emulator software. This software must perform a number of functions, the first of which is to permit you to enter the emulation mode. From there, many of the emulators let you run concurrent PC and 3270 modes, controlled through a toggle switch. One key, designed as a toggle, shifts the PC environment back and forth between PC and 3270 modes.

The emulator software has an important feature, the transfer utility set, which appears with varying degrees of success on early emulators. An emulator should be able to bring files down from the host to the PC and return them to the host when processing is completed. The transfer utilities should support whatever environment is necessary. This point is key: you must make certain that the software supports not only the two-way transfer, but also the desired mainframe environment—TSO or VM/CMS, or both.

How the information is displayed should also be taken into account. Compare the emulated display with the 3270 to see that status lines, or comments, are the same and that all the characters are compatible. Some differences can occur in the character sets, so designers must choose representative characters.

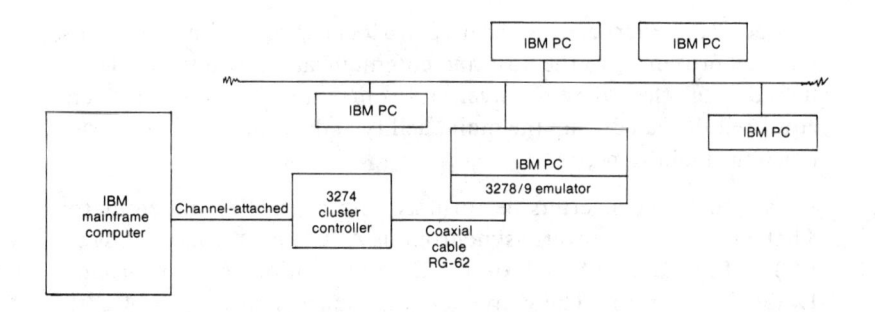

*Fig. 15.2. 3270 emulator on a networked PC.*

The emulator should be totally compatible with your present system. You should be able to disconnect the coax and connector from the 3270 terminal and plug the cable directly into the emulator board on the PC. Then when you turn on the system and start the emulator software, you will be connected to the mainframe.

## Protocol Converters

Protocol converters can be used as terminal interface units, replacing IBM 3270 controllers. These converters permit both the direct connection of PCs to the host and the retention of 3270 functionality. An IBM 3101 display terminal emulation program must be run on the PC to complete the emulation.

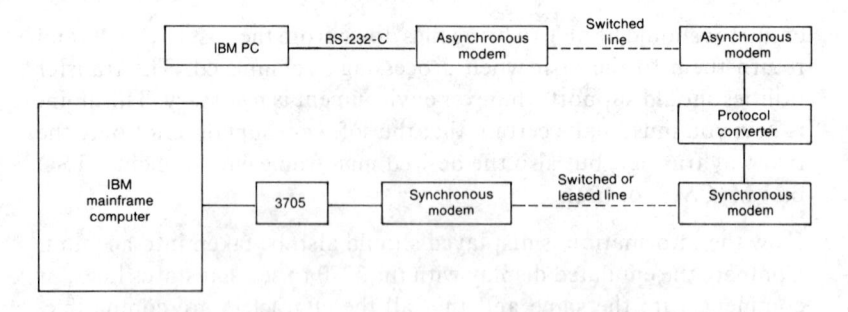

*Fig. 15.3. Protocol converter.*

Protocol converters can also be used in a local system, with PCs in close physical proximity to the host and communicating with it over leased lines through the protocol converter. From remote locations a modem-equipped PC can dial up the main facility and, through the converter, reach the mainframe.

These protocol converters perform as both controller and emulator. That is, they must convert asynchronous ASCII protocol (used by the PC) to IBM Binary Synchronous Communications or Synchronous Data Link Control. The converters also must map into the PC the functional characteristics of the 3270 terminal.

The IBM 3270 series operates in batch mode. The host mainframe sends a batch of data, called a screen image, to the terminal. Reading and editing are performed locally at the terminal. Then the edited screen is uploaded back to the host for storage.

For the PC using a protocol converter to emulate a 3270, the converter must execute the functions of the 3270 and send the appropriate commands to the PC. Interaction with the asynchronous terminal involves translating the 3270 screen-formatting commands, the keyboard commands, and the data-handling commands.

# Networking with the Emulator

We have looked at the emulator as an intelligent terminal, with one emulator card per PC. As part of a local area network, a single emulator card can serve the network so that any PC on that network can emulate a 3270 terminal and interface with the mainframe.

The PC with the emulator card in it becomes an emulation server for the entire network. Any PC on the network can do a virtual call to the server. Then the logic in the server will internet the PC to the mainframe. Besides reducing the amount of emulation hardware you must buy, this arrangement means that you need only one coaxial cable and one connection (channel) for the entire network. The number of controller ports used on the mainframe side is also reduced. The emulation server is analogous to a 3274 controller, with the server entering the mainframe through a 3705 back end. One server may be able to handle as many as 16 to 32 virtual circuits concurrently.

The network server, which supports both file server and print server functions, can also perform at the same time the duties of emulation server. Once the emulation circuit board is made resident, the emulator server runs like any other software package. Of course, the emulator settings must not conflict with any other devices within the server.

For example, if you have a modem in a PC, a 3270 emulator board, and a network interface card, you must know the interrupts and all the I/O channels being used by each. If some of the interrupt settings are identical for two or more boards, the system will not function properly.

Most emulators permit the concurrent use of other communications software, including networking software, as long as the interrupts and channels aren't duplicated. The emulator software should permit the changing of channels so that conflicts can be avoided. If a certain address is already used for communications, you should be able to reset the emulator address to an alternative so that the communications programs don't collide with each other.

The network sets up its own communication system, managed by the network interface card and the network software. The PC's three parallel ports (LPT1, LPT2, and LPT3), and its two serial ports (COM1 and COM2) are not affected by the network. But other devices, such as printers, modems, and emulators, use these ports and must be properly directed.

Some emulators cannot be shared by networking PCs. In these cases one PC can act as the "mainframe connection"—a single PC that is equipped with the emulator hardware and software. The person using that PC becomes a traffic manager, downloading and uploading data for the entire network.

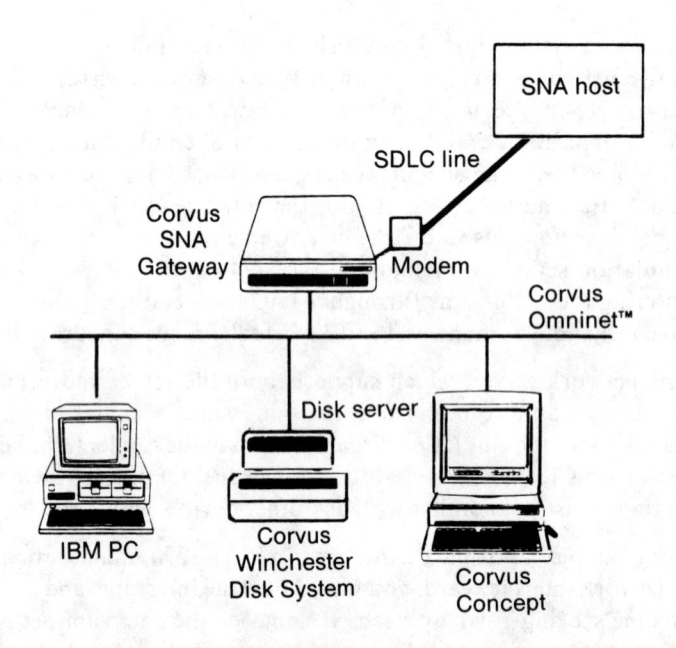

*Fig. 15.4. The Corvus SNA Gateway uses dual processors, an MC68000, and a Z80A. The Z80A supports SDLC and the RS-232 access to the SNA system. The MC68000 handles processing for the higher SNA protocols. Gateway software permits multiple active sessions with a variety of logical unit types. With the SNA Gateway, PCs can emulate 3278 Model 2 display stations. Reprinted by permission of Corvus Systems, Inc.*

# Using the Emulator-Equipped PC

For an analyst, or for anyone else whose position requires that many jobs be done concurrently, emulators can be quite efficient. Perhaps an analyst works on the mainframe, writing and maintaining programs. In addition, he may be needed to support local microcomputer users and their applications software. With an emulator-equipped PC that taps into a local area network, the analyst can perform all the functions and reach out to many physical locations.

Suppose that the analyst is working on a project on the mainframe in a 3270 mode and somebody comes in with a question about a spreadsheet. The analyst touches a couple of keys and brings up the application.

After assisting the person, the analyst then returns to 3270 mode. With electronic mail this process is even better. A question can be asked through a PC-conveyed memo. The sender references the appropriate files, which the analyst can call up from the central hard disk. He can then send back a response. Though the two users may be miles apart, the interaction is the same as if they were sitting next to one another.

Another interesting feature of the PC and terminal emulator is that you can capture a complete session. Later, at the end of the session, you can decide whether to keep it. But at the end of a session on a dumb terminal, the session is gone. If you want to know what you did or you want to remember a particular piece of information, you have to run the session again from the start. With the PC you capture the session and review it as you wish. You can store the whole session for later viewing or analysis.

Many terminal operators—the people in planning, finance, accounting, and inventory—extract bits and pieces from large files. Typically, these operators look through thousands of pages of output but actually manipulate just a few pages of it. With a 3270 emulator the operators are able to extract information and manipulate it locally on their PCs. The small computational work is taken down to the local level. This setup reduces the workload on the mainframe, which can then support more operators and be more accessible to them.

With this arrangement the host system is benefited by downloading menial tasks that don't require mainframe power. The mainframe is best used to store very large files and data bases. Of course, the mainframe excels at running large programs and handling extensive computational tasks, such as executing large compiles. All other work should be run on the PC, if possible.

At the local level, operators can manipulate the data with personal computer programs. These are usually much easier to use than comparable mainframe programs. And PC software is not only easier to use but often more powerful as well. Mainframe programs usually lack the sophistication of the smaller programs that are written for the PC.

Engineers can bring down subroutines from their files and manipulate these subroutines on the text editor, maybe even run a compatible compiler on the PC level. When a subroutine checks out, an engineer

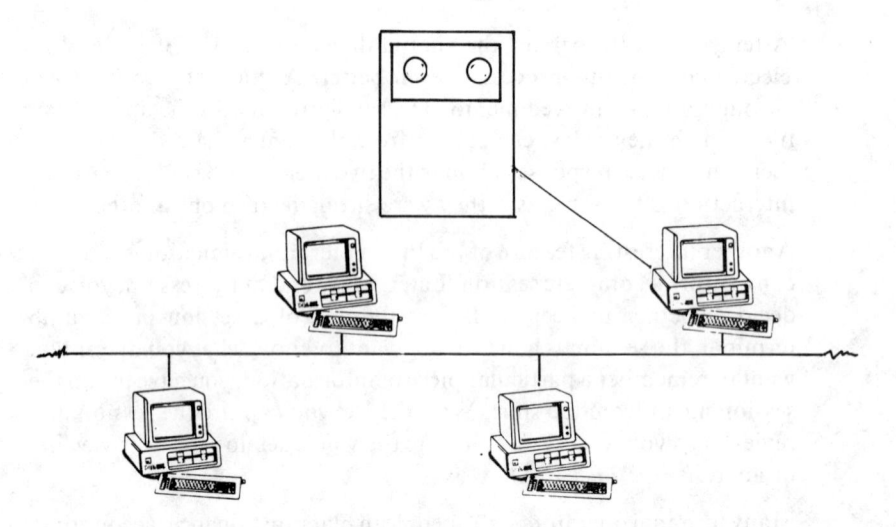

*Fig. 15.5. The PC-to-mainframe connection retains the advantages of distributed processing while integrating PC activity with other corporate processing.*

can put it into mainframe and do the final run that costs so many hundreds of dollars per hour of computation time. The user saves time in manipulating the program, which, of course, saves dollars, too.

Sometimes part of the processing is done on the host mainframe, and another part is downloaded to the PC for processing. Let's suppose that you've got a computer program that generates all its numbers in English engineering units, such as pounds, feet, inches, and so on. You're doing work for a government agency that has decided to convert to metric—a trend that's happening with increasing frequency. The agency wants the report printed in metric units.

You have several choices. You can do all the calculation by hand. Or you can modify your primary program that generated the numbers. You can leave the primary program alone and run a conversion program on the mainframe to put the file into proper form. Or you can let the PC handle the work. You can capture the output onto your PC and write a conversion program that reads that output, then gives the metric equivalents. Using the PC in this way is good management of resources. You can take data in its original form and have it manipulated for a special purpose by your local machine. You can reformat data and merge it into a document or spreadsheet, all done locally on your PC.

## Backup on the PC

In a corporate data processing environment, the mainframe computing system provides the primary data storage facility. Yet even with all the mainframe's sophisticated data protection and backup procedures, sole reliance on this system has some drawbacks. Mainframe hard disk devices are reliable but not immune to head crashes. Nothing is quite as horrifying as to find out that a head crash occurred on the track where your data happened to be located. Of course, everything is archived or backed up regularly. But suppose that the major editing which you did yesterday was wiped out by a head crash, shortly before the data was due to be backed up.

Besides head crashes, mainframe data is subject to other threats. Disk space on mainframes is always a scarce commodity. Invariably, the amount of data expands to fill the disk faster than new disks can be installed. In one instance a company moved its computing resources from one computer to another. By mistake, all the archived tapes from the old machine were placed on scratch status, which means that they could be erased and reused. Consequently, vast amounts of important data were lost.

The threat of disasters like these is why old-line engineers still swear by punch cards. Punch card readers can be found in the main engineering building of many large companies. And punch card decks are still used as a personal backup system. But many of these users began wishing a long time ago for a safe equivalent to punch cards that would eliminate the problems of these bulky media. Then the PC arrived. With a handful of floppies, a user can now have both control and backup and not be concerned with how the mainframe data is handled or mishandled.

Obviously, personal archiving can get you into trouble. You should always work with the program that is on the mainframe, not with your personal backup. Otherwise, local backup systems create the risk of having multiple versions, overwriting other people's work, and experiencing many of the multiuser problems we've discussed in earlier chapters. Then, too, personal archiving may violate company security.

Nonetheless, a system of personal archiving, when properly used, can be an important benefit of the PC-to-mainframe connection.

## Downtime Equals Loss

Many multibillion dollar corporations have trouble keeping communications working reliably between terminals and host mainframe computers. Downtime may have any number of causes. In one instance a backhoe operator dug through a cable and shut down a data processing department for two days. Most problems tend to be less radical, involving only a few hours of downtime now and again. But accumulated downtime is a serious mainframe-related problem. One study in a major corporation showed that the host computer was unavailable from 10 to 20 percent of the time. A more representative figure may be as low as 5 percent. That 5 percent, however, seems to be concentrated during peak hours, thus magnifying the effect.

The costs of downtime can mount up with an unreliable communications network. Companies often don't see these costs because they don't show up on any ledger sheet. The costs are real, nevertheless.

In contrast, the PC rarely has downtime, certainly nothing like that of mainframe systems. If the mainframe goes down, you'll probably have an entire staff sitting around with little to do. But if you have copies of mainframe files and programs sitting on a network server, the real effect of mainframe downtime can be minimized.

## IBM's Micro-to-Mainframe Machines

IBM has made a major move into the micro-to-mainframe world with two products. One is the PC with built-in 3270 emulation capability. The other is the XT/370, an IBM PC/XT that is essentially a desktop mainframe.

The 3270/PC operates in either PC or 3270 mode, and a single keystroke allows the user to switch between modes. This PC can communicate with several mainframe systems: IBM System/370, IBM 308X, or the 43XX processor through an IBM 3274 controller. Besides providing access to the mainframe computer, the 3270/PC permits information to be displayed in seven user-defined windows as well as moved to different windows. Data can be downloaded from the mainframe and stored locally for processing on the PC.

The 3270/PC uses a different display unit and different keyboard from those of the standard PC. The display, an IBM 5272, is a high-resolution, color unit that supports up to eight colors. The keyboard is a combination of the PC and 3270 keyboards. The 3270/PC has 122 keys, with PC-specific keys in blue to distinguish them from the 3270 keys.

The XT/370 is a PC/XT with three special-purpose circuit boards. One board permits 3277 display terminal emulation and lets the machine connect to an IBM 3774 controller. The second board adds 524K of memory and up to 4M of virtual memory. And the third board has two Motorola 68000 microprocessors and an Intel 8087 numeric co-processor. The processors and the chip emulate parts of the 370 instruction set.

## For the Future

IBM's heavy involvement in the PC-to-mainframe arena will have a profound effect. Emulation products and gateways into SNA that have been developed by the hardware industry have significant price advantages over the IBM machines. But IBM's machines have more features—and an IBM logo.

One of the large deficiencies in the mainframe connection has been in the area of compatible applications software. Some work has been done on integrating PC programs with different mainframe systems. Some programs run on a PC and on a mainframe using compatible data base formats. For the most part, though, data bases created on a PC are not compatible with mainframe environments, and vice versa. The appearance of new hardware is certain to encourage software houses to develop applications programs that fill this gap.

The desktop mainframe that IBM calls the XT/370 can run a great deal of mainframe software without any conversions. That is, the programs have no compatibility problems. Still some monetary conversion seems inevitable. A mainframe applications package frequently costs $50,000 or more. Prices on existing mainframe software will undoubtedly come down, at least for the XT/370-tailored versions. At the same time, new software will appear that is developed specifically for this machine.

The microcomputer is finally a solid fixture in the corporate world. This computer has the power to do real work, the communications line to integrate that work, and now the word of IBM that the PC really belongs.

# 16
## Electronic Mail

When people are asked why they're installing a local area network, rarely does someone answer "electronic mail." Electronic mail is usually considered a secondary benefit, if it's considered at all. Yet this situation will change very soon. Anticipating the change, network developers and communications suppliers have been pouring considerable resources into developing mail capabilities.

By itself, electronic memoing is an enormously useful productivity tool. But it is only one of the features of electronic mail. Network pioneer Robert Metcalfe of 3Com refers to electronic mail as "the single most significant contributor to office productivity—more important even than spreadsheets and word processing."

## Defining Electronic Mail

Electronic mail is a message that is encoded as electrical impulses and passed over transmission lines. The message may be a memo, letter, file, graph, or a combination of any of these. Most of the problems and delays of getting a physical document from one person to another are eliminated by electronic mail. Like a telephone call, the message becomes available to the addressee as soon as it is sent. But unlike a telephone call, both parties do not need to be available simultaneously for communication to succeed. Thus, electronic mail effectively eliminates "telephone tag," where two parties invariably attempt to communicate when one of them is out of the office.

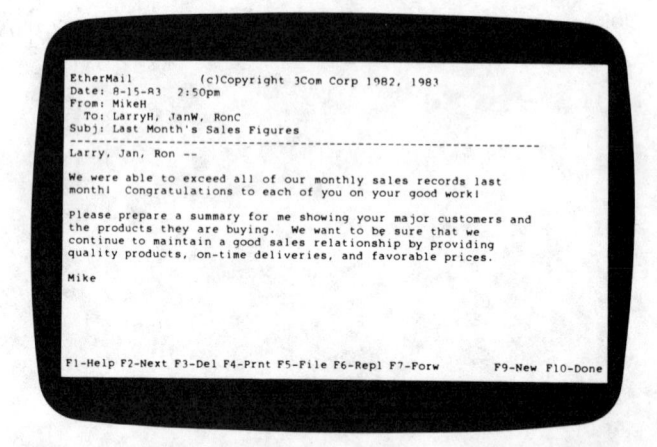

*Fig. 16.1. An electronic mail message. Reprinted by permission of 3Com Corp.*

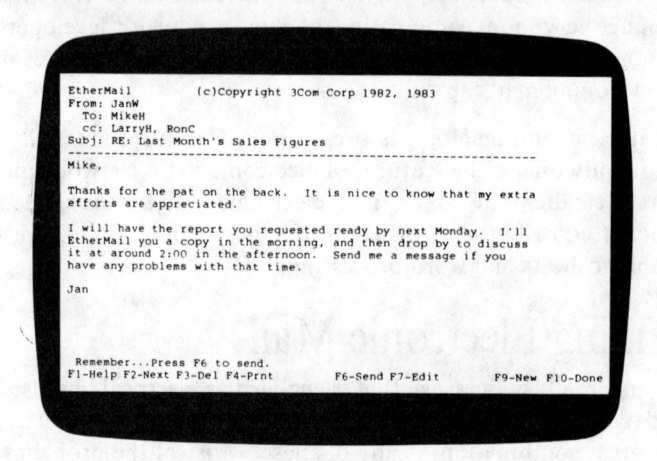

*Fig. 16.2. An electronic mail response. Reprinted by permission of 3Com Corp.*

A computer-based message system (CBMS), such as the local area network, has many advantages over terminal-based electronic delivery systems. Local area network electronic mail lets you create, send, receive, and store messages. Mail can be sent to individuals or groups. In addition to supporting direct communications, the CBMS allows computers to store the messages for reference, forwarding, and a variety of other purposes.

Local area networks that are user-defined, not device-defined, have another advantage in a mail system. A user-defined system permits a user with a password to logon to any convenient PC. That PC will have the same access privileges, file directories, and *mail address* as the user's own workstation. The local area network user can therefore send and receive personal messages from any place in the network, as long as the proper password is given. Unauthorized people cannot read personal mail or send messages using a false name.

## Using Electronic Mail

The primary component of the electronic mail system is a "mailbox," one for each mail user on the network. The mailbox is an area on the central hard disk reserved for each user. This mailbox serves as the central message holder and has both "in" and "out" baskets. For a message to be sent, a link is established between the sender's "out" basket and the addressee's "in" basket.

After the message has been sent, the addressee is informed that mail is in his "in" box. Some mail packages require that the user query the system to find out whether mail is waiting; other packages send notification to the addressee's status line as soon as the mail is posted or whenever the addressee logs onto the network. When the addressee calls for the mail, the sender is informed of successful delivery. Any user can put mail into a personal mailbox. No one, however, can open a mailbox and read or delete its contents without knowing the mailbox owner's name and password.

Most mail packages include an editor for memo writing. Longer documents can be written on the user's word-processing software, if that is more convenient.

Some tricks are available for using a mail system efficiently. For instance, when several users are sent a document, a new copy of that

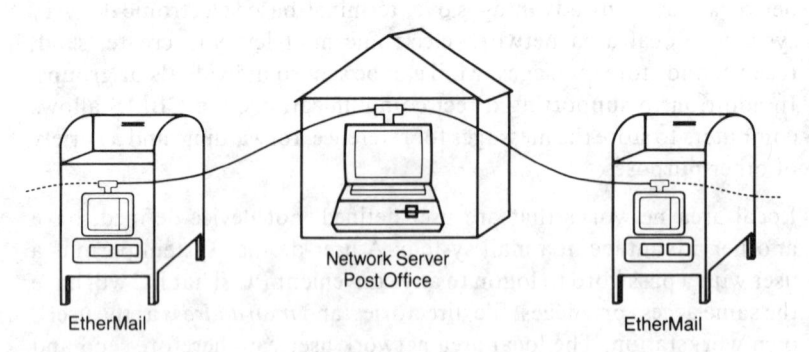

*Fig. 16.3. The network server acts as the "post office," or central distribution point, for electronic mail messages. Reprinted by permission of 3Com Corp.*

document is made for each user. With large documents, you can save disk space by sending a message to read a document with a particular file name, instead of actually copying the file and putting it into the mail system.

Mailboxes usually permit you to scan the contents of the mailbox. A display will show the date, source, and title of each message so that more important messages can be read first. For labeling messages a common system is useful; you can then tell quickly what kinds of messages are in the mailbox. A message title may be prefixed with a label, such as Rprt, Doc, Memo, Personal, or Graph. As an added refinement, some mail systems let you search for mail. For example, a menu might list all the mail sent by John or all messages labeled Rprt.

Since mail may be retained in mailboxes, you need a method for learning the current status of each mailbox. Mail can be flagged as already read, as awaiting reply, as save until a certain date, and so on.

# Evaluating Electronic Mail

Electronic mail packages are usually offered as optional software supplied by the network vendor. As yet, not many hardware-independent mail packages are available. When vendors offer a variety of mail systems, you should be able to choose a system that best suits your own needs.

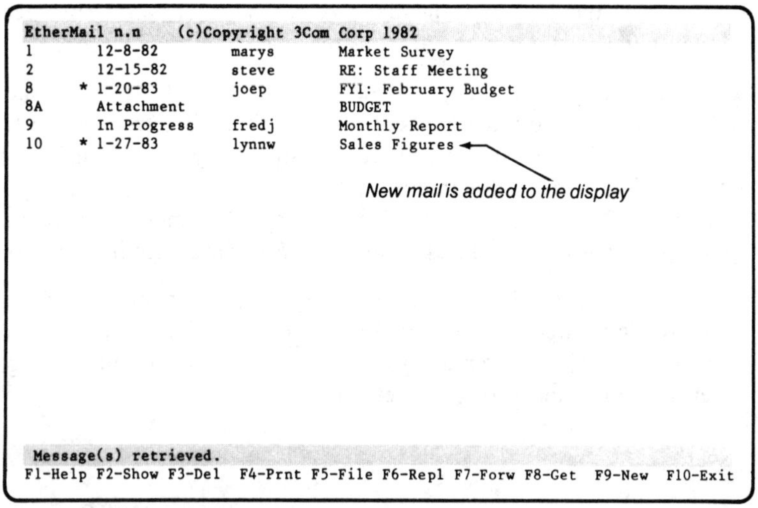

```
EtherMail n.n    (c)Copyright 3Com Corp 1982
1        12-8-82      marys      Market Survey
2        12-15-82     steve      RE: Staff Meeting
8      * 1-20-83      joep       FYI: February Budget
8A       Attachment              BUDGET
9        In Progress  fredj      Monthly Report
10     * 1-27-83      lynnw      Sales Figures ←
                                          New mail is added to the display




Message(s) retrieved.
F1-Help F2-Show F3-Del  F4-Prnt F5-File F6-Repl F7-Forw F8-Get  F9-New  F10-Exit
```

*Fig. 16.4. Getting new mail. Electronic mail menus should have some way of identifying new mail, such as with an asterisk. Reprinted by permission of 3Com Corp.*

In selecting a mail package, you should expect to find some features typically found in other software packages. These features can be evaluated just as they would be for any software. The "user friendly" features, though, should be given special consideration because of the wide range of people who will be using electronic mail. Commands should be simple and close to natural language. The package should be menu-driven, and the menus should be readable. An on-line help system is also an asset.

Beyond these basic features, electronic mail does have some special requirements. A mail package should have one menu that lists all the items in the mailbox. The system should permit messages to be read in any order, as well as read and forwarded with additional remarks if necessary. The ability to create distribution lists and to flag messages for "delayed send" are also desirable features.

Mail can be archived in each user's personal mailbox. The owner can pull out mail, read it, delete it, forward it, or save it. You should be able to store messages back into the mailbox. Messages should be protected so that they aren't automatically deleted once they've been read.

Most electronic mail packages include some kind of editor, either line or full screen. You shouldn't expect the same power in a mail editor that you'd want in a regular word processor; simplicity is more important. For creating a mail document that is long or complex, use your conventional word processor. Then put that document into the mail system, appending the addressee and any other message information.

A mail package should permit interfacing to applications programs so that any file created on the network can be sent through the electronic mail system. Ideally, the mail system should also permit interfacing to other local area and wide area networks.

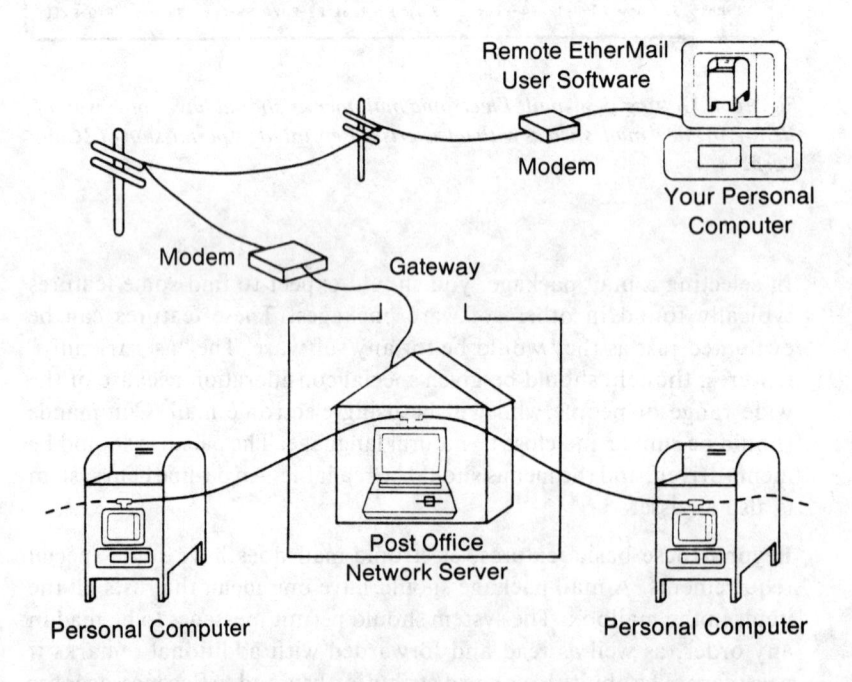

*Fig. 16.5. Using remote mail, a person at a remote location with a PC and a modem can contact the network and deliver and receive messages. Reprinted by permission of 3Com Corp.*

Some electronic mail packages have an "express mail" feature. When express mail is sent, the addressee is immediately notified on the status line of the PC that mail is waiting. A "remote mail" feature lets a remote PC user with a modem and telephone send mail to the local area network.

## An Intraoffice Study

Local area networks with PCs are now introducing people to the intraoffice capability of electronic mail. In this case, electronic mail replaces telephone functions more than it replaces U.S. mail functions. But besides replacing telephones, intraoffice electronic mail also replaces memos, messages, and meetings.

The value of electronic mail is much greater for large networks than it is for small ones. For this reason the results of small-scale evaluations of electronic mail may be misleading. The problem lies in the critical mass phenomenon. The typical mistake made in electronic mail evaluations is that they are based on a small, controlled setting.

Let's suppose that we put five people—Bill, Janet, Frank, Ted, and Ken—in a pilot study. Each is given a PC workstation with electronic mail capability. Over a month's time, we observe communications patterns to see whether electronic mail capability does improve communications.

Here are just five people in the middle of an organization with 1,000 employees. Each of these five can send messages only to the other four, representing something like .03 percent of the five employees' total communication needs. The result of such a study would undoubtedly show that the electronic mail system is actually an inconvenience for them because they are operating below critical mass.

With electronic mail, critical mass is the point where most of the communications for a given user can be routed through electronic mail channels. You must be able to use electronic mail for a high percentage of your communications, whether intraoffice or interoffice, or both. Otherwise, no realistic message distribution (communication) channels exist, and electronic mail becomes just another technology without an application.

# Interoffice Mail

Intraoffice electronic mail, when implemented on a company-wide basis, has proved extremely successful in improving communications. The next logical step is to interconnect company mail networks with other companies and distant facilities in an internet mail system. As telecommuting and dispersed personnel bases become more common, the need for dependable communications with remote sites is increasing.

The primary reasons for internetting are to establish communications among additional groups of users and to route these communications through a single multipurpose device—the PC. Of course, internetting doesn't require electronic mail, but mail does significantly enhance the communications capability of the internet.

Internetting still has some technical problems to be resolved, as discussed in Chapter 14. Internet mail, in particular, requires extensive addressing capability to support the person-to-person nature of the communications.

Internetting with electronic mail between identical networks is relatively straightforward. Some network protocols even support internetting with special features. The Ethernet specification, for example, requires that every Ethernet NIC be assigned a unique address. Across dissimilar networks, however, the problems increase. Mail-handling gateways can help dissimilar networks send mail to one another, but within limits. The networks must use similar naming conventions and message formats before mail can be sent reliably.

# Other Applications

True electronic mail is limited to those systems that transmit messages directly from the sender to the receiver. Many users find it expedient to use general mail service systems, such as Mailgram, along with a local area network mail system. Combinations of electronic mail and document delivery are now available when computer-to-computer messaging is not possible or practical. Through such combinations some of the advantages of electronic mail can be extended even to correspondents without electronic mail capability.

Both the increased use of broadband cable TV for two-way communications and the interconnection of multichannel systems with PBX and local area network systems will further spur the use of electronic mail. In the future, voice mail and computer conferencing will become compatible with a broad group of devices and will therefore become widely used. Integration of mail systems will make electronic mail a universal communications medium, its functionality growing in proportion to the numbers of interconnected users.

Many applications for electronic mail are only just now being explored. Others are yet to be discovered. The convergence of electronic mail technologies will contribute toward the development of an integrated electronic mail system. As such a system evolves and as electronic mail is integrated with traditional data processing, electronic mail will become the communications pipeline for critical corporate information.

# Glossary

**Access**—To retrieve data from permanent magnetic storage and bring that data into electronic memory. Computers can manipulate data only when it is in electronic memory.

**Algorithm**—A special method used to solve a particular problem. On a contention network, for example, an algorithm is used to reschedule transmissions after a collision.

**Analog**—A system based on a continuous ratio, such as voltage or current values. (See also **Digital**.)

**Analog transmission**—A communications scheme that uses a continuous signal, which is varied by amplification. Broadband networks use analog transmissions. (See also **Digital transmission**.)

**Applications software**—A program or set of programs that performs a specific task for the computer user. Word processor and spreadsheet programs are examples of applications software.

**ARCnet**—Attached Resource Computer Network. A local area network scheme designed by Datapoint. ARCnet provides intercommunication among networked devices at a rate of 2.5Mbit/sec.

**ASCII**—American Standard Code for Information Interchange. This is the coded character set used internally by the IBM PC and most other microcomputers.

**Asynchronous (Async)**—A method of data communication in which transmissions are not synchronized by a clocking signal. Sets of data are defined by start-stop bits. Local area networks transmit asynchronously.

**Attenuation**—Loss of signal strength. On a local area network, attenuation will prevent successful communication when cable lengths exceed their maximum range.

**Background task**—A job processed in a subordinate status to foreground tasks. Some network operating systems permit a microcomputer to function as both a network server and workstation. Often the network duties are carried out as background tasks while the local user's instructions are executed in foreground.

**Backup**—A duplicate copy of a program or data file. A backup of data should be made as protection against corruption or loss of the original.

**Bandwidth**—The capacity of a communications channel. Bandwidth is typically stated as bits per second (bit/sec) or cycles per second (Hertz). As a measure of the rate at which information can be passed across a network, bandwidth is therefore an indication of network speed.

**Baseband system**—A communications method in which the information-bearing signal is placed directly onto the cable in digital form. Since the I/O of the microcomputer is also digital, no translation is necessary for a baseband system at the sending or receiving end.

**Baseband coax**—A single channel medium for carrying baseband transmissions.

**Batch mode**—Running a program without user interaction. In networking, batch mode often refers to batch transfers whereby an entire file is downloaded from a central machine, such as a network server or host mainframe computer. The file is manipulated locally, then returned to the central device.

**Baud**—An imprecise unit of measure, roughly equivalent to bits per second.

**Bisynchronous (Bisync)**—Binary synchronous. A protocol developed by IBM for mainframe data transmissions. The transmission method is controlled by a clocking signal.

**Bit**—Binary digit. The basic unit of information used in computer systems. A bit is either 0 or 1.

**Bridge**—A device that matches circuits and is used to connect identical local area networks through store and forward buffers that check addresses and may regulate bandwidth.

**Broadband system**—A communications method characterized by a large bandwidth. The bandwidth is usually split, or multiplexed, to provide multiple communications channels. A broadband system uses analog transmissions. Since the microcomputer is a digital device, a modem is required at either end of the transmission cable to convert the digital signal to analog and back again.

**Broadcast**—A transmission technique in which all attending stations receive the transmission. Messages are broadcast onto local area networks by the sending workstation, but only the addressee accepts and reads the message.

**Buffer**—A temporary data storage facility.

**Bus**—A path for electrical signals; also a type of network topology with a single cable onto which all devices attach. The cable ends are terminated with resistors.

**Byte**—A unit of measure, usually eight bits. (Ten-bit bytes are occasionally used, but should be predefined.)

**Cache**—A buffer between the CPU and the magnetic storage device. Data can be retrieved from magnetic storage and held in the cache in anticipation of the data's use by the CPU. A cache increases the speed of system operations because data acquisitions are faster from the cache than from magnetic storage.

**Carrier Sense Multiple Access (CSMA)**—A contention network access scheme. Workstations monitor the network and may transmit any time the cable appears to be clear—that is, when no carrier is sensed, or "heard," on the network.

**Chip**—(Slang) A silicon wafer imprinted with integrated circuits. Often used to mean CPU.

**Coaxial cable**—Two-conductor cable in which the conductors have the same axis. The center conductor carries the signal while the outer conductor, a tubular braid of wire, provides the ground. The outer conductor also shields the signal against electrical interference. Same as Coax.

**Collision**—A garbled transmission, which results from simultaneous transmissions by two or more workstations onto the same network cable.

**Communication link**—An electrical and logical connection between two devices. On a local area network, a communication link is the point-to-point path between sender and addressee.

**Contention**—An access method for sharing a network cable, based on "first come, first served."

**Controller**—A device that communicates with the host computer and relays information between the host computer and terminals.

**Coprocessor**—A microprocessor that is installed in a system to handle specific tasks, thereby reducing the workload of the CPU.

**CPU**—Central Processing Unit. The microprocessor that provides processing capability, or "intelligence," for a microcomputer.

**CRC**—Cyclic redundancy checking. A common method of checking for errors in a received message.

**Cross talk**—Signal interference created by emissions passing from one cable element to another.

**CSMA-CD**—Carrier Sense Multiple Access with Collision Detection. A contention scheme, which includes a method of recovery in the event of a collision. When a collision is detected, transmitting stations cease transmission and wait a predefined interval before retransmitting.

**Data**—Information. (See **Data communications**.)

**Data communications**—The passage of information in the form of electrical impulses representing alphanumeric characters. Data communications contrast with both voice and video communications.

**Datagram**—A message comprised of packets of information.

**Data integrity**—The condition in which data (information) is uncorrupted and usable. Computer data is normally stored and transmitted in volatile form for easy manipulation. Such storage, whether electrical or magnetic, is subject to a number of threats, and great care must be exercised to maintain data integrity.

**Dedicated**—Reserved for a single function. A dedicated network server, for example, cannot be used for any purpose other than network serving.

**Default value**—A definition that is selected when no other definition is specified. Default values are utilized for disk drives, printers, programs, and many other software and hardware variables as a convenience to the user.

**Diagnostics**—Programs or routines that test computer hardware and software to determine whether they are operating properly.

**Digital**—A system based on discrete states, typically the binary conditions On or Off.

**Digital transmission**—A communications system that passes information encoded as pulses. Baseband networks use digital transmissions, as do microcomputers.

**Direct connect**—In local area networking, the process of attaching a workstation to the network cable without an intervening multiplexer. Direct connect is accomplished via a network interface card.

**DMA**—Direct memory access. A high-speed method of transferring data from a peripheral device directly into the microcomputer's memory.

**Download/upload**—The transfer of an entire data file (or program) between computers. Transferring a file from a host to a remote computer is downloading. Transferring from a remote computer to a host is uploading. (See **Batch mode**.)

**Emulation**—The duplication of the functional capability of one device in another device. For example, an IBM PC may be made to emulate a dumb terminal for communications with a host mainframe computer.

**Ethernet**—A local computer network protocol designed by Xerox. Ethernet specifications include a bus topology, baseband coax medium, and 10Mbit/sec data rate.

**ECMA**—European Computer Manufacturers Association.

**FDM**—Frequency division multiplexing. A technique in which a communications medium is divided into parallel channels. Each is allocated a different frequency band. This technique is used to give broadband coax its multichannel capability.

**Fiber optics**—Glass or plastic fibers that carry information by modulating a visible signal.

**Foreground task**—A job that is done in priority status before subordinate, or background, tasks are executed. In multitasking, a network server usually performs local workstation routines in foreground while executing network tasks in background.

**Gateway**—A device that connects two dissimilar networks. A gateway has its own processor and memory and may perform both protocol and bandwidth conversion.

**Hard disk**—Also called a fixed disk or Winchester disk.

**Host computer**—A machine that provides the processing power for attached terminals. The host computer is usually a mainframe or minicomputer.

**Host-to-terminal**—A network scheme in which a central controlling machine, the host, serves multiple dumb terminals. Also known as a master/slave scheme.

**IEEE**—Institute of Electrical and Electronic Engineers. One of several groups whose members are drawn from industry and who attempt to establish industry standards. The IEEE 802 committee has published numerous definitive documents on local area network standards.

**Internet**—"Between networks," or the process of sending traffic from one network to another. Same as internetwork.

**Interrupt**—A signal that can break into the execution of a program with a new command.

**I/O**—Input/output.

**I/O port**—A circuit that receives data from the main processor or provides data to the processor. The IBM PC can have up to 65,536 I/O ports.

**ISO model**—The International Standards Organization's Open System Interconnection model. A set of guidelines for network design, divided into seven distinct layers.

**K**—Kilobyte. A unit of measure for computer memory equal to 1,024 bytes.

**Jumper**—An electrical conductor that connects two points in a curcuit.

**LAN**—Local area network.

**Layer**—A discrete set of communications functions capable of interfacing with adjacent sets in a hierarchical structure. (See also **ISO model**.)

**Local area network**—A geographically confined computer-based communications system. The network may be used to indicate any combination of hosts, terminals, microcomputers, and other attached devices. In this book, unless otherwise noted, the term is used to mean a "microcomputer local area network." (See also **Peer-to-peer**.)

**Lock**—A method of preventing simultaneous access of data. A lock may be advisory, as with a semaphore, in which case the user may override. Such advisory locks warn the user that a file is in use but do not prevent its access. Some operating systems provide "hard locks," which cannot be overridden.

**Logon/logoff**—The process of activating or deactivating a local microcomputer as a network entity. Logon procedure for a local area network requires the starting (booting) of a network user program, often followed by keyboard entry of a logon name and a password. Same as login/logout.

**Logical**—A functional description that may differ from the physical description. A network, for example, may be configured so that a logical local drive C for one workstation is physically volume F on a disk server's partitioned hard disk.

**Mainframe**—A large computer.

**Mapping**—Assigning a hard disk volume to a particular logical disk drive.

**Megabyte**—A unit of measure equal to 1,000,000 bytes.

**Memory dump**—A captured image of part of the internal memory of a microcomputer. Memory dumps are generally used for software diagnostics.

**Menu**—A display that lists the choices available to the user and allows selection of a choice by entering one or two keystrokes.

**Menu-driven**—A software program in which all information necessary for its operation is displayed in a menu. This typically restricts the available options but makes the program easier for a novice to use.

**Microcomputer**—A microprocessor-based computing system with enough power to perform computations, including the ability to modify its own programs. The microcomputer has its own memory and I/O circuitry. Usually, processing power is limited to a single CPU.

**Modem**—MOdulator/DEModulator. A device that converts digital signals from a computer to modulated signals for transmission over a telephone line. At the receiving end, another modem converts the modulated signals back to digital signals and passes them to a receiving computer.

**Motherboard**—The main circuit board of a computer system, into which may be plugged smaller boards to expand the functions of the system. Same as system board.

**Multitasking**—The concurrent handling of multiple jobs by a single CPU. On a network server, multitasking usually means that the server can be used in foreground as a local workstation while network tasks are carried on in background.

**Multiuser**—A system in which multiple users share a single CPU. In common usage, multiuser indicates a host-to-terminal system whereas a local area network indicates a peer-to-peer system.

**Multiple access**—The condition in which multiple users can open the same file simultaneously. Same as concurrent access.

**Multiplexing**—Supporting simultaneous multiple transmissions on a single medium.

**Network**—A communications system that consists of attached devices.

**Network interface card (NIC)**—A circuit board that permits direct connection of a microcomputer to a network cable. The network side of the NIC usually has a BNC twist connector, and the microcomputer side plugs in the computer bus. NICs often have a transmitter, encoder/decoder circuitry, memory buffer, and sometimes a coprocessor.

**Operating system**—A software program that manages the hardware/software interface of a computer.

**OSI**—Open System Interconnection. The seven-layer ISO model of local area network guidelines.

**Overwrite**—To write (store) data on a magnetic disk in the same area where other data has been stored. In the process, the original data is destroyed. In a local area network, overwrites occur most often when two people access the same data, update the data, then attempt to write the updates to disk. The network operating system may be unaware that the data has been modified, and may store the two updates in the same space. The last person to store data will overwrite the first person's data.

**Packet**—A set of data with addresses and control codes attached to it so that it may be transmitted on a computer network.

**Packet switching**—The transmission of packetized data across a shared medium. The circuit is available to other transmissions as soon as the packet has been sent. Other packets, though part of the same message, may be transmitted across different circuits if necessary. This transmission method is commonly used on local area networks.

**Parameter**—A definable variable.

**Parity**—An error detection scheme for data communications based on an odd or even number of 1 bits. If odd parity is specified, an extra bit is added to make the total number of 1 bits odd. If even parity is specified, the extra bit is used to make the total even. Parity is checked after a transmission is received and, if parity is inconsistent, a transmission error has occurred.

**Password**—A security tool used to identify authorized network users and to define their privileges within the network. Passwords are normally requested during the logon procedure after the logon name is entered by the user.

**Peer-to-peer**—A network scheme which assumes that connected devices have local processing power. In a peer-to-peer system the network operating system distributes some network functions to workstations and unburdens the network server whenever possible.

**Peripheral**—A device, such as a printer or disk drive, that is connected to a computer and controlled by it.

**Polling**—A system of regularly checking the status of attached devices. When the polled device has a request, it is accepted and executed.

**Protocol**—A set of defined parameters for establishing and controlling communications. In a local area network, major protocols cover the hardware level (Ethernet, ARCnet, etc.), and transport level (XNS, IP/TCP, etc.).

**Queue**—A waiting line in which jobs are stored, pending processing. A common queuing device is a print spooler, which holds data sent for printing. The spooler feeds the data to the printer as the printer can use it.

**RAM**—Random-access memory. A Read/Write memory space, any area of which can be accessed in a nonsequential manner. Normally, RAM refers to electronic memory.

**RAM disk**—An area of electronic memory that is configured by a software program to emulate a disk drive. Data stored in a RAM disk can be accessed more quickly than data stored on a physical disk drive.

**Read**—To access a data file and examine its contents without making a modification.

**Read-Only**—A privilege designation that permits a user to open the file but not modify it.

**Read/Write**—A privilege designation that permits a user to open and/or modify a file.

**Repeater**—A network device used to amplify and pass along an attenuated signal.

**Resident program**—A program that, once loaded into memory, remains there until the system is powered down or until it is reset. The resident program is readily available to the user or other programs.

**Response time**—The interval necessary to answer a request, usually measured at the user interfaces; in other words, the time from the issuance of a keyboard request until the receipt of the answer on the display.

**ROM**—Read-only memory. Often designated as firmware, a ROM is a memory chip with a software program permanently embedded in its circuits.

**RS-232-C**—A common protocol for connecting microcomputer system components. On the IBM PC, an RS-232-C is the serial data interface to modem-based communications.

**Screen buffer**—A memory area that contains the screen characters and attributes.

**Scrolling**—The process of adjusting the display upward or downward.

**Serial transmission**—A data transmission method in which each bit in a byte is sent sequentially, one at a time. When the data arrives at its destination, the bits are reassembled into 8-bit bytes.

**Serial port**—A computer data channel, usually an RS-232-C interface, on a computer. A serial port allows serial data into and out of the computer. The port converts parallel data to serial data and serial data to parallel data.

**Server**—A hardware and software device that acts as an interface between a local area network and a peripheral device. The server receives requests for peripheral services and manages the requests so that they are answered in an orderly, sequential manner.

**SNA/SDLC**—Systems Network Architecture/Synchronous Data Link Control. A communication method commonly used to transmit data from an IBM host computer to a 3274 or 3276 controller.

**Software**—The instruction programs that tell a computer what to do.

**Spooler**—A software program that will take data which is addressed to a peripheral and store that data in memory. The spooler will release the data to the peripheral as the data can be used. Once the spooler is loaded, the CPU is free to continue processing while the peripheral is served by the spooler. Print spoolers, which hold files for printing, are the most common type of spoolers.

**Synchronous**—A transmission controlled by a clock pulse acted on by the sender and receiver.

**Star**—A local area network topology in which cables radiate from a central network processor. Workstations are attached to the cables, one workstation per cable.

**Terminal**—A user interface device that lacks built-in processing capability. Terminals normally have a keyboard and a display, and attach to a host computer for processing and data storage facilities.

**Token passing**—A network access scheme in which a special packet is circulated among workstations. Any workstation wishing to transmit captures the token by setting a bit on the token. When the workstation has completed its transmission, the station releases the token and control of the network by resetting the bit to "free" status.

**Topology**—The physical layout of a local area network. Some common topologies are Bus, Ring, and Star.

**Transient program**—A program that is loaded into memory, executes a specific function, then releases the memory space occupied by the program. Unlike a resident program, the services of a transient program are no longer available once the program has been exited.

**Traffic**—The volume of messages sent over a shared medium. Traffic is often used as a rough measure of the amount of cable utilization (such as heavy, light, etc.).

**Transparent**—Any process that is not noticeable to the user during normal operation.

**TSO**—Time-sharing option. A widely used multiuser system on large IBM host computers.

**User**—A computer operator.

**Virtual**—The effective condition. Virtual memory, for example, may function as main memory but provides greater storage by utilizing a portion of disk storage as if virtual memory were electronic memory.

**Virtual circuit**—A logical data transmission path between sender and addressee. The virtual circuit exists only during the transmission.

**VM/CMS**—Virtual Machine/Conversational Monitor System. A widely used multiuser system on IBM host computers.

**Twisted pair**—Transmission cable composed of two braided wires.

**Volume**—In a local area network, a partitioned area of a shared hard disk. Volumes are similar to local disk drives and may be used in a similar manner.

**Window**—A 24-line segment of data from a larger display screen or from another program also resident in memory.

**Winchester**—A hard disk.

**Write**—To store data to disk.

# Vendor Directory

## Networks

Corvus Systems, Inc.
2029 O'Toole Avenue
San Jose, CA 95131
(408) 946-7700

Davong Systems, Inc.
217 Humboldt Court
Sunnyvale, CA 94086
(408) 734-4900

Destek Group
830 C E. Evelyn Avenue
Sunnyvale, CA 94086
(408) 737-7211

Gateway Communications, Inc.
16782 Redhill Ave.
Irvine, CA 92714
(714) 261-0762

Interlan, Inc.
3 Lyberty Way
Westford, MA 01886
(617) 692-3900

Nestar Systems, Inc.
2585 East Bayshore Road
Palo Alto, CA 94303
(415) 493-2223

Novell, Inc.
1170 North Industrial Park Drive
Orem, UT 84057
(800) 453-1267

Orchid Technology
47790 Westinghouse Drive
Fremont, CA 94539
(415) 490-8586

Tecmar, Inc.
6225 Cochran Road
Cleveland, OH 44139
(216) 349-0600

3Com Corp.
1390 Shorebird Way
Mountain View, CA 94043
(415) 961-9602

Ungermann-Bass, Inc.
2560 Mission College Blvd.
Santa Clara, CA 95050
(408) 496-0111

## Network Operating Systems

Digital Research, Inc.
P.O. Box 579
Pacific Grove, CA 93950
(408) 649-3896

LANTech
9635 Wendell Rd.
Dallas, TX 75243
(214) 340-4932

Novell, Inc.
0170 North Industrial Park Drive
Orem, UT 84057
(800) 453-1267

SofTech Microsystems, Inc.
16885 West Bernardo Dr.
San Diego, CA 92127
(619) 451-1230

## Security

Analytics Communications Systems
1820 Michael Faraday Dr.
Reston, VA 22090
(703) 471-0892

Boole & Babbage, Inc.
510 Oakmead Parkway
Sunnyvale, CA 94086
(800) 222-6653

Digital Pathways
1060 E. Meadow Circle
Palo Alto, CA 94303
(415) 493-5544

Fischer Innis
4175 Merchantile Ave.
Naples, FL 33942-9990
(800) 237-4510
(813) 793-1500 (in Florida)

IMM Corporation
100 N. 20th St.
Philadelphia, PA 19133
(215) 569-3880

LeeMAH
729 Filbert St.
San Francisco, CA 94133
(415) 434-3780

Merritt Software, Inc.
P.O. Box 1504
Fayetteville, AR 72702
(501) 442-0914

Norell Data Systems
3400 Wilshire Blvd.
Los Angeles, CA 90010
(213) 258-1653

Racal Milgo Information Systems
6950 Cypress Rd.
Plantation, FL 33318
(305) 584-4242
"Datacryptor II"

TelTech
Software Development Division
548 Fifth Ave.
New York, NY 10036

## Multiuser Applications Software

American Planning
4600 Duke St., Suite 423
Alexandria, VA 22304
(800) 368-2248
(Business applications software)

Bluebird Systems
6352 Corte Del Abeto, Suite A
Carlsbad, CA 92008
(Business applications software)

Cypher
121 Second St.
San Francisco, CA 94105
(415) 974-3675
"Revelation" (DBMS)

# VENDOR DIRECTORY

DataAccess
8525 S.W. 129th Terrace
Miami, FL 33156
(305) 238-0012
"DataFlex" (DBMS)

Microrim
1750 112th Ave. N.E.
Bellevue, WA 98004
(206) 453-6017
"R:Base Series" (DBMS)

Open Systems, Inc.
430 Oak Grove
Minneapolis, MN 55403
(612) 870-3515
(Business applications software)

Software Connections
1800 Wyatt Dr., Suite 17
Santa Clara, CA 95054
(408) 988-3704
"DataStore" (DBMS)

Ryan-McFarland Corporation
Corporate Sales Headquarters
609 Deep Valley Dr.
Rolling Hills Estates, CA 90274
(213) 541-4828
"RM/COBOL"

Sunburst Software Ltd.
2696 University Ave., Suite 250
Provo, UT 84604
(801) 374-5223
(Accounting software)

TCS Software, Inc.
3209 Fondren Rd.
Houston, TX 77063
(713) 977-7505
(Accounting software)

## Cable and Connectors

Anixter
2375 Zanker Rd.
San Jose, CA 95131
(408) 946-6470

Belden Corp.
P.O. Box 1980
Richmond, IN
(317) 983-5200

Trompeter Electronics, Inc.
8936 Comanche Ave.
Chatsworth, CA 91311
(213) 882-1020

## Terminal Emulation

AST Research, Inc.
2121 Alton Avenue
Irvine, CA 92714
(714) 863-1333

CXI
10011 North Foothill Boulevard
Cupertino, CA 95014
(408) 725-1881

Digital Communications Associates, Inc.
303 Technology Park
Norcross, GA 30092
(404) 448-1400

IBM
Entry Systems Division
P. O. Box 2989
Delray Beach, FL 38444

# Index

3.2 megabyte floppy, 5
300-baud modem, 125
3270 emulation, 192, 193, 202
3270 terminals, 65, 80
3270/PC, 202
3274 cluster controller, 73
3278 terminal, 83
3279 terminal, 193
3287 printer, 83
3Com Corp., 52, 61, 70, 72, 80, 164, 205
43XX, 193, 202
68000-based network, 77
68000-based server, 161
80186 chip, 83
802 committee, 19
8086, 71
8088 microprocessor chip, 9, 133
access methods, 60
access privileges, 106
access scheme, 8, 24
    Carrier Sense Multiple Access, 25
    Collision Detection, 25
    deterministic, 26
    performance, 26
    token passing, 25
=access time, 133
    access to data, 13
    acoustic coupler, 183
    add-on modules, 93
    administration, 111
    alarm system, 142
    alternatives for sharing data, 49
    Americare Service Program, 72
    Anixter, 153, 156
    Apple II, 75
    Apple III, 75
    application, 68
    Application layer, 16
    application programmer
    concerns, 109
=applications software, 37, 95, 203
    ARCnet, 19, 25, 30, 55, 61

ARCnet protocols, 88
ASCII data, 85
assigning users, 115
AST Research, 193
async modem, 183
AT&T, 182
attenuation, 180
audit trail, 144, 169
automatic locking, 44, 45, 91
B-35, 184
B-Plus tree, 104
background environment, 40
backup, 201
    file, 119
    procedure, 121
    redundancy, 23
bad sectors, 121
balance of resources, 7
bandwidth, 19
baseband, 177
baseband coaxial cable, 27
baseband network, 8
baseband-to-broadband, 83, 185
baseband-to-baseband, 85
BASIC, 108
BASIC with multiuser support, 109
batch transfers, 8, 66
batch mode, 196
BI-286, 109
binary data, 85
Binary Synchronous Communications, 17
binding, 17
BLOSSOM, 93
BNC connector, 157
bottlenecks, 127
bottom-up approach, 178
break-ins, 139
bridge, 83, 136, 178, 185
    benefits, 180
broadband, 177
broadband cable TV, 213
broadband coaxial cable, 27

231

broadband network, 8
BSC, 193
Business BASIC 2, 109
Business BASIC 3, 109
business support systems, 182
CA, 79
cable bottleneck, 134
cable connectors, 157
cable distribution, 152
    conduit, 153
    inexpensive method, 154
    moisture protection, 156
    over-ceiling cable tray, 153
    surface raceway, 153
    under-floor duct, 153
cable handling, 154
cable information, 155
cable radiation, 149
cable testing, 160
cable type, 65
cable, 3
    baseband coaxial, 27
    broadband coaxial, 27
    fiber-optic, 28
    least expensive, 27
    twisted pair, 27
caching, 127
CAD, 126
CAD/CAM, 163
call-back security, 142, 150
Carrier Sense Multiple Access scheme, 25
Carrier Sense Multiple Access with Collision Detection, 61
categories of software, 97, 99
CBMS, 207
CCITT, 182
CD, 79
central computing resource, 102
central network disk, 48
central processor, 9, 37
central storage, 3, 12
centralized backup facility, 122
centralized control, 38
channel capacity, 28
channel services, 55
choice of network, 60
choice of printers, 138
classified access schemes, 143
client program, 54
closed system, 22
closed topology, 64
clustered local networks, 178
COBOL, 108
collision avoidance, 79
Collision Detection, 25, 73
collision statistics, 134
common data base, 126
communications, 213
    hardware, 51
    links, 17

software, 97
compatibility, 61
computer-aided design, 126
computer-based message system, 207
Concept computer, 73
concurrent access, 36
    hazards, 37
Concurrent CP/M, 55, 89
conduit, 153, 154
configuration, 34
Constellation, 10
Consultative Committee for International Telegraph and Telephone, 182
contention scheme, 25
control, 62
controller ports, 197
coprocessor, 66
coprocessor boards, 134
copy-protected diskette, 95
corrosion of uncapped cable, 156
Corvus Systems, 10, 52, 61, 72, 198
Corvus Winchesters, 75
cost, 62
cost control, 174
cost of re-creating data, 141
CP/M, 52, 89
CP/M-86, 4, 53, 67, 78
crashed files, 120
CRC messages, 172
cross talk, 162
Crypt, 146
cryptanalysis, 145
CSMA scheme, 25
CSMA-CD, 61, 70, 82, 91, 102, 172, 189
    longevity, 26
CXI, 193
data base management systems, 47, 97
data base software, 97
Data Encryption Standard, 146
data protection, 33
data safety, 12
data security, 12, 67
    alarm system, 142
    call-back, 150
    diskless PC, 147
    encryption, 145
    encryption keys, 146
    locks, 142
    on-line coders, 147
    passwords, 143
    personal identification, 143
    remote access, 143
data security systems, 139
data transfers, 127
Data-Link layer, 16
DataAccess, 99
Dataflex, 99
Datapoint, 61
DataStore, 99, 102, 105

# INDEX

daughterboard, 94
Davong Systems, 30, 61, 88
dBASEII, 108
DBMS, 97, 104
DCA, 193
deadlock, 47, 101
DEC Rainbow, 67, 75
DEC VAX minicomputer, 12, 71, 133
deciphering equipment, 145
decryption, 145
dedicated cable, 22, 64, 152
dedicated network, 182
dedicated processor, 65
dedicated server, 39
dedicated wires, 24
default area, 77
default file locking, 37
defining users, 106
delayed send, 209
delete access, 106
DES, 146
DESNET, 75
Destek, 61, 75
deterministic access method, 26
device log, 122
device-defined networks, 207
diagnostic routines, 62
diagnostics, 167
    in hardware, 172
dial-up line, 183
Digital Research, 55
directories, 116
disk cache, 89
disk caching, 127
disk emulation, 36
disk error, 171
disk server, 32, 36, 38
disk server network, 102
disk sharing, 30
disk space, 201
diskless PC, 142, 147
    software problems, 148
dissimilar systems, 68
distance limitation, 64
Distributed Bus, 21
    reliability, 23
distributed control, 38
distributed file system, 57
distributed processing, 12
Distributed Star, 23
document file, 119
documentation, 63
DOS, 89
dot-matrix printers, 188
downtime, 202
DR NET
    features, 55
drive technology, 132
dumb terminals, 11

dynamic updating, 105
ECMA, 20
efficient software, 107
ELAN, 80
ELAN Voice System, 81
electrical interference, 27, 63, 161
electromagnetic media, 140
electronic mail, 34, 199, 205
    features, 209
    value of, 211
electronic memoing, 205
electronic memory
    speed, 128
electronic memory storage system, 128
emulator card, 196
emulator-equipped PC, 193
encryption, 139, 142, 145
encryption keys, 146
encryption security devices, 67
end-to-end distances, 64
end-to-end encryption, 145
environment, 63
equal access to data, 102
error codes, 169
error detection, 17
EtherMail, 72
EtherNet, 11, 19, 24, 55, 61, 83, 212
    performance, 71
    topology, 71
EtherPrint, 72
EtherSeries, 52, 70, 80
European Computer Manufacturers Association, 20
evaluating an emulator, 193
evaluation criteria, 61
expansion, 151
expansion buses, 68
exposed cables, 153
express mail, 211
faceplates, 152
fair access to resources, 102
faster processing, 133
fault tolerance, 66, 160, 161
FCB, 37
fiber-optic cable, 28, 149, 163
file control block, 37
file names, 119
file organization, 114
file retrieval, 130
file server, 36, 38, 52, 197
file specification utility, 33
file structure, 128
file-access privileges, 118
file-by-file tape backup, 120
files on the network, 117
fire-retardant cable, 159
first-come-first-served, 26
flat directory, 129
flexibility, 64, 122
floppy disk backup storage, 122

floppy diskette technology, 5
foreground processing, 39
foreground/background, 40
forms-handling capability, 137
functionality, 59
future standards, 26
G/NET, 52, 79, 184
gateway, 16, 65, 178, 181
    design, 182
Gateway Communications, 52, 61, 79, 133, 179, 184, 193
General Electric Instrumentation Service Co., 79
government standards, 67
graphics applications, 108
graphics software, 97
ground loop, 164
grounding, 163
growing the network, 135
handling information, 112
hard disk, 9, 127
hard disk backup, 12
hard disk bottleneck, 131
hard disk interface, 133
hard disk storage, 131
hardware failure, 171
hardware layers, 19
hardware listing, 123
hardware settings, 123
hardware-independent operating systems, 51
head crashes, 201
heavy traffic conditions, 26, 125
heavy-duty printers, 137
helical spiral, 155
hierarchical directory, 129
hierarchical disk storage, 77
hierarchy, 17
high data rates, 163
high-level protocols, 20
high-performance peripherals, 136
high-speed modems, 189
host-to-terminal network, 3
host-to-terminal protocol, 19
hostile conditions, 63
HUBs, 86
I/O request, 55
IBM, 193, 203
IBM 308X, 193
IBM 5272, 203
IBM Binary Synchronous Communications, 196
IBM compatibility, 194
IBM mainframe computers, 20
IBM PC/XT, 9, 131, 161, 202
IBM System/370, 193
IBM PC Cluster, 66
ID badge, 143
IEEE, 19, 61, 70, 188
image backup, 120
improperly used locks, 47
incompatible personal computers, 68
independent processes, 40

informal cable installation, 153
Information Builders, 99
information sharing
    —among dissimilar devices, 85
    hazards of, 43
initial planning, 112
installation, 63
installation log, 152
installation planning, 151
Institute of Electrical and Electronic Engineers, 19
integrated data base, 107
Intel
    80186, 133
    8087, 203
    82586, 172
interdepartmental traffic, 136
interface compatibility, 64
interface requirements, 64
interfacing mail to applications programs, 210
interference, 65, 161
Interlan, 61, 84, 193
interleaving, 132
internal failure, 171
International Standards Organization, 16, 20, 65
internet, 136
Internet Protocol/Transmission Control Protocol, 20
internetting, 16, 65, 177, 178, 185, 212
    addressing, 187
    hardware, 178
    protocol, 181
interoffice mail, 212
interrupt-driven logic, 89
intradepartmental file sharing, 136
IP, 181
IP/TCP, 20
ISO, 16
isolated PCs
    different data, 111
    lost opportunity, 111
jamming signal, 25
keeping track of file activity, 104
key word, 143
kinking and bending cable, 155
languages, 108
LANOS, 75
Lantech Systems, 57
Layer 1, 16
Layer 2, 16
Layer 3, 16
Layer 4, 16
Layer 5, 16
Layer 6, 16
Layer 7, 16
layout, 64
levels of security, 142
levels within a directory, 129
Liaison, 53
    features, 54
link encryption, 145

# INDEX 235

load balancing, 186
local area network
    advantages, 192
    alternatives to, 8
    as communications devices, 11
    components, 3
    definition, 2
    diagnostics, 168
    disadvantages, 192
    longevity of technology, 26
    size, 24
    speed, 19
local area network server, 181
local operating system, 30
local processing capability, 9
local storage, 126
local storage devices, 148
local-to-wide area gateways, 188
locally maintained software, 123
locator services, 55
lock time, 46
locked environment, 48
locking, 43, 57
    automatic, 44
    concept, 44
    manual, 44, 46
    record, 45
    shareable files, 47
    transaction, 45
    types, 44
    utilities, 34, 52
locks, 91, 142
login utility, 33
loop-backs, 168
LOOPLOCK utility, 93
low-traffic conditions, 61
machine configuration, 122
magnetic media, 120
mail address, 207
mail utility, 34
mail-handling gateways, 212
mailbox, 207
Mailgram, 212
mainframe, 192
mainframe applications, 101
mainframe connection, 197
mainframe downtime, 202
mainframe-to-PC migration, 101
maintenance log, 123
management function, 38
managing resources, 7
manual file locking, 44, 46
master-slave protocol, 182
mean-time-between-failures hours, 137
media-independent operating system, 53
megabits per second, 2
Merritt Security, 147
message path, 127
message units, 17

micro-to-mainframe machines, 202
micro-to-micro network, 3
microprocessor, 4, 9, 66
Microsoft BASIC, 108
mirror-image backup, 121
modems, 188
modulation techniques, 17
moisture effects, 156
monitor, 35
Motorola 68000, 133, 203
Motorola 6801 microprocessor, 73
MP/M-II, 55
MS-DOS, 82
MTBF hours, 137
multi-accessed network software, 99, 100
Multibus, 76
multichannel technology, 27
multilevel password protection, 77, 82
MultiLink, 30, 88
multiple hard disks, 131
multiple machine types, 68
multiple servers, 70, 130
multiplexer, 10
multiprocessor versus single-processor, 8
multistrand wire, 27
multitasking, 29, 68
multitasking kernel, 89
multitasking operating system, 56
multitasking servers, 39
multiuser, 11, 13, 29, 57, 131
    software, 95, 105
    tools, 108
naming conventions, 119
National Bureau of Standards, 146
NCC, 167, 168
Nestar Systems, 61, 85
Net/One, 82, 185
Net/Plus, 84
NETDIR, 93
NetWare, 52, 79, 109, 170, 171
    S, 77
    X, 77
network
    addresses, 152
    applications software, 75
    cables, 27
    cabling, 65
    controls, 38
    features, 69
    interface card, 3, 68
    interface unit, 82, 185
    layer, 187
    management, 17
    manager, 112, 173
    monitors, 167
    operating system, 4, 20, 29, 30, 91
    overhead, 38
    performance, 125
    selection checklist, 60

    server, 70, 197
    speed, 66
    status utilities, 57
    traffic, 61
    utilization, 126
Network Control Center, 168
Network layer, 16
network-deliverable, 100
network-to-network interfaces, 16
networked software, 99, 100
networking
    applications, 9
    arguments for and against, 4
    organizational benefit, 6
networking range, 180
networking software, 97
NIC, 3
NIU, 82, 185
nonstandard networks, 15
nonshareable, 34
Norell Data Systems, 146
Novell, 52, 77, 109, 170
object-code compatibility, 53
off-the-shelf software, 102
ohms of resistance, 160
Omninet, 52, 55
    capabilities, 75
    popularity, 72
    third-party support, 73
on-board intelligence, 82
on-line coders, 147
on-line help facility, 71, 209
Open Systems Interconnection, 16
    model, 65
open topology, 64
optimizing disk access, 128
Orchid Technology, 61, 91, 129, 133
order-entry, 47
organizational control, 38
organizing the network, 117
OSI, 145
    model, 16, 30, 65
OUT, 105
over-ceiling cable tray, 153, 154
overwriting, 34, 43
p-System, 4, 52, 54, 67
packet buffer, 71
packet format, 181
packets, 17, 30
parallel interface, 76
Pascal, 89
password, 38, 144
    assignment, 144
    level, 79
    protection, 39
    utility, 33
PBX network, 8
PBX system, 66, 177
PC DOS, 4, 30, 52, 57, 109, 133

PC installation, 151
PC-Focus, 99, 101
PC-to-mainframe communications, 192
PCnet, 91
    BLOSSOM, 129
PCnetPLUS DISKLESS, 93
peer-to-peer communications, 19
peer-to-peer network, 3, 9
peer-to-peer operating system, 54
PerComNet, 57
perfect local area network, 15
performance, 39, 130, 132, 157, 180
performance degradation, 9
peripheral sharing, 75, 92
peripherals, 7, 10
personal archiving, 201
personal identification, 142
personnel records, 107
Physical layer, 16
physical devices, 35
physical layout, 63
physical security, 67, 142
pipelining, 89
pipes, 34, 91
PLAN 2000, 85
PLAN 4000, 85
plan for networking, 60
plenum cable, 159
Plexus, 58
Point-Four Systems, 109
point-to-point link, 17
polling scheme, 10
portability, 54
preconfiguring the system, 57
Presentation layer, 16
print queuing, 86
print server, 197
print server software, 72, 83
print serving utility, 32
print spool utility, 32
print spooler, 56
printer buffer, 32
printer ports, 77
printer sharing, 30, 86
printer strategy, 137
printing, 93
Printronix MVP, 137
private, 34
proNET, 52
proprietary transceiver logic, 80
protection, 56
    against cable radiation, 142, 149
Proteon, 52
protocols, 16, 17, 64, 86, 181
    converters, 65, 195
public, 34
public data network, 183
public key, 146
punch card readers, 201

# INDEX

queue, 34, 52, 102
Quick*NET, 100
RAM cache, 89
RAM disk, 91, 129
random accessing, 108
random seek, 128
raw bit rate, 127
read-ahead scheme, 128
read-only, 33, 36, 47
read/status request, 170
read/write, 33, 36, 46
reading data simultaneously, 48
reality rating, 67
rebooting, 40, 172
Recommendation X.25, 182
reconfiguring the network, 55, 151
record file locking, 45
record locking, 93
reducing the load, 125
redundancy, 66
reliability, 137
remote access, 143
remote command execution capability, 92
remote connections, 188
remote mail, 211
removable cartridge tape drive, 120
removable Winchester hard disk cartridges, 120
repeater, 179
requester, 56
response time, 2
retransmissions, 26
retry statistics, 134
RF modems, 28
Ring, 21, 22
risk analysis, 140
root directory, 130
rotational latency, 131
routing, 186
RS-232, 17, 76, 84, 184
RS-422, 17, 76, 184
safeguarding network operations, 40
schematic diagram, 152
search directories, 53
secret key, 146
security, 139
    in login, 144
selecting a mail package, 209
self-test, 168, 173
semaphore, 44, 103
sequential accessing, 108
sequential searching, 53
serverless network, 56
servers, 4, 35
    differences between, 36
Session layer, 16
seven-layer model, 18
shareable, 34
shared DOS mode, 91
shared environment, 49

sharing resources
    advantages, 5
    disadvantages, 4
shared transmission medium, 60
shell, 77
shell structure, 53
shielded wiring, 63
shielding, 67
shielding conduit, 149
signal interception, 149
signal radiation, 67
single network, 136
single point of failure, 38
single-user environment, 107
SNA, 19, 20, 82
    gateway, 70
    protocol, 182
SNA/SDLC, 193
socket services, 55
SofTech Microsystems, 51, 53
software, 52, 208
    driver, 35
    layers, 19
    use, 45
Software Connections, 99, 102
speed, 66
spike, 163
spreadsheet software, 97
stand-alone operations, 48
    constraints, 49
    machines, 13
standard coaxial cable, 155
standardization, 15, 19, 119
    CSMA-CD, 26
Star topology, 21
    disadvantages for local area network use, 22
    speed, 77
Star-Wired Ring, 23
station-dependent login, 33
status information, 169
status lines, 195
status report, 79
steering connection, 13
stepper motor, 132
storage space, 131
streaming tape, 120
    backup, 86
subdirectory, 130
support, 61
surface raceway, 153
synchronization error, 171
Synchronous Data Link Control, 196
syntax, 18
system calls, 36
system documentation, 152
Systems Network Architecture, 19, 82
tailoring the network, 112
tamper-detection, 105
tape backup systems, 120

TCS Software, 100
tech support equipment, 169
technician's point of view, 59
Tecmar, 61, 80
Telenet, 182, 183
telephone tag, 206
terminal emulations, 85
terminal interface units, 195
terminal network, 8
terminal-to-host network, 9
theft, 141
thick Ethernet, 72
thin Ethernet, 72
throughput, 138
TI Professional, 75
time-out errors, 172
time-sharing terminals, 192
token, 26
Token Bus, 21, 23
token passing, 26, 61
    longevity, 26
tool-crimp connector, 157
top-down approach, 178
topology, 19, 20, 54, 63, 64
    similarities, 21
Touch-Tone decoder, 82
traffic statistics, 150
transaction file locking, 45, 47
Transcriptor, 147
transfer utility, 17, 194, 195
    rate, 131
translation of formats, 18
transmission errors, 136
transmission media, 21
transparency, 55
transparently networked software, 100
Transport layer, 16
triax, 155
Trompeter Electronics, 159
TSO, 195
twinax, 155
twisted-pair cable, 27, 73, 155, 158
Tymnet, 182, 183
U.S. Bureau of Standards, 20
U.S. Department of Defense, 20
U.S. government ratings, 67
unauthorized access, 141, 207
unauthorized taps, 140
unbinding, 17
under-floor duct, 153, 154
underground installations, 157
uNETix-DFS, 57
Ungermann-Bass, 61, 82, 185
UNIX, 57, 67
unnetworked software, 99, 100
update access, 106
updating shared files, 48
upgrading single-user DBMS software, 101
use of software, 45

user control of locking, 46
user education, 112
user passwords, 13
user privileges, 33
user profile, 33
user software, 35
user-access scheme, 117
user-defined networks, 207
user-dependent login, 33
using electronic mail, 207
utility, 30
    definition, 32
    disk serving, 32
    file specification, 33
    locking, 34
    login, 33
    mail, 34
    password, 33
    print serving, 32
    print spool, 32
utilization strategy, 126
vandalism, 141
verbal semaphore, 101
video and voice transmissions, 62
virtual diskettes, 32, 34
virtual files, 57
VisiCalc, 100
VisiWord, 100
VM/CMS, 195
voice coil drives, 133
voice coil positioning, 132
volume, 34, 37, 70
vulnerability, 140
"what if" calculations, 138
wicking effect, 159
wide area networks, 178
    interface module, 184
Winchester hard disk, 9
window programs, 46
windows, 202
wiring arrangements
    Distributed Bus, 21
    Ring, 21
    Star, 21
    Token Bus, 21
WNIM, 184
word-processing software, 97
wrench-crimp connector, 157
X.25 gateway
    card, 184
    networks, 182
    options, 183
    stand-alone processor, 184
Xerox, 20, 61, 72
Xerox Network System, 19, 30, 84, 187
XNS, 19, 187
XT/370, 202
Z80 processor, 73, 147
Z80B processor, 79

# NEW TECHNIQUES FOR PROFESSIONALS

## IBM PC UPDATE

---

### INNOVATIVE... INFORMATIVE... USEFUL

That's what today's professionals are saying about *IBM PC UPDATE*.

And well they should. No other monthly periodical offers PC users as much quality information as *UPDATE* packs into every issue. Designed for today's professionals, *UPDATE* is a dynamic, valuable resource.

INNOVATIVE... and unique, *UPDATE*'s segmented approach provides convenience. Each clearly defined section is easy to find and offers practical information on one of *UPDATE*'s featured topics: word processing, spreadsheets, data base management, and integrated software.

INFORMATIVE... articles keep you up-to-date on the latest hardware and software releases and provide useful information on important existing products.

USEFUL... skill-building information helps you improve productivity and increase your proficiency on the PC. Monthly columns give you expert advice for maximizing the potential of applications programs such as dBASE, WordStar, 1-2-3, Symphony, and Framework.

Read *IBM PC UPDATE*. This is one publication today's professional can't afford to miss.

### SUBSCRIBE TODAY

---

**ORDER FORM**

**IBM PC UPDATE**
**New Techniques for Professionals**

| | Price | Qty. | Extension |
|---|---|---|---|
| 12 issues (inside the United States) | $48.00 | | |
| 24 issues (inside the United States) | $72.00 | | |
| 12 issues (outside the United States) | $68.00 | | |
| 24 issues (outside the United States) | $92.00 | | |

**que**

Que Corporation
7999 Knue Road
Indianapolis, IN 46250
317/842-7162
800/227-7999

Subtotal _____
*Shipping & Handling ($1.50) _____
Indiana Residents Add 5% Sales Tax _____
**GRAND TOTAL** _____

**Method of Payment**

Check ☐   VISA ☐   MasterCard ☐   AMEX ☐

Card Number _____ Exp. Date _____

Cardholder Name _____

Ship to _____

Address _____

City _____ State _____ ZIP _____

All prices subject to change without notice.

NIBMPC-8511

# More Computer Knowledge from Que

| | | |
|---|---|---|
| **LOTUS SOFTWARE TITLES** | 1-2-3 for Business | $16.95 |
| | 1-2-3 Financial Macros | 19.95 |
| | 1-2-3 Macro Library | 19.95 |
| | 1-2-3 Tips, Tricks, and Traps | 16.95 |
| | Using 1-2-3 | 19.95 |
| | Using 1-2-3 Workbook and Disk | 29.95 |
| | Using Symphony | 19.95 |
| | Symphony: Advanced Topics | 19.95 |
| | Symphony Macros and the Command Language | 22.95 |
| | Symphony Tips, Tricks, and Traps | 21.95 |
| **WORD-PROCESSING TITLES** | Improve Your Writing with Word Processing | 12.95 |
| | Using DisplayWrite | 18.95 |
| | Using Microsoft Word | 16.95 |
| | Using MultiMate | 18.95 |
| | Using the PFS Family: FILE, WRITE, GRAPH, REPORT | 14.95 |
| | Using WordPerfect | 18.95 |
| | Using WordStar 2000 | 17.95 |
| **IBM TITLES** | IBM PC Expansion & Software Guide | 29.95 |
| | IBM's Personal Computer, 2nd Edition | 17.95 |
| | Networking IBM PCs: A Practical Guide | 18.95 |
| | PC DOS User's Guide | 16.95 |
| | PC DOS Workbook | 14.95 |
| | Using PC DOS Version 3 | 21.95 |
| **APPLICATIONS SOFTWARE TITLES** | dBASE III Advanced Programming | 22.95 |
| | dBASE III Handbook | 17.95 |
| | Multiplan Models for Business | 15.95 |
| | R:base 5000 User's Guide | 19.95 |
| | Using AppleWorks | 16.95 |
| | Using Dollars and Sense | 14.95 |
| | Using Enable | 17.95 |
| | Using Excel | 19.95 |
| **COMPUTER SYSTEMS TITLES** | Apple Favorite Programs Explained | 12.95 |
| | Commodore Favorite Programs Explained | 12.95 |
| | Introducing the Apple IIc: Applications and Programming | 12.95 |
| | MS-DOS User's Guide | 16.95 |
| | The HP Touchscreen | 19.95 |
| | The HP 110 Portable: Power to Go! | 16.95 |
| | Using NetWare | 24.95 |
| **PROGRAMMING AND TECHNICAL TITLES** | Advanced C: Techniques and Applications | 19.95 |
| | Common C Functions | 17.95 |
| | C Programmer's Library | 19.95 |
| | C Programming Guide, 2nd Edition | 19.95 |
| | CP/M Programmer's Encyclopedia | 19.95 |
| | C Self-Study Guide | 16.95 |
| | Turbo Pascal for BASIC Programmers | 14.95 |
| | Understanding UNIX: A Conceptual Guide | 19.95 |
| | Understanding XENIX: A Conceptual Guide | 19.95 |

Que Order Line: **1-800-428-5331**

All prices subject to change without notice.

# MORE COMPUTER KNOWLEDGE FROM QUE

## IBM PC Expansion & Software Guide

Nowhere will you find a more complete listing of hardware manufacturers and software vendors who support IBM products. This comprehensive book gives you up-to-date information about 7,666 products from 2,087 vendors.

Be informed. Keep this best-seller next to your PC for quick and easy reference.

## Understanding XENIX: A Conceptual Guide

*by Paul N. Weinberg and James. R. Groff*

Another superbly written book by the authors of the highly acclaimed *Understanding UNIX: A Conceptual Guide*. A comprehensive overview, this book describes the major features and benefits of XENIX, the multiuser operating system of the future. Includes the IBM PC AT and Tandy Models 16 and 6000.

## Using DisplayWrite

*by Deborah and Walton Beacham*

An excellent guide for mastering DisplayWrite. Clear, step-by-step instructions augment a practical approach to using all of DisplayWrite's features. An indispensable tool for all DisplayWrite users.

## PC DOS User's Guide

*by Chris DeVoney*

Master PC DOS with this best-seller from Que. This easy-to-use guide covers both the simple and advanced features of PC DOS, Version 2.0. A valuable asset to your PC library.

*Another extremely useful book from one of the better publishers in the field.*

Bruce W. Marcus, Book Editor
*THE STOCK MARKET MAGAZINE*
April, 1984

| Item | Title | Price | Quantity | Extension |
|---|---|---|---|---|
| 169 | IBM PC Expansion & Software Guide | $29.95 | | |
| 170 | Understanding XENIX: A Conceptual Guide | $19.95 | | |
| 158 | Using DisplayWrite | $16.95 | | |
| 30 | PC DOS User's Guide | $16.95 | | |

**Book Subtotal** \_\_\_\_
Shipping & Handling ($1.75 per item) \_\_\_\_
Indiana Residents Add 5% Sales Tax \_\_\_\_
**GRAND TOTAL** \_\_\_\_

**Method of Payment:**

☐ Check    ☐ VISA    ☐ MasterCard    ☐ American Express

Card Number _____ Exp. Date _____

Cardholder Name _____

Ship to _____

Address _____

City _____ State _____ ZIP _____

All prices subject to change without notice.

NIBMPC-8511

FOLD HERE

Place
Stamp
Here

Que Corporation
7999 Knue Road
Indianapolis, IN 46250